S\
THE M

There are more than one hundred and fifty
Rough Guide travel, phrasebook and music titles,
covering destinations from Amsterdam to Zimbabwe,
languages from Czech to Thai, and music from
World to Opera and Jazz

Forthcoming titles include

Cuba • Dominican Republic • Las Vegas
Sardinia • Switzerland

Rough Guides on the Internet

www.roughguides.com

Rough Guide Credits

Text editors: Kieran Falconer & Cameron Wilson
Series editor: Mark Ellingham
Typesetting: Helen Ostick
Cartography: Nichola Goodliffe

Publishing Information

This first edition published September 1999 by
Rough Guides Ltd, 62–70 Shorts Gardens, London WC2H 9AB

Distributed by the Penguin Group:

Penguin Books Ltd, 27 Wrights Lane, London W8 5TZ
Penguin Books USA Inc., 375 Hudson Street, New York, NY10014, USA
Penguin Books Australia Ltd, 487 Maroondah Highway,
PO Box 257, Ringwood, Victoria 3134, Australia
Penguin Books Canada Ltd, 10 Alcorn Avenue,
Toronto, Ontario M4V 1E4, Canada
Penguin Books (NZ) Ltd, 182–190 Wairau Road,
Auckland 10, New Zealand

Typeset in Bembo and Helvetica to an original design by Henry Iles.
Printed in Spain by Graphy Cems.

© Margo Daly
384pp includes index
A catalogue record for this book is available from the British Library.
ISBN 1-85828-453-8

The publishers and authors have done their best to
ensure the accuracy and currency of all the information
in *The Rough Guide to Sydney*, however, they can accept
no responsibility for any loss, injury or inconvenience
sustained by any traveller as a result of information or
advice contained in the guide.

SYDNEY

THE MINI ROUGH GUIDE

by Margo Daly

with contributions by
Matt Buchanan, Stephen Nicholls &
Alison Cowan

We set out to do something different when the first Rough Guide was published in 1982. Mark Ellingham, just out of university, was travelling in Greece. He brought along the popular guides of the day, but found they were all lacking in some way. They were either strong on ruins and museums but went on for pages without mentioning a beach or taverna. Or they were so conscious of the need to save money that they lost sight of Greece's cultural and historical significance. Also, none of the books told him anything about Greece's contemporary life – its politics, its culture, its people, and how they lived.

So with no job in prospect, Mark decided to write his own guidebook, one which aimed to provide practical information that was second to none, detailing the best beaches and the hottest clubs and restaurants, while also giving hard-hitting accounts of every sight, both famous and obscure, and providing up-to-the-minute information on contemporary culture. It was a guide that encouraged independent travellers to find the best of Greece, and was a great success, getting shortlisted for the Thomas Cook travel guide award, and encouraging Mark, along with three friends, to expand the series.

The Rough Guide list grew rapidly and the letters flooded in, indicating a much broader readership than had been anticipated, but one which uniformly appreciated the Rough Guide mix of practical detail and humour, irreverence and enthusiasm. Things haven't changed. The same four friends who began the series are still the caretakers of the Rough Guide mission today: to provide the most reliable, up-to-date and entertaining information to independent-minded travellers of all ages, on all budgets.

We now publish more than 150 titles and have offices in London and New York. The travel guides are written and researched by a dedicated team of more than 100 authors, based in Britain, Europe, the USA and Australia. We have also created a unique series of phrasebooks to accompany the travel series, along with an acclaimed series of music guides, and a best-selling pocket guide to the Internet and World Wide Web. We also publish comprehensive travel information on our Web site: **www.roughguides.com**

Help Us Update

We've gone to a lot of effort to ensure that this first edition of *The Rough Guide to Sydney* is as up-to-date and accurate as possible. However, if you feel there are places we've underrated or over-praised, or find we've missed something good or covered something which has now gone, then please write: suggestions, comments or corrections are much appreciated.

We'll credit all contributions, and send a copy of the next edition (or any other Rough Guide if you prefer) for the best letters. Please mark letters: "Rough Guide Sydney Update" and send to:

Rough Guides, 62–70 Shorts Gardens, London WC2H 9AB, or Rough Guides, 375 Hudson St, New York, NY 10014.

Or send email to: **mail@roughguides.co.uk**

Online updates about this book can be found on Rough Guides' Web site (see opposite)

The Author

Margo Daly was born in Sydney where she studied Communications at the University of Technology; she has an MA in Writing from Sheffield Hallam University. She is the co-author of *The Rough Guide to Australia* and has contributed to Rough Guides to *France*, *Paris*, *Thailand*, *Europe* and *More Women Travel*. She is the co-editor, with Jill Dawson, of the Sceptre fiction anthology *Wild Ways: New Stories of Women on the Road*.

Acknowledgements

At the Rough Guides, a huge thank you to Kieran Falconer and Cameron Wilson for tireless editing and loads of valuable input, to Nichola Goodliffe for fabulous maps, and Jo Mead for overseeing the whole project. Thanks to all those who I plagued with questions especially Katinka Carr and David Bock at the Australian Museum: Elsie Hastings at the Olympic Co-ordination Authority; Judith Mayer and Caroline Muirhead at YHA NSW; Lyndsey Thompson at the Fish Markets; Jo Holder at the S. H. Ervin Gallery; and Greg Bond at the NPWS, La Perouse. Big thanks to Matthew Buchanan, a girl's best friend; Tony Nesbitt for help with sport; Michael Schofield for contributing the horse-racing section; Brad Miller and Kate Daly for the study and the sojourn in Melbourne; Justine Scott McCarthy for refuge in London; Rosanna Arcuili for the Leichhardt home; Beth Yahp; Janine Daly for cocktail input and much more; Stephen Nichols; Alison Cowan; Michael and Brigitte Daly for a reintroduction to Pearl Beach; Mary Daly, Gabe Kessler and Ella Rose for the Hunter Valley road-trip, and as always Margaret and Tony Daly.

CONTENTS

Listings

Excursions from Sydney

Contexts

Sydney 2000: The XXVII Olympics

Introduction

I t might seem surprising that Sydney, established in 1788, is not Australia's capital. Yet the creation of Canberra in 1927 – intended to stem the intense rivalry between Sydney and Melbourne – has not affected the view of many Sydneysiders that their city remains the *true* capital of Australia, and certainly in many ways it feels like it. The city has a tangible sense of history in the old stone walls and well-worn steps in the backstreets around The Rocks, while the sandstone cliffs, rocks and caves amongst the bushlined harbour still contain Aboriginal rock carvings, evocative reminders of a more ancient past.

Flying into Sydney provides a thrilling close-up snapshot of the city as the aeroplane swoops alongside sandstone cliffs and golden beaches, revealing toy-sized images of the Harbour Bridge and the Opera House tilting in a glittering expanse of blue water. Towards Mascot airport the red-tiled roofs of suburban bungalows stretch ever southwards, blue squares of swimming pools shimmering from grassy backyards. The night views are nearly as spectacular, skyscrapers topped with colourful neon lights, Olympic sculptures glowing softly on the great gearstick of the Sydney Tower, while the illuminated white shells of the Opera House reflect on the dark water as ferries crisscross to Circular Quay.

Sydney has all the vigour of a world-class city, and a population of five million people; yet on the ground you'll find it still possesses a seductive, small-town, easy-going charm. The furious development in preparation for the year 2000 Olympics, heralded as being something of Sydney's coming-of-age ceremony alarms many locals, who love their city just the way it is. It's not so much the greatly improved transport infrastructure, or the $200 million budget to improve and beautify the city streets and parks, but the rash of luxury hotels and apartments adding themselves, often contentiously, to the beloved harbour foreshore. It's a setting that perhaps only Rio de Janeiro can rival: the water is what makes the city so special, and no introduction to Sydney would be complete without paying tribute to one of the world's great harbours. Port Jackson is a sunken valley which twists inland to meet the fresh water of the Parramatta River; in the process it washes into a hundred coves and bays, winds around rocky points, flows past the small harbour islands, slips under bridges and laps at the foot of the Opera House.

Taken together with its surrounds, Sydney is in many ways a microcosm of Australia as a whole – if only in its ability to defy your expectations and prejudices as often as it confirms them. A thrusting, high-rise business centre in the **CBD**, a high-profile gay community in **Darlinghurst**, inner-city deprivation of unexpected harshness, with the highest Aboriginal population of any Australian city, and the dreary traffic-fumed and flat suburban sprawl of the **Western Suburbs**, are as much part of the scene as the beaches, the bodies and the sparkling harbour. But all in all, Sydney seems to have the best of both worlds – if it's seen at its gleaming best from the deck of a harbour ferry, especially at weekends when the harbour's jagged jaws fill with a flotilla of small vessels, racing yachts and cabin cruisers, it's at its most varied in its **neighbourhoods**, not least for their lively café and restaurant scenes. Getting away from the city centre and exploring them is an essential part of Sydney's pleasures.

A short ferry trip across to the leafy and affluent North Shore accesses tracts of largely intact bushland, with bush-walking and native animals and birds right on the doorstep. In the summer the city's hot offices are abandoned for the remarkably unspoilt ocean and harbour **beaches** strung around the eastern and northern suburbs. Day-trips away offer a taste of virtually everything you'll find in the rest of Australia. There are magnificent **national parks** and native wildlife – Ku-Ring-Gai Chase and Royal being the best known of the parks, each a mere hour's drive from the centre of town. North of the centre the **Central Coast** is great for surfers, and has more enclosed waters for safer swimming and sailing. Inland, the **Blue Mountains** offer tea rooms, scenic viewpoints and isolated bushwalking. On the way, and along the **Hawkesbury River**, are historic colonial towns. Inland to the northwest is the **Hunter Valley**, Australia's oldest and possibly best-known wine-growing region, amongst pastoral scenery.

When to visit

Since Sydney has such wonderful beaches, the **best time** to come is **between early October and Easter**, the official swimming season, when the beaches are patrolled, and outdoor swimming pools reopen.

The sunny **springtime** months of September and October are when the wild flowers are in bloom, and the smell of blossoms such as jasmine fill the warming city streets, while the bush is alive with critters not yet reduced to summer torpidity. The sweltering hot **summer months** are mid-December, January and February; Christmas can

Sydney's climate

| | °F | | °C | | Rainfall | |
| | Average daily | | Average daily | | Average monthly | |
	MAX	MIN	MAX	MIN	IN	MM
Jan	78	65	26	18	3.5	89
Feb	78	65	26	18	4.0	102
March	76	63	24	17	5.0	127
April	71	58	22	14	5.3	135
May	66	52	19	11	5.0	127
June	61	48	16	9	4.6	117
July	60	46	16	8	4.6	117
Aug	63	48	17	9	3.0	76
Sept	67	51	19	11	2.9	74
Oct	71	56	22	13	2.8	71
Nov	74	60	23	16	2.9	74
Dec	77	63	25	17	2.9	74

often see 40°C in the shade, though it's been known to be cool and overcast; average summer temperatures are 25°C. Sydney is subtropical, with high and very oppressive humidity in summer building up to sporadic torrential rainstorms. This is party time, combining high summer with Christmas and New Year festivities and January's Sydney Festival, culminating in the Gay and Lesbian Mardi Gras street parade in late February/early March.

April, when the Royal Agricultural Show hits town, is anecdotally – and actually – the rainiest month. May is a contrastingly glorious time when you can bet on dry sunny weather and blue skies as Sydney heads for its mild **winter**

months of June, July and August. Don't expect bare trees and grey skies - native trees are evergreen and the skies are usually a less intense blue. Temperatures are rarely less than 10°C, colder during the night, and decidedly chilly the further you go west, with frost on the plains heading to the Blue Mountains – where there are rare light snowfalls. Bring the usual coats, scarves, gloves and woolly hat if you want to go to the mountains in winter; it gets cool at night in summer too. A jumper and jacket should keep you warm enough in the city, where the cafés continue with their outdoor seating, with braziers to radiate some heat.

BASICS

Getting there from Britain and Ireland

The market for flights between Britain and Australia is one of the most competitive in the world, and in real terms prices have never been lower. Modern aircraft offer **direct flights** to Sydney in 22–23 hours – with Qantas, British Airways, Singapore or Malaysian. Other airlines involve changing flights for connecting planes, and potentially long waits in between, which can make the journey last up to 36 hours. However, it often costs no more to break the journey in such **stopover** points, typically in Southeast Asia, New Zealand and or North America, or even Argentina, South Africa or Japan – so that it need not be the tedious, seat-bound slog you may have imagined. Some airlines usually have great special deals as well which include discounted or free flights en route or in Australia itself. All direct scheduled flights to Australia depart from London's two main airports, Gatwick and Heathrow. There are no direct flights from Ireland. Airtours offer **charter flights** and **package holidays** to Sydney from London Gatwick or Manchester, from November to April only.

Fares, flights and air passes

Most of the discount and specialist agents listed below can quote fares on scheduled flights. For the latest prices and special deals, check out the ads in the travel pages of the weekend newspapers, London's listing magazine *Time Out,* the free listings magazine *TNT,* or Teletext or Ceefax. We've included **Web sites** where available with our airline list below – it's worth checking out these sites for "On-line specials" available via **Internet auctions**. However, **booking ahead** as far as possible is still the best way to secure the most reasonable prices, and it is almost invariably cheaper to buy tickets through **agents** (see opposite) rather than through airlines themselves.

High season differs slightly from airline to airline, but the most expensive time to travel to Sydney is always the two weeks before **Christmas** until mid-January; prices also go up from mid-June or the beginning of July to the middle of August coinciding with the peak European holiday times. **Shoulder seasons** are mid-January to March and mid-August to November; while the **low-season** runs from April to mid-June. Discounted fares to Sydney can start as low as £499 for a charter flight via another stop. Fares for a direct flight vary from £700 to £1000. Another option is a **round-the-world** (RTW) ticket; prices range from around £750 for a simple London–Bangkok–Sydney–LA–London deal to well over £1000 for more elaborate plans. With a British Airways, Qantas, Air New Zealand or Singapore Airlines ticket, further discounts are available on **internal flight passes** in Australia.

Airlines and agents

Airlines

Aerolineas Argentinas ©0171/494 1001
Air New Zealand ©0181/741 2299; *www.airnz.co.nz*
Airtours ©01706/260 0000

Alitalia ✆0171/602 7111; *www.alitalia.it*
All Nippon Airways (ANA) ✆0171/355 1155; *www.ana.co.jp*
British Airways ✆0345/222111; *www.british-airways.com*
Garuda Indonesia ✆0171/486 3011; *www.garuda.co.id*
Japan Airlines ✆0345/747700; *www.jal.co.jp*
KLM ✆0990/750900; *www.klm.nl*
Lauda Air ✆0171/630 5924; *www.laudaair.com*
Malaysia Airlines ✆0171/341 2020;
www.malaysiaairlines.com.my
Olympic Airways ✆0171/409 3400
Qantas ✆0345/747767; *www.qantas.com.au*
Singapore Airlines ✆0181/747 0007; *www.singaporeair.com*
South African Airways ✆0171/312 5000; *www.saa.co.za*
Thai Airways ✆0171/499 9113; *www.thaiair.com*
United Airlines ✆0845/844 4777 *www.ual.com*

Flight agents

Austravel ✆0171/734 7755; *www.austravel.net*
Bridge the World ✆0171/734 7447
Campus Travel ✆0171/730 8111; *www.campustravel.co.uk*
Flightbookers ✆0171/757 2468; *www.flightbookers.net*
The London Flight Centre ✆0171/244 6411
Quest Worldwide ✆0181/547 3322
STA Travel ✆0171/361 6262; *www.statravel.co.uk*
Trailfinders ✆0171/938 3366; Dublin ✆01/677 7888
The Travel Bug ✆0171/835 2000; *www.travel-bug.co.uk*
USIT Dublin ✆01/602 1700; *www.usit.ie*

Packages and tours

Packages are a good option for those worried about spi-ralling costs or who want to enjoy quality hotels at a cheap-er price. An Airtours 14-night high season package, includ-ing return flights and staying at the four-star *Gazebo Hotel* in Elizabeth Bay (see p.143) costs £1149. There are plenty of more flexible tours which combine Sydney with other areas of Australia; Travel Bag offers some good tour options, plus some action and eco-oriented trips including the Great Barrier Reef.

Specialist package and tour operators

Australia Travel Centre Dublin ©01/874 7747
Jetabout ©0181/741 3111
Qantas Holidays ©0990/673464
Travel Bag ©0171/287 5556 or 497 0515
Travelmood ©0171/258 1234

Getting there from the US and Canada

From Los Angeles it's possible to fly nonstop to Sydney in fourteen and a half hours. Qantas, United, Canadian Airlines and Air New Zealand all operate direct flights. Flying on an Asian airline will most likely involve a stop in their capital city (Singapore, Tokyo, etc) and if you're travelling from the West Coast of North America you'll probably find their fares on the Pacific route somewhat higher than their American or Australasian competitors.

Many of the major airlines offer deals whereby you can make **stopovers** either at **Pacific Rim** destinations such as

Tokyo with Japan Airlines, Honolulu with Canadian Airlines or Kuala Lumpur with Malaysia Airlines or at a number of exotic South Pacific locations with Air New Zealand. Either there will be a flat surcharge on your ticket ($60 per stop, in the case of Singapore Airlines, with a maximum of four stops) or they may offer you a higher priced ticket allowing you to make several stops over a fixed period of time. But the best deal will probably be a Circle Pacific or a **round-the-world** (RTW) ticket from a discount outfit like High Adventure Travel.

Airlines and agents

Airlines
Air New Zealand US ✆1-800/262-1234;
Canada ✆1-800/563-5494; *www.airnz.com*
Canadian Airlines US ✆1-800/426-7000;
Canada ✆1-800/665-1177; *www.cdnair.ca*
Cathay Pacific ✆1-800/233-2742; *www.cathay-usa.com*
Japan Airlines ✆1-800/525-3663; *www.jal.co.jp*
Malaysia Airlines ✆1-800/552-9264; *www.malaysiaairlines.com*
Qantas ✆1-800/227-4500; *www.qantas.com.au*
Singapore Airlines ✆1-800/742-3333; *www.singaporeair.com*
United Airlines ✆1-800/538-2929; *www.ual.com*

Discount flight agents and consolidators
Air Brokers International US ✆1-800/883-3273 or 415/397-1383; *www.airbrokers.com*
Austravel US ✆1-800/633-3404, fax 212/983-8376; *australia-online.com/austravel*)
Council Travel US ✆1-800/226-8624, 888/COUNCIL or 212/822-2700; *www.ciee.com*
Educational Travel Center US ✆1-800/747-5551 or 608/256-5551; *www.edtrav.com*
High Adventure Travel US ✆1-800/350-0612 or 415/912-5600; *www.highadv.com*

Now Voyager US ✆212/431-1616; *www.nowvoyagertravel.com*
Pacific Experience US ✆1-800/233-4255
STA Travel US ✆1-800/777-0112 or 212/627-3111;
www.sta-travel.com
Travel Cuts CANADA ✆1-800/667-2887 or 416/979-2406;
www.travelcuts.com

Fares and flights

Most of the consolidators and discount agents listed above can quote and offer the best fares on scheduled flights, though you can go direct through airlines. We've included **Websites** where available with our airline list above – it's worth checking out these sites for "On-line specials" available via **Internet auctions**, the latest way to sell last-minute seats. If you travel a lot, **discount travel clubs** are another option – the annual membership fee may be worth it for benefits such as cut-price air tickets and car rental. Many airlines offer youth or student fares to **under-26s**.

However, **booking ahead** as far as possible is still the best way to secure the most reasonable prices. Fares vary significantly according to season – generally **high season** is Dec–Feb, **low season** April–Aug, and other times are **shoulder**. The highest prices are over Christmas and New Year; booking as far in advance as possible is highly recommended.

Sample lowest standard **scheduled fares** for low/high seasons are: from Chicago ($1325/$1825), New York ($1380/$1880), LA or San Francisco ($1000/$1500); Seattle ($1240/$1740), Montréal or Toronto (CDN$1965/$2465), and Vancouver (CDN$1670/CDN$2170). There are also deals on Qantas involving free or low-price internal flights. To see more of the world, a sample **RTW ticket** could consist of LA–Sydney–Bangkok–Delhi–Bombay–London–LA ($1880).

Charter flights to Australia offer fares that slightly undercut scheduled flights but are offset by more restrictions.

Sydney on the Net

Online listings www.citysearch.com.au
The ultimate Sydney online guide to arts and entertainment, music, movies, eating, shopping, with links to tourist attractions and accommodation.

Read all about it! www.smh.com.au
Read selected daily pages of the *Sydney Morning Herald*.

Best of the fest www.sydneycity.nsw.gov.au
A useful list of festivals and events.

Dance till you drop www.mardigras.com.au
The official Gay and Lesbian Mardi Gras site with links to other gay and lesbian sites.

Package tours

Several of the operators below, such as United Vacations, offer city stopovers, providing, for example, three nights' accommodation, and perhaps a day-tour, starting at around US$325 on top of your ticket. Organized tours of Australia, which inevitably take in Sydney, can cost from US$3300 for a typical two-week tour taking in the usual cultural/historical/natural sights.

Tour Operators

AAT King's ℗1-800/353 4525; *www.world.net/travel /australia/austtour*
Abercrombie and Kent International Inc ℗1-800/323-7308 or 630/954 2944, fax 954 3324; *www.abercrombiekent.com*
ATS Tours ℗1-800/423 2880, fax 310/643 0032
Australian Pacific Tours ℗1-800/290-8687, fax 416/234 8385

Austravel ✆1-800/633 3404; *australia-online.com/austravel*)
Down Under Direct/Swain Australia Tours ✆1-800/642 6224;
www.swaintours.com
Goway Travel ✆1-800/387 8850; *www.goway.com*
International Gay and Lesbian Travel Association ✆1-
800/448 8550; *www.iglta.org*
Newmans Vacations ✆1-800/468 2665; *www.newmans.com*
Qantas Vacations ✆1-800/641 8772;
www.quantasvacations.com
United Vacations ✆1-800/351 4200

Getting there from New Zealand

New Zealand–Australia routes are busy and competition is fierce, resulting in an ever-changing range of deals and special offers; your best bet is to check the latest with a specialist travel agent (opposite). Flying time from Auckland to Sydney is around three and a half hours.

Ultimately, the price you pay for your flight will depend on how much flexibility you want; many of the cheapest deals are hedged with restrictions – typically a maximum stay of thirty days and an advance-purchase requirement. The cheapest return **fares from Auckland** to Sydney are with Thai Airways (from NZ$470), but these tend to be heavily booked. Qantas and Air New Zealand each have daily direct flights to Sydney (both NZ$680). Flying from **Wellington** or **Christchurch** adds an extra NZ$150–200. Prices peak primarily from December to mid-January.

There's a huge variety of **packages** to Sydney available; call any of the travel agents listed below. The holiday subsidiaries of airlines such as Air New Zealand, Ansett and Qantas package short **city-breaks** (flight and accommodation) and **fly-drive** deals for little more than the cost of the regular airfare.

Airlines and agents

Airlines
Air New Zealand ✆09/357 3000; *www.airnz.co.nz*
Ansett Australia ✆09/796 409; *www.ansett.com.au*
Ansett New Zealand ✆09/302 2146; *www.ansett.com.nz*
Malaysia Airlines ✆09/373 2741; *www.malaysiaairlines.co.my*
Qantas ✆09/357 8900; *www.qantas.com.au*
Thai Airways ✆1300/651 960; *www.thaiair.com*
United Airlines ✆09/379 3800; *www.ual.com*

Specialist travel agents
Budget Travel ✆09/366 0061, free call ✆0800/808 040
Destinations Unlimited ✆09/373 4033
Flight Centre ✆09/309 6171; ✆03/379 7145; ✆04/472 8101
STA Travel ✆09/309 0458; ✆03/379 9098; ✆04/385 0561; *www.statravel.co.nz*
Thomas Cook ✆09/379 3920

Visas and red tape

All visitors to Australia, except New Zealanders, require a visa or Electronic Travel Authority (ETA). **Visa application forms** are obtained from the Australian High Commissions, embassies or consulates listed opposite; citizens of the US can also get them from the embassy Internet sites. **Three-month tourist visas**, valid for multiple entry over one year, are issued free and processed over the counter, or are returned in three weeks by mail. However, the new computerized system, **Electronic Travel Authority (ETA)** can speed things up: passengers give their details to airline or travel agents who transmit them to Australia, with confirmation taking only a few minutes. You must also be flying on a major airline, and travel agents charge to process the visas.

Longer visas, working visas and extensions

Visits from three to six months incur a fee (UK £18; US $33). If you think you might stay more than three months, it's best to get the longer visa before departure, because once you get to Australia **visa extensions** cost A$145. You may also be asked to prove you have adequate funds to support yourself. If you're visiting immediate family who live in Australia apply for a **Close Family Visa**, which has fewer restrictions.

Twelve-month **working holiday visas** – with the stress on casual employment – are easily available to British, Irish, Canadian, Dutch, Japanese and Koreans aged 18–25 (in some cases up to 30). You must arrange the visa before you arrive in Australia; the processing fee is £60 in the UK and CDN$150 in Canada.

Australian Embassies and Consulates

UK Australia House, Strand, London WC2B 4LA; ✆0171/379 4334, fax 240 5333.
IRELAND Fitzwilton House, Wilton Terrace, Dublin 2; ✆01/676 1517, fax 678 5185.
US 1601 Massachusetts Ave NW, Washington, DC 20036; ✆202/797-3000, fax 797-3168; International Building,150 E 42nd St, 34th floor, New York, NY 10117-5612; ✆212/351-6500, fax 351-6501.
CANADA Suite 316, 175 Bloor St E, Toronto, Ontario M4W 3R8; ✆416/323-1155, fax 323-3910.

Customs and quarantine

The duty-free allowance on entry is one litre of alcohol and 250 cigarettes or 250g of tobacco. Australia has strict quarantine laws that apply to fruit, vegetables, fresh and packaged food, seed and some animal products, among other things; expect to be welcomed into the country with the ritual on-board pesticide spray.

VISAS AND RED TAPE

Money, costs and banks

If you've stopped over from Southeast Asia you'll obviously find Australia, with its high Western standard of living, expensive on a day-to-day basis. Fresh from Europe or the US you'll find prices comparable and often cheaper, particularly for accommodation and eating out.

Currency

Australia's currency is the Australian dollar, or "buck", divided into 100 cents and shown on currency tables as AU$. Plastic notes with forgery-proof clear windows come in $100, $50, $20, $10 and $5 denominations, along with $2, $1, 50¢, 20¢, 10¢ and 5¢ coins. **Exchange rates** fluctuate around an over-the-counter rate of AU$2.54 for £1; AU$1.58 for US$1; AU$1.05 for CDN$1. For the most current exchange rates, consult the useful currency converter Web site: *www.oanda.com*

Costs

The absolute minimum daily budget for food, accommodation and transport alone is AU$40 if you stay in a hostel, eat in the cheapest cafés, restaurants and travel by public transport. Add on a minimal social life and you're looking at at least AU$55. Staying in decent hotels, eating at moderate restaurants, and paying for tours and nightlife, double your budget to at least AU$100–150 per day.

Travellers' cheques and plastic

Travellers' cheques are the best way to bring your funds into Australia, as they can be replaced if lost or stolen. Australian dollar travellers' cheques are ideal as theoretically they're valid as cash, though smaller businesses may be unwilling to take them and some banks will still charge to change them. Travellers' cheques in US dollars and pounds sterling can be changed at banks, Bureaux de change and international hotels; banks should be able to handle all major currencies.

Credit cards can come in very handy as a backup source of funds, and they can even save on exchange-rate commissions. Mastercard and Visa are the most widely recognized; you can also use Amex, Bankcard and Diners Club. In addition, with an **international debit card** you may be able to pay for goods via EFTPOS (Electronic Funds Transfer at Point of Sale) and gain direct access to your home funds via **ATM machines** displaying the Cirrus-Maestro symbol.

Banks and exchange

The major banks, with branches countrywide, are Westpac, ANZ and the Commonwealth and National banks; their main branches, all with foreign currency counters, are mostly in the CBD, around Martin Place. **Banking hours** are Monday to Thursday 9.30am to 4pm and Friday 9.30am to 5pm. **Bureaux de change** are found in both the domestic and international airport terminals, and in the city centre; only a few in the city are open on the weekend, and solely the ones at the airport late at night, so try to exchange your currency during weekdays.

Emergency cash can be wired to Western Union, 182 George St, City ✆9241 2372; daily 8.30am–5pm.

MONEY, COSTS AND BANKS

15

Banks and exchange

American Express 92 Pitt St ℭ9239 0666. Mon–Fri
8.30am–5.30pm, Sat 9am–noon. Lost or stolen travellers'
cheques ℭ9271 1111.
ANZ Bank 20 Martin Place ℭ9227 1911.
Commonwealth Bank 48 Martin Place ℭ9378 2000.
National Australia Bank 300 Elizabeth St ℭ9215 6789.
Singapore Money Exchange Shop 10, Eddy Ave, Central
Station ℭ9281 4118. Mon–Sat 9am–7pm, Sun 9am–6pm.
Thomas Cook Ground floor, QVB Building, cnr George and
Druitt streets (no phone). Mon–Wed & Fri 9am–6pm, Thurs
9am–9pm, Sat 9am–4pm, Sun 11am–5pm.
Travelex Australia 37–49 Pitt St ℭ9241 5722. Daily
8am–6.45pm.
Westpac Bank AMP Centre, 50 Bridge St ℭ13 2032.

Opening hours and holidays

OPENING HOURS AND HOLIDAYS

Business and post office hours are generally Monday to
Friday 9am–5pm. Shops and services are generally open
Monday to Saturday 9am to 5pm and until 9pm on
Thursday night. The major retailers and several shopping

malls in the city also open on Sunday between 11am and 5pm, and big supermarkets generally open seven days from 8am until 8 or 9pm, closing around 4pm on Sundays. There are several 24-hour convenience stores/supermarkets in the inner city and suburbs.

Tourist attractions – museums, galleries and historic monuments – are open daily, usually between 10am and 5pm, generally only closing on Christmas Day and Good Friday; specific opening hours are given throughout the Guide.

Public holidays

When an official holiday falls at the weekend, there may be an extra day off immediately before or after. The school holiday dates, when accommodation gets booked up and prices rise are given on p.240.

New Year's Day

Australia Day (January 26 or Monday following)

Good Friday

Easter Monday

Anzac Day (April 25, or if Sat or Sun,
   Monday following)

Queen's Birthday (first Monday in June)

Bank Holiday (first Monday in August)

Labour Day (first Monday in October)

Christmas Day

Boxing Day (Dec 26)

OPENING HOURS AND HOLIDAYS

THE GUIDE

THE GUIDE

Introducing the city

Port Jackson, more commonly known as **Sydney Harbour** carves Sydney in two halves, linked only by the **Sydney Harbour Bridge** and Harbour Tunnel. The **South Shore** is the hub of activity, and it's here that you'll find the **city centre** and most of the things to see and do. Many of the classic images of Sydney are within sight of **Circular Quay**, making this busy waterfront area on Sydney Cove a good point to start discovering the city, with the **Opera House** and the expanse of the Royal Botanic Gardens to the east of Sydney Cove. It's also near the historic area of **The Rocks** to the west, and prominent museums and art galleries. From Circular Quay south as far as King Street is the **Central Business District** (CBD), with pedestrianized Martin Place at its centre. Just east of Martin Place, **Macquarie Street** is Sydney's civic streetscape, lined with fine colonial sandstone buildings including the NSW Parliament House. Beyond Macquarie Street the open space of **The Domain** stretches to the Art Gallery of New South Wales. To the south of the Domain, **Hyde Park** is very much the formal city park, overlooked by churches and the Australian Museum and with a solemn war memorial.

Park Street divides Hyde Park into two; heading west along it you reach the ornate **Town Hall**, around which

Sydney's shopping heart is focused, including the glorious Queen Victoria Building. Watching over it all is the AMP Centrepoint Tower, with 360° views from the top. The city's two main thoroughfares of **George and Pitt streets** stretch downtown to the increasingly down-at-heel **Central Station** and the area known as **Haymarket**, where a vibrant **Chinatown** sits beside the entertainment area of **Darling Harbour** – major museums and attractions around here include the Sydney Aquarium, the Powerhouse Museum, a casino and the fish markets.

East of the city centre, following **William Street** uphill past Hyde Park, is **Kings Cross**, Sydney's red-light district and major travellers' centre, full of accommodation, strip joints and late-night cafés. The adjacent waterfront area of **Woolloomooloo** is home to some lively pubs. North and east of "the Cross" you move gradually upmarket, with the **Eastern suburbs** stretching along the harbour to Watsons Bay, meeting the open sea at **South Head**.

....

**The telephone code for Sydney and all the area
covered in this book is ©02.**

....

Running south from the head are the popular and popu-lous Eastern Beaches, from **Bondi** through **Coogee** to Maroubra ending at **La Perouse** and the expanse of **Botany Bay**. Further southbrings you to surf territory at **Cronulla** and the **Royal National Park** across Port Hacking.

From the southeast corner of Hyde Park, **Oxford Street** steams through the gay, restaurant, club and bar strip of **Darlinghurst**, becoming increasingly upmarket through gentrified **Paddington** which has **Centennial Park** as its playground.

South of Oxford Street, opposite Paddington, **Surry Hills** is another up-and-coming area, with plenty of action on **Crown Street**. The nearby Sydney Cricket Ground and Fox Studios are twin focal points at **Moore Park**. On the western side of Surry Hills is Central Station; and heading west brings you to Sydney University, surrounded by the café-packed and youthful areas of **Newtown** and **Glebe.** West of Glebe, ugly **Parramatta Road** heads to Italian dominated **Leichhardt** and ever westwards to the **Blue Mountains**.

The bushclad **North Shore** of the harbour is very much where the old money is. There are some wonderful spots to reach by ferry, from **Taronga Zoo** to **Manly**. North of Manly the **Northern Beaches** stretch up to glamorous **Palm Beach** which looks across to several national parks, including **Ku-Ring-Gai Chase**. Flowing towards Pittwater and Broken Bay is the sandstone-lined **Hawkesbury River**. North of here, the Central Coast is a weekend beach playground for Sydneysiders, while the **Hunter Valley** is the place for wine tasting.

Arrival

The classic way to arrive in Sydney is, of course, by ship, cruising near the great coathanger of the Harbour Bridge to tie up at the docks alongside Circular Quay. Unfortunately you're not likely to be doing that, and the reality of the functional airport, bus and train stations is a good deal less romantic.

BY AIR

Sydney's **Kingsford Smith Airport**, commonly referred to as "Mascot" after the suburb where it's located, is barely

Airport buses

State Transit

Airport Express buses (℃13 1500). Green-and-yellow buses linking the domestic and international terminals ($2.50), and shuttling to and from the city centre, Kings Cross, Glebe and Bondi on four different routes: #300, #350, #351, #352. Fares are $6 one-way and $10 return (valid two months). Operating daily between 5am and 11pm. Tickets can be bought on board and at the NSW Travel Centre in the international terminal, where you can also buy tourist bus passes – the Sydney Pass (p.26) includes return airport–city transfer.

Shuttle services – Sydney Area

Jetbus (℃0500/886 008). To and from the eastern beaches: Bondi, Coogee, Randwick, etc, $8 one-way.
Kingsford Smith Transport/Sydney Airporter (℃9667 3221). Drop-offs to the door of your hotel or hostel in the area bounded by Kings Cross, Darling Harbour, Glebe and Double Bay. $6 one-way, $11 return.

Northern Beaches and Central Coast

Central Coast Airbus (ring for times ℃4332 8655). Scheduled #747 service to the Central Coast ($18) via the northern suburbs, Ku-Ring-Gai Chase and Berowra.
Northern Beaches Airport Shuttle (℃9913 9912, fax 9970 5248). Service to northern beaches' accommodation – Manly, Whale Beach and Palm Beach. Book in advance giving the day, time and flight and they will designate a waiting point. Manly $20 per person, Palm Beach $30.

8km south of the city (flight arrivals and departures ℃1900/9180, 75¢ per min; Airport Travellers Information ℃9669 111). Domestic and international terminals are on opposite sides of the airport, linked by the free Long-Term Car Park Shuttle Bus (every 30min) or you can take the Airport Express bus for $2.50. See the box opposite for details of **airport buses**. The **Airport Link Underground Railway** is due to open in May 2000, connecting Sydney Airport to the city circle train line. The journey will take just over ten minutes, with a frequency of every seven minutes at peak times. A **taxi** ride from the airport to the city centre or Kings Cross costs $20–25, depending on traffic.

Bureau de change offices at both terminals are open daily from 5am until last arrival, with rates comparable to major banks, and a large, efficient **tourist information centre,** the New South Wales Travel Centre (see p.27), is open the same hours, on the ground floor section of the international terminal. It can do stand-by hotel **accommodation** deals and sells tourist passes which can be used on the Airport Express bus. A range of hostels advertise on an adjacent notice board with free phones for direct reservations. Nearby are a bank of **car hire** stands.

BY TRAIN AND BUS

All local and interstate **trains** arrive at **Central Station** on Eddy Avenue, south of the city centre. From here, and neighbouring **Railway Square** you can hop onto nearly every major bus route, and from within Central Station you can take a CityRail train to any city or suburban station.

All interstate **buses** to Sydney arrive and depart from Eddy Avenue and Pitt Street bordering Central Station. The area is well set-up with decent cafés, a 24-hour police station, a huge YHA hostel, and the **Sydney Coach Terminal**, on the corner of the two (daily

Tourist passes

Tourist bus passes can be bought on board Explorer buses, at the airport, at tourist information offices, State Transit Info booths and railway stations.

Sydney Explorer Pass

The red **Sydney Explorer** (daily 8.15am–5.25pm; every 15min) takes in all the important sights in the city and inner suburbs; you can hop on and off at any of the 24 stops. The blue **Bondi & Bay Explorer** (daily 9.15am–4.20pm; every 25min) covers the waterside eastern suburbs with 19 stops from Kings Cross to Coogee. Choose either service on a one-day **Sydney Explorer Pass** ($25), which comes with a map and description of the sights, and includes free travel on any State Transit bus within the same zones as the Explorer routes. A two-day **Twin Ticket** ($45) allows you to use both bus services over 2 days in a 7-day period.

Sydney Pass

The Sydney Pass is valid for all buses and ferries including the Explorer services, the ferry and JetCat to Manly, the RiverCat to Parramatta and a return trip to the airport valid for two months with the Airport Express bus. It also includes four harbour cruises and travel on trains within a central area. Choose a 3-, 5- or 7-day version to use within a 7-day period for $70, $95 and $110 respectively.

6am–10pm; ✆9281 9366). The terminal has telephones and luggage lockers ($4, $6 or $8 per 24hr). The **Traveller's Information Service** here (✆9669 5111) sells Sydney Passes, arranges harbour cruises and tours, and can make **hotel bookings** at stand-by rates. A range of hostels advertise on an adjacent notice board with free phones for direct reservations; many of them provide free pick-ups.

Information

The **New South Wales Travel Centre** at the international airport terminal (✆9667 6050; daily 5am until last arrival), offers the most comprehensive tourist information service. Staff can arrange car rental and onward travel – it's licensed to sell train and bus tickets – and book hotels (but not hostels) anywhere in Sydney and NSW free of charge. The **accommodation bookings** here are at stand-by rates, so it's possible to get a good deal – but only face to face (no telephone bookings). Most hostels advertise on an adjacent notice board; there's a free phone line for reservations.

The main central tourist office is the **Sydney Visitor Centre** in The Rocks at 106 George St near Circular Quay (daily 9am–6pm; ✆9255 1788; also see p.44), offering a similar range of literature; they have a self-service budget accommodation booking board with free phones directly linked to the listed hotels. Otherwise tourist information is supplied by the **Darling Harbour Visitor Information Centre** (daily 9.30am–5.30pm; ✆9286 0111), next to the IMAX cinema; **Sydney Visitors Information** (Mon–Fri 9am–5pm; ✆9235 2424), a small information kiosk at Martin Place; or the **Manly Visitor Information Centre** (daily 10am–4pm; ✆9977 1088) by the ocean beach, on South Steyne. The City of Sydney Council has introduced the **City Host Programme** with three information kiosks open daily at Circular Quay, Martin Place and Town Hall, with staff providing brochures, maps and information.

For information on Sydney Harbour National Park, the series of bush-covered foreshore lands and islands around the harbour, and other national parks around Sydney, the **National Parks and Wildlife Service** (NPWS) have an information centre and bookshop at Cadman's Cottage, 110 George St, The Rocks (daily 9am–5pm; ✆9247 5033).

Publications and maps

Ask at the tourist offices overleaf for *Sydney: The Official Book of Maps*, a free booklet with excellent maps of Sydney, and the surround, plus a CityRail and ferry plan. The *Sydney Airport Arrivals Guide* is also useful. Several free monthly **listings magazines** are worth picking up at tourist offices: *This Week in Sydney* is probably the best for general information, while *Index* is good for details of cultural activities. Sydney Council publish a useful quality monthly magazine, *The Official Sydney Events Guide* which can be bought at newsagents for $2.95 but is often given away in hotels. To get under the skin of Sydney read Friday's *Sydney Morning Herald* for its "Metro" listings supplement. *TNT Magazine* is the best of an array of publications aimed at **backpackers**, while **hostel notice boards** themselves act as an informal network, advertising everything from cars to camping gear. The National Parks and Wildlife Service produce a very handy detailed free foldout map, *Sydney Harbour National Park,* which provides excellent detail of the harbour, showing all the main sites, ferry routes and bushwalks; pick it up from Cadman's Cottage (see above).

Tours in the city and around

Tours to specific destinations around Sydney are detailed in the relevant chapter.

AAT Kings ©9252 2788. One of the largest operators, its big-group bus tours cover city sights, wildlife parks, the Blue Mountains, Jenolan Caves, the Hawkesbury River and the Hunter Valley. Admissions and hotel pick-ups and drop-offs included.

CityRail ©9217 8812. Day-trips by rail can be very good value, generally covering all transport and entry fees – trips include the Blue Mountains and the Hawkesbury River.

Cycle Tours Australia free call ©1800/353 004. Five-hour guided bike tour of Sydney including the beaches, price ($45) includes bike, equipment and ferry.

National Parks and Wildlife Service (©9247 5033). Offer some great regular tours of the harbour's islands (see p.35) and the Quarantine Station near Manly (p.125), as well as more sporadic bushwalking and special interest tours. Drop in to the information centre at Cadman's Cottage (opposite).

Rocks walking tours ©9247 6678. The 1hr 15min guided walks in the stone streets of The Rocks begins at the former Sailors Home, now tourist office, at 106 George St. Mon–Fri 10.30am, 12.30pm & 2.30pm, Sat & Sun 11.30am & 2pm; $12.

Sydney Aboriginal Discovery Tours ©9566 4816. Tours around Sydney Harbour – bushwalks and cruises – with the local Aboriginal people who run this outfit. Only available to groups.

continues over

Sydney Harbour Seaplanes free call ℂ1800/803 558. A Hollywood-style service but for a group, a fifteen-minute scenic flight becomes affordable at $180 for the whole plane, which takes six, or individuals can go up for $50 per person at scheduled times.

Unseen Sydney Walking Tours ℂ9555 2700. This 1hr 30min night-time ghost tour is well worth the money, led by an entertaining, storyteller with a good sense of humour. The highlight is the final drink in the *Hero of Waterloo*. Tues, Thurs–Sun at 6.30pm, meeting at an appointed place in Circular Quay; $15.

City transport

Sydney's public transport network is reasonably good, though the system relies heavily on buses and traffic jams can be a problem. There are buses, trains, ferries, a light rail system and the city monorail to choose from, plus plenty of taxis. If you're staying for more than a few days, a weekly Travelpass (p.37) is a worthwhile investment.

> **For public transport information, routes and timetables call the Bus, Train, Ferry InfoLine**
> ℂ13 1500. **Daily 6am–10pm.**

BUSES

Within the central area, **buses,** hailed from yellow-signed bus stops, are the most widespread mode of transport. **Tickets**, costing from $1.20 for up to two sections, $2.50 (the most typical fare) for up to nine sections and rising to

Useful bus routes

You should arm yourself with the very useful free **Sydney Buses Network Map** showing all STA bus routes; we have given the bus numbers in the text which you can then consult on the Network Map. You can get the map and other bus **information**, **timetables** and **passes** from these handy booths near CityRail stations and ferry terminals:

Wynyard CityRail, Carrington St. Mon–Fri 8am–6pm, Sat 9am–2pm.

Circular Quay CityRail, cnr of Loftus and Alfred streets. Mon–Fri 8am–8pm, Sat & Sun 9am–6pm.

Town Hall CityRail, outside Queen Victoria Building, York St. Mon–Fri 8am–6pm, Sat 9am–2pm.

Bondi Junction CityRail, bus interchange. Mon–Fri 7.15am–5pm, Sat 7.30am–2.30pm.

Manly Wharf Mon–Fri 7am–6pm, Sat & Sun 8am–4pm.

Bus Routes

With few exceptions buses radiate from the centre: major interchanges are located at Railway Square near Central Station, especially for the southwest routes; at Circular Quay for a range of routes; from York and Carrington streets outside Wynyard Station for the North Shore; and Bondi Junction Station for the Eastern suburbs and beaches. Other important depots are outside the Queen Victoria Building (QVB) on York St, at the corner of Argyle and Kent streets, Millers Point near The Rocks, and outside Milsons Point CityRail, by the northern end of the Harbour Bridge, and at Manly Wharf. There are two west–east bus routes, the #400, from Burwood through to Bondi Junction via the airport and the #370 which runs from Leichhardt to Coogee Beach.

$4.60 according to the distance travelled, can be bought on board from the driver. There are different sections for each bus route, rather than a section being a specific distance, which are explained at the back of the relevant bus time-table. TravelTen tickets and other travel passes (see box p.37) provide substantial discounts; these must be validated in the green ticket reader by the front door.

....

**For details on any of these bus routes,
phone ☎13 1500. Daily 6am–10pm.**

....

TRAINS

Trains are operated by **CityRail** (see colour map no. 1), and speedily cover most of the city but you will need to transfer to a bus or ferry to get to most harbourside or beach destinations. There are five main train lines, each of which stops at Central and Town Hall stations. Trains run from around 5am to midnight, with **tickets** starting at $1.60 on the City Loop underground and for short hops; you can save money by buying off-peak returns after 9am and all weekend.

....

**No excuses will be accepted if you don't have a ticket
or have overridden your fare, with fines at a steep $150.**

....

LATE-NIGHT TRANSPORT

Trains finish around midnight, as do most regular buses, though several bus services running towards the eastern and northern beaches, such as the #380 to Bondi Beach, the #372 and #373 to Coogee and the #151 to Manly, run through the night. Otherwise a pretty good network of **Nightrider buses** follow the train routes to the suburbs, departing from Town Hall Station (outside the Energy Australia building on George Street; map 5, B8). You can use return train tickets, Railpasses and Travelpasses on board the nightbuses or else buy a ticket from the driver. Security guards patrol night-time trains; if the train is deserted at any time, sit in the carriage nearest the guard, marked by a blue light.

STA FERRIES

Sydney's distinctive green-and-yellow **ferries** are the fastest means of transport to most places around the harbour. Even if you don't want to go anywhere, a ferry ride is a must, for it gives you a chance to get out on the water and see the city from the harbour. There's also a **hydrofoil**, the JetCat, which goes to Manly; the speedy catamaran gets you there in half the time, but with less charm.

There are five commuter wharves at Circular Quay (map 5, C3) with ferries going off in various directions from each; cruises depart from Wharf 6. Ferries generally operate until early evening except for the JetCat and ferries to Neutral Bay and Balmain which continue to between 11.30pm and midnight. Except for the Manly Ferry, services on Sunday are greatly reduced and often finish earlier. Timetables for each route are available at Circular Quay.

One-way fares are $3.20 ($4 for the Manly Ferry); return fares are doubled. The JetCat to Manly is $5.20, while the RiverCat to Parramatta is $5. Travelpasses and FerryTen tickets can be a good deal – see box on p.37.

See the colour harbour map on p.10 and the plan on p.34 for at-a-glance ferry routes.

STA FERRIES

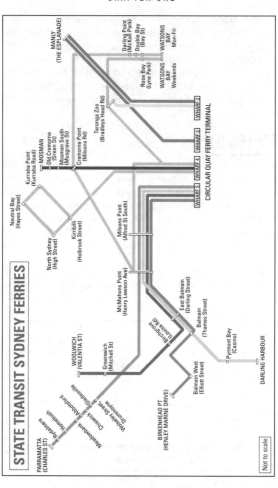

STATE TRANSIT SYDNEY FERRIES

Not to scale

Harbour Cruises

Almost all **harbour cruises** leave from Wharf 6, Circular Quay and some from Darling Harbour. However, apart from the running commentary, most offer nothing that you won't get on a regular harbour **ferry** for a lot less: the best of the ordinary trips is to **Manly**. The **Australian Travel Specialists** at Jetty 2 and 6, Circular Quay, the Harbourside Shopping Centre at Darling Harbour, and Manly Wharf (©9247 5151) book all cruises.

Sydney Harbour Ferry Cruises – run by State Transit – seem to offer the best value: choose between the Morning River Cruise (daily 10am & 11.15am; 1hr; $12), the recommended Afternoon Harbour Cruise to Middle Harbour and back (Mon–Fri 1pm, Sat & Sun 1.30pm; 2hr 30min; $17.50), or the Harbour Lights Cruise in the evening (Mon–Sat 8pm; 1hr 30min; $15).

Captain Cook Cruises at Jetty 6 (©9206 1111) all involve lunch, dinner or morning or afternoon tea; a luncheon cruise will set you back $44. They also have a hop-on, hop-off Sydney Harbour Explorer (9.30am–3.30pm; $20) circuiting between Circular Quay, the Opera House, Watsons Bay, Taronga Zoo and Darling Harbour.

Matilda Cruises, based at the Aquarium Wharf, Darling Harbour (©9264 7377), offer various cruises; all depart from Darling Harbour but pick up from Circular Quay later. Its **Sail Venture** trips are on sailing catamarans: and range from two-hour Coffee or Luncheon Cruises ($24–48), to a four-course Dinner Cruise (7pm; 3hr 30min; $90). Their hop-on hop-off 1hr **Rocket Harbour Express Cruise**, commences from Darling Harbour, stopping at the Opera House, Circular Quay and Taronga Zoo, and whizzing past Watsons Bay for a look (every

continues over

HARBOUR CRUISES

30min 9.30am–4.30pm; $16). The **Matilda Ferry** service shut-
tles between Darling Harbour, the casino and Circular Quay
($3.25).

There are also several more romantic sailing trips to consider.
The Bounty (office at 29 George St, The Rocks; ✆9247
1789), offers outings on a replica of Captain Bligh's ship
made for the film starring Mel Gibson. Embarking at
Campbells Cove for various cruises, most involving food and
entertainment; brunch is cheapest (Sun 10–11.30am; $45).
With **Sydney by Sail** (bookings ✆9552 7561), there are shorter yacht sails on Port Jackson ($49; 1hr 30min) and longer
ones going further into surrounding inlets ($89; 3hr).
Departures, from Darling Harbour's National Maritime
Museum include admission to the museum. **Sail Svanen**
(✆9698 4456), moored at Campbells Cove, with day luncheon
sails on the harbour for $79, or longer overnight sails to
Broken Bay($240).

MONORAIL

The **Monorail** (✆9552 2288) is essentially a tourist
shuttle designed to loop around Darling Harbour every
3–5 minutes, connecting it with the city centre. The
elevated view of the city, particularly from Pyrmont
Bridge, makes it worth investing $2.50 (day-pass $7) and
ten minutes to do the whole circuit with its seven
stops (Mon–Wed 7am–10pm, Thurs–Sat 7am–midnight, Sun 8am–10pm except May–October Thurs
until 10pm).

LIGHT RAIL

The high-tech **Sydney Light Rail** (SLR; ✆9660 5288)
runs from Central Station to the Pyrmont peninsula with

Travelpasses

There's a vast array of commuter **travelpasses** available, sold at most **newsagents** and at **train stations**. The best one for tourists is the weekly **Green Travelpass** (below). Off-peak means Mon–Fri after 9am and any time at weekends and public holidays.

Buses, trains and ferries

Weekly **Travelpasses** buy unlimited use of buses, trains and ferries and can begin on any day of the week. The **Red Travelpass** ($23) is valid for the city and inner suburbs, and inner harbour ferries but not the Manly Ferry or the RiverCat beyond Meadowbank. Better value is the **Green Travelpass** ($29), which allows use of all ferries – except JetCats before 7pm. **DayRover tickets** ($16 off-peak; $20 peak) give unlimited travel on all services offered by CityRail and State Transit.

Buses and trains

Cityhopper tickets give one day's unlimited train and bus travel in the area between Central Station, Darling Harbour, Redfern, Moore Park, Kings Cross and North Sydney for $6.60 (off-peak $5.40).

Buses and ferries

Weekly travelpasses for buses and ferries (starting with first use rather than on the day of purchase) consist of the **Blue Travelpass** ($20), which gives you unlimited travel on buses in the inner-city area and on inner harbour ferries – not Manly or Parramatta; the **Orange Travelpass** ($26), which gets you further on the buses and is valid on all ferries; and the **Pittwater Travelpass** ($37) which gives unlimited travel on all buses and ferries. A **DayPass** provides all-day bus and ferry transport as far afield as you like for $12.

continues over

Buses

TravelTen tickets represent a 45 percent saving over single fares by buying ten trips at once; they can be used over a space of time and for more than one person. The blue version ($8.80) lets you ride up to two sections per validation (Central Station to Circular Quay is one section, for example, and Queen Street Woollahra to Bondi Junction is two), while a Red TravelTen ($17.60) allows you to travel up to nine sections per ride (Leichhardt to Town Hall is five sections). **BusTripper** offers a day's unlimited bus travel for $7.80.

Ferries

FerryTen tickets, valid for ten single trips, start at $19 for Inner Harbour Services, go up to $30 for the Manly Ferry, and peak at $44 for the JetCat services.

Trains

Rail Weekly tickets allow unlimited travel between any two nominated stations, with savings of about 20 percent on the price of five return trips.

ten stops en route, linking Central with Chinatown, Darling Harbour, Star City Casino, Pyrmont's Sydney Fish Market and Wentworth Park. The 24-hour service operates at five- to seven-minute intervals during peak periods and every ten to twelve minutes at other times. Tickets are purchased at vending machines by the stops; Central Station to Convention is Zone One and Pyrmont Bay to Wentworth Park is Zone Two (single Zone One ticket $2, return $3; single Zone Two ticket $3, return $4; day-pass $6; weekly ticket $16). TramLink tickets combine a rail ticket to Central Station with an SLR ticket; price depends on which CityRail station you buy your ticket from.

TAXIS

All taxis are licensed and metered. They are mostly white-coloured cars, sometimes station wagons. You can flag them down in the street when their rooftop light is on or book them over the telephone. Drivers do not expect tips and often need directions. Taxicompanies include ABC ℭ13 2522; De-Luxe ℭ9361 8222; Legion ℭ13 1451; Premier ℭ13 1017; RSL ℭ13 1581; and Taxis Combined Services ℭ9332 8888. You can catch a pricey but fun **water taxi** from the pier at Campbells Cove, The Rocks (map 5, C2), or book one to pick you up at any wharf or pier with Taxis Afloat ℭ9955 3222.

Harbour Bridge and The Rocks

The Rocks, immediately beneath the Sydney Harbour Bridge, is the heart of historic Sydney. On this rocky outcrop between Sydney Cove and Walsh Bay, Captain Arthur Phillip proclaimed the establishment of Sydney Town in 1788, the first permanent European settlement in Australia. Within decades, however, the area had become little more than a slum of dingy dwellings, narrow alleys and dubious taverns and brothels. In the 1830s and 1840s, merchants began building fine stone warehouses here, but as the focus for Sydney's shipping moved to Woolloomooloo, the area again fell into decline. By the 1870s and 1880s, the notorious Rocks "pushes", gangs of "larrikins" (louts), mugged passers-by when they weren't beating each other up. The narrow street named Suez Canal (map 5, C3) was a favourite place to jump out from. Some say the name is a shortening of Sewers' Canal, and indeed the area was so filthy and rat-ridden that whole streetfronts had to be torn down in 1900 to contain an outbreak of bubonic plague.

The Rocks remained a run-down, depressed and depress-

Rocks information and tours

The best place to start your **tour** of The Rocks is the **Sailors' Home**, at 106 George St (daily 9am–6pm; map 5, C2); built in 1864 to provide decent lodgings for visiting sailors as an alternative to the area's brothels and inns. The building housed sailors until the early 1980s but is now the **Sydney Visitor Centre** supplying tourist information about the history and sights of The Rocks along with a re-creation of the sailors' sleeping quarters; pick up a guided tour leaflet or arrange to go on a guided walking tour (see p.29).

The small sandstone house next to the information centre, at 110 George St, is **Cadman's Cottage** (map 5, C3), the oldest private house still standing in Sydney, built in 1816 for John Cadman, ex-convict and Government coxswain. It's now the **National Parks and Wildlife Service** bookshop and information centre (daily 9am–5pm).

ing quarter until the 1970s, when there were plans to raze the remaining cottages, terraces and warehouses to make way for office blocks. However, due to the foresight of a radical building workers' union which opposed the demolition, the restored and renovated historic quarter is now one of Sydney's major tourist attractions. Despite a passing resemblance to a historic theme park, it's worth exploring.

There are times when the old atmosphere still seems to prevail: Friday and Saturday nights can be thoroughly drunken – so much so that there's a prominent police station and officers patrolling on horseback. New Year's Eve is also riotously celebrated here, as fireworks explode over the harbour.

**The area covered in this chapter
is shown on colour map 5.**

THE SYDNEY HARBOUR BRIDGE

Map 5, C1 & map 10, C5 Lookout point daily 10am–5pm; $2; 5min walk from Cumberland St then 200 steps. Circular Quay CityRail or ferry.

The awe-inspiring **Sydney Harbour Bridge** has spanned the water dividing north and south Sydney since 1932. It's hard to imagine the view of the harbour without the castle-like sandstone pylons anchoring the bridge to the shore and the crisscross of steel arch against the sky. At 503m, it was the longest single span arch bridge in the world when it was built. As the NSW Premier, J.T. Lang, of the Labor party, prepared to cut the ribbon, further excitement was provided by the dashing horseman and Royalist fanatic, Francis de Groot, who galloped up like a cavalryman and cut the opening ribbon with a saber declaring "I open this bridge in the name of the Majesty the King and all the decent citizens of NSW" in protest at Lang's Socialist leanings.

Residents of the north of England might find the bridge familiar: the much tinier Tyne Bridge in Newcastle-upon-Tyne, built in 1929, was the model for Sydney Harbour Bridge. Construction costs for the altogether huger Sydney project weren't paid off until 1988, and there's still a $2 toll to drive across, though, payable only when heading south; you can walk or cycle it for free. Pedestrians should head up the steps to the bridge from Cumberland Street (map 5, B3), reached from The Rocks via the Argyle Steps off Argyle Street (map 5, B3), and walk on the eastern side (the western side is the preserve of cyclists).

The bridge demands full-time maintenance, protected from rust by continuous painting in trademark steel-grey. One of Australia's best-known comedians, Paul Hogan of *Crocodile Dundee* fame, worked as a rigger on "the coathanger" before being rescued by a New Faces talent quest in the 1970s. To check out Hoge's vista, you can now

Climbing the bridge

Bridge Climb take small, specially equipped groups (max 10) to the top of the bridge (℡9240 1111; tours every 10–20min 7.45am–3.05pm extended to 4.25pm during Daylight Savings; over 12s only; special night-time tours available; $98). Though the experience takes three hours, only two hours is spent on the bridge, gradually ascending and pausing while the guide points out landmarks and offers interesting background snippets. The hour spent checking in and getting kitted up at the "Base" at 5 Cumberland St, The Rocks (map 5, C2), makes you feel as if you're preparing to go into outer space, as do the grey *Star Trek*-style suits specially designed so that you blend in with the bridge – no colourful crawling ants to spoil ground-level views. It's really not as scary as it looks – there's no way you can fall off, fully harnessed as you are, and this can calm a normal fear of heights. The only thing you're allowed to take up are your glasses, attached to your suit by special cords – everything from handkerchiefs to caps are provided and similarly attached. This precaution also means you can't take your camera with you. You do get one group photo on top of the bridge (free with the price of the climb), but the group – of jolly strangers, arms akimbo – crowds out the panoramic background. To get a good shot showing yourself with the splendours of the harbour behind, you'll need to fork out from $12.95 to $24.95 extra.

follow a rigger's route and climb the bridge without getting arrested – once the favoured illegal occupation of drunken uni students. If you can't stomach (or afford) the climb, there's a **lookout point** actually inside the bridge's southern pylon where, as well as gazing out across the harbour, you can study a photo exhibition on the bridge's history.

THE ROCKS

Just exploring the narrow alleys and streets hewn out of the original rocky spur is the chief delight of **The Rocks**, a voyage of discovery that involves climbing and descending several stairs and cuts to different levels. Down the steps from the Sydney Visitor Centre a stroll north along Circular Quay West brings you to **Campbells Cove** (map 5, C2), where **Campbell's Storehouses** is fairly representative of The Rocks' focus on eating and shopping for souvenirs, clothing and arts and crafts in beautifully restored sandstone warehouses, once part of the private wharf of the merchant Robert Campbell, built in 1839 to hold everything from tea to liquor. A replica of Captain Bligh's ship, the *Bounty*, is moored here between cruises (see p.36), adding a Disneyish atmosphere, while a luxury hotel, the *Park Hyatt*, overlooks the whole area. Going past the hotel to Dawes Point Park under the Harbour Bridge brings you to **Dawes Point** (map 5, C1), a favourite spot for photographers, separating Sydney Cove, on the Circular Quay side, from Walsh Bay and several old piers, one of which houses the wonderfully sited Wharf Theatre (see p.221; map 5, B1). Heading back to Campbells Cove, you can climb the Customs Officer's Stairs to Hickson Road where you can browse in the **Metcalfe Stores** (map 5, C2), another warehouse-turned-shopping complex, this time dating from around 1912. Exit from the old bond stores onto George Street, where at weekends you can further satisfy your shopping urge at the shaded **Rocks Market** (see p.263), which takes over the Harbour Bridge end of the street with more than a hundred stalls selling everything from Australiana to antiques.

There's more shopping at the **Argyle Stores** (map 5, C3), on the corner of Argyle and Playfair streets, a complex of decidedly more tasteful and upmarket boutiques in a beautifully restored set of former bond stores arranged around an inner courtyard; on the top floor you can take in great views from the bar of *bel mondo* (see p.171), also accessed from Gloucester Walk. The Argyle Stores is just near the impressive **Argyle Cut** (map 5, B3), which slices through solid stone to the more residential area of **Millers Point**. The Cut took eighteen years to complete, carved first with chisel and hammer by convict chain gangs who began the work in 1843; when transportation ended ten years later the tunnel was still unfinished, and it took hired hands to complete it in 1859. Up the **Argyle Steps** and along the narrow brick pedestrian walkway of peaceful **Gloucester Walk** takes you to the tiny **Foundation Park**. It's quite a delight to stumble across – remains of cottage foundations discovered in architectural digs have formed the basis for an arrangement of sculptural installations representing Victorian furniture. You can follow Gloucester Walk back to the northern end of George Street for a drink at *The Mercantile*, one of Sydney's best Irish watering holes. Gloucester Walk also leads to the pedestrian entrance of the Harbour Bridge on **Cumberland Street**, the location of a couple of classic old boozers, the *Glenmore* and the *Australian*.

....

**For these, and more pub favourites
in The Rocks, see p.194.**

....

From the latter, head down **Gloucester Street**; at nos. 58–64 is the **Susannah Place Museum** (Sat & Sun only 10am–5pm; $6; map 5, B3), a row of four brick terraces built in 1844 and continuously occupied by householders until 1990; it's now a "house museum" (including a re-created corner store) which traces the domestic history of Sydney's working class.

THE ROCKS

45

MILLERS POINT

Looking west towards Darling Harbour, mostly residential **Millers Point** is a reminder of how The Rocks used to be – many of the homes are still government or housing association-owned and there's a surprisingly real community feel so close to the tourist hype. Of course, the area has its upmarket pockets, like the very swish *Observatory Hotel* on Kent Street, but for the moment, the traditional street-corner pubs and shabby terraced houses on the hill are reminiscent of the raffish atmosphere once typical of the whole area, and the peaceful leafy streets are a delight to wander in.

You can reach the area through the Argyle Cut or from the end of George Street, heading onto **Lower Fort Street**. The **Colonial House Museum**, at no. 53 (daily 10am–5pm; $1; map 5, B2), takes up most of a residential 1883 terrace house where local character Shirley Ball has lived for over fifty years; her collection is crammed into six rooms, and includes period furnishings, hundreds of photographs of the area, etchings, artefacts and models. If you continue to wander up Lower Fort Street don't pass up the opportunity to have a bevvy in the **Hero of Waterloo** at no. 81 (map 5, B2), built from sandstone excavated from the Argyle Cut in 1844, then peek in at the place of worship for the military stationed at Dawes Point fort from the 1840s, the **Garrison** (or Holy Trinity Church, as it's officially called; daily 9am–5pm; map 5, B2) on the corner of Argyle Street. Next to the church, the volunteer-run **Garrison Gallery Museum** (Tues, Wed, Fri & Sat 11am–3pm, Sun noon–4pm; free) is housed in what was the parish schoolhouse. Australia's first Prime Minister, Edmund Barton, was educated here and the collection of photographs, complete with images of ragged barefoot children and muddy dirt roads gives a good indication of the conditions of his tutelage. Near the church, Argyle Place has some of the area's prettiest terrace houses.

OBSERVATORY PARK

Map 5, B3. Circular Quay CityRail or ferry.

Opposite the Garrison church, climb up the steps on Argyle Street to **Observatory Park** with its shady Moreton Bay figs, park benches and lawns, for a marvellous hilltop view over the architecture below and the whole harbour in all its different aspects – glitzy Darling Harbour, the new Glebe Island Bridge in one direction and the old Harbour Bridge in the other, gritty container terminals, ferries gliding by – and on a rainy day enjoy it from the bandstand which dominates the park. It's also easy to reach the park from the Bridge Stairs off Cumberland Street by the Argyle Cut.

Also in the park is the **National Trust Centre**, located in a former military hospital (1815), with a café (Tues–Fri 11am–3pm, Sat & Sun 1–5pm), and a specialist bookshop (Tues–Fri 9am–5pm, Sat & Sun noon–5pm) where you can pick up leaflets about other historic buildings and settlements in New South Wales. The rear of the building houses the **S.H. Ervin Gallery** (Tues–Fri 11am–5pm, Sat & Sun noon–5pm; free), the result of a 1978 bequest of a million dollars to devote to Australian art; changing thematic exhibitions are of scholarly non-mainstream art, focusing on subjects such as Aboriginal or women artists.

The Observatory

Map 5, B3. Museum and gardens daily 10am–5pm; free. Nighttime telescope viewings, times vary seasonally; 2hr; booking essential, usually up to a week in advance, on ☏9217 0485; 2hr; $8.

The Italianate-style **Observatory** from which the park takes its name marked the beginning of an accurate time standard for the city when it opened in 1858, calculating the correct time from the stars and signalling it to ships in the harbour and Martin Place's GPO by the dropping of a time ball in its tower at 1pm every day. Set amongst some very pretty gardens, the Observatory has been a **museum of astronomy** (daily 10am–5pm; $5) since 1982 and the excellent, modern museum is well worth a visit. A large section is devoted to the **Transit of Venus**, the rare astronomical event (about twice every century), which prompted Captain Cook's 1769 voyage of exploration, during which time he charted Australia's east coast. The extensive exhibition of astronomical equipment, both archaic and high-tech, includes the still working telescope installed under the copper dome to observe the 1874 Transit of Venus. Another highlight, in the "Stars of the Southern Sky" section are animated videos of Aboriginal creation stories. Every evening you can view the southern sky through telescopes and learn about the Southern Cross and other southern constellations (there's also a small planetarium which is only used during night visits when the sky is not clear enough for observation).

Around the Opera House

At the southern end of Sydney Cove, sandwiched between Sydney's first settlement, The Rocks, and its modern emblem, the Opera House, **Circular Quay** is the launching pad for harbour and river ferries and sightseeing cruises. Less attractively, it's also the terminal for buses from the eastern and southern suburbs, and a major suburban train station to boot, with the ugly 1970s Cahill Expressway also spoiling the views. Always bustling with commuters during the week, "The Quay", as the locals call it, is crammed with people simply out to enjoy themselves at the weekend. Restaurants, cafés and fast-food outlets stay open until late and buskers entertain the crowds, while vendors of newspapers and trinkets add to the general hubbub. It's a popular stroll from the Quay to the Opera House and the Royal Botanic Gardens (see p.53) just beyond, licking an ice cream or stopping for some oysters and a beer at a waterfront bar. The sun reflecting on the water and its heave and splash as the ferries come and go make for a romantic setting. All the necessities for a picnic in the Botanic Gardens, including bubbly andfresh prawns, can be purchased at the Quay.

**The area covered in this chapter is shown
on colour map 5.**

Besides ferries, Circular Quay still acts as a passenger terminal for ocean liners, though it's been a long time since the crowds waved their hankies regularly from the **Sydney Cove Passenger Terminal**, looking for all the world like the deck of a ship itself. To reach it, head past the **Museum of Contemporary Art** to Circular Quay West; take the escalator and the flight of stairs up for excellent views of the harbour. The rest of the terminal is now given over to swanky restaurants.

Behind the quay on **Alfred Street**, you can check out contemporary craft and Aboriginal culture in the recently renovated **Customs House** or peruse the exhibits at the nearby **Justice and Police Museum**.

See p.35 for a selection of cool cruises starting from
Circular Quay.

Writers' Walk

For intellectual stimulation, you need only look beneath your feet as you stroll along Circular Quay: the inscribed bronze pavement plaques of **Writers' Walk** provide an introduction to the Australian literary canon. There are short biographies of writers ranging from Miles Franklin, author of *My Brilliant Career*, Booker Prize winner Peter Carey and Noble Prize awardee Patrick White, to the feminist Germaine Greer, as well asquotable quotes on what it means to be Australian. Notable literati who've visited Australia also feature: Joseph Conrad, Charles Darwin and Mark Twain.

THE SYDNEY OPERA HOUSE

Map 5, E2. Guided tours daily 9am–4pm, every 30–40min; 1hr; $9; tickets from the Lower Concourse. Circular Quay CityRail or ferry.

The **Sydney Opera House**, such an icon of Australiana that it almost seems kitsch, is just a short stroll from Circular Quay, by the water's edge on Bennelong Point. It's best seen in profile, when its high white roofs, at the same time evocative of full sails and white shells, give the building an almost ethereal quality. Despite its familiarity, or perhaps precisely because you already feel you know it so well, it's quite breathtaking at first sight. The shimmering effect is created by thousands of white tiles carefully fitted together to cover the sails: much like bathroom tiles, they need frequent regrouting to keep the building waterproof. Inside the shell is a large Concert Hall (seating 2690), used for symphony concerts, chamber music, opera and dance, a smaller Opera Theatre for opera, ballet and dance, and two theatres, the Drama Theatre and the Playhouse, plus restaurants, bars, a cinema, an Aboriginal artists' gallery and a library.

For information on performances at the Opera House see p.218.

Now almost universally loved and admired, it's hard to believe quite how controversial a project this was during its long haul from plan, as a result of an international competition in the late 1950s, to completion in 1973. The building's twenty-fifth birthday was recently celebrated with free concerts and the announcement of a $66 million ten-year plan to renew and modify the interior, refocusing media attention on past mistakes. For sixteen years, construction was plagued by quarrels and scandal, so much so that the Danish architect, **Jørn Utzon**, who won the competition,

THE OPERA HOUSE

51

was forced to resign in 1966 after nine years of working on the project. Some say he was hounded out of the country by politicians and xenophobic architects. Seven years and three Australian architects later the interior was finished, but it has always been felt to be acoustically – and aesthetically – imperfect even though the final price tag was

"The Toaster"

The latest controversy to surround the Opera House has been the ugly **East Circular Quay apartments** erected alongside it, obscuring one of the world's great buildings, spoiling a wonderful view, and depriving some very majestic Moreton Bay figs their sunlight in the adjoining Botanical Gardens. Dubbed **"the toaster"** by locals, and described by Robert Hughes, the expat Australian art critic and historian, author of *The Fatal Shore*, as "that dull brash, intrusive apartment block which now obscures the Opera House from three directions", no one can understand how the building, universally considered an eyesore, was approved by Sydney Council.

Despite huge public protests before and during construction work still went ahead. The public temper towards the project is seen clearly in the letters pages of the *Sydney Morning Herald*, where it is a constant *bête noire*. So hated are the apartments that there have been calls for the Prime Minister to dip into the Federation Fund, amassed for the 2001 celebrations of a century of Federation, to buy and demolish the building. The price of destruction would be high: the Sydney Lord Mayor, Frank Sartor, estimates it would cost $400 million to purchase and pull down the building. It has cost developers $200 million to build the 237-unit complex and apartments have been selling with prices ranging from $2.2 to $5.55 million. The loathed building will have bars and restaurants and even a cinema to attract public goodwill.

$102 million − well over ten times the original estimate. Utzon, was invited, either in a gesture of goodwill, or as a sincere attempt to finally realize his full design, by the NSW Premier to be the principal consultant on the interior modification, which would have given him the final authority for all design decisions. However, the offer came too late: Utzon, in his eighties and living in Mallorca, was reluctant to travel and declined the invitation.

The building is particularly stunning when floodlit and, once you're inside, the huge windows come into their own as the dark harbour waters reflect a lustrous image of the night-time city − interval drinks certainly aren't like this anywhere else.

On Sunday afternoons there are always free outdoor concerts on one of the forecourts, ranging through jazz, classical, folk and rock (✆9250 7111 for details, or pick up the *Sydney Opera House Diary* from tourist offices); Sundays are further enlivened by the **Tarpeian Markets** (10am–4pm) in the forecourt with an emphasis on crafts.

THE ROYAL BOTANIC GARDENS

Map 5, E5. Daily 7am–sunset; free. Guided tours daily 10.30am; 1hr–1hr 30min. Circular Quay or Martin Place CityRail.

The **Royal Botanic Gardens**, established in 1816, occupying a huge waterfront area east of Circular Quay, is sandwiched between the Opera House and The Domain. Around the headland from Bennelong Point, Farm Cove was where the first white settlers struggled to grow vegetables for the hungry colony. Today's cultivation is a bit more diverse than a few spuds and there are examples of trees and plants from all over the world, although it's the huge, gnarled native **Moreton Bay figs** that stand out. The gardens provide some of the most stunning **views** of Sydney Harbour and are always crowded with workers at lunchtime, picnickers on fine weekends, and lovers beneath the trees or in the popular café/restaurant. Dusk brings fruit bats flying overhead in noisy groups and the odd rioting posse of possums.

Many **paths** run through the gardens. A popular and speedy route is to start at the northern gates near the Opera House and stroll along the waterfront path to the gates which separate it from The Domain, through here and up the **Fleet Steps** to Mrs Macquaries Chair (see p.72). In the north of the park, the original residence of the governor of NSW can be visited, and nearby you can listen to lunchtime recitals at the Conservatorium. Below the music school, the remaining southern area of the gardens has a Herb Garden, a cooling Palm Grove established in the 1860s, a popular café by the duckponds, and the **Sydney Tropical Centre** (daily 10am–4pm; $5; map 5, E5) – a striking glass pyramid and adjacent glass arc respectively housing native tropical plants and exotics.

At the southeast entrance, off Mrs Macquarie's Road, free **guided tours** of the gardens commence from the **visitors centre** (daily 9.30am–4.30pm).

Government House and the Conservatorium

Government House: interior Fri–Sun 10am–3pm; free guided tour 45min; grounds daily 10am–4pm.

Within the northern boundaries of the park, the sandstone mansion glimpsed through a garden and enclosure is the Gothic Revival-style **Government House** (built 1837–45; map 5, E3), seat of the governor of New South Wales, and still used for official engagements by the governor who now lives in a private residence. The stately interior has limited opening hours but you are free to roam the grounds.

Further south of Government House, just inside the gardens at the end of Bridge Street, the **Conservatorium of**

Music (map 5, E4) is housed, with modern additions, in what was intended to be the servants' quarters and stables of Government House. Public opinion in 1821, however, said the imposing castellated building was far too grand for such a purpose and a complete conversion, including the addition of a concert hall, gave it a loftier aim of training the colony's future musicians. Conservatorium students have traditionally given free lunchtime recitals every Tuesday and Friday at 1.10pm during term time.

CUSTOMS HOUSE

Map 5, C4. Circular Quay CityRail or ferry.

Alfred Street, immediately opposite Circular Quay, has the architectural gem, the sandstone and granite **Customs House**. First constructed in 1845 and redesigned in 1885 by the colonial architect James Barnet, to give its current Classical Revival-style facade, the building was neglected for many years. However, over $20 million was spent on refurbishing the exterior and completely transforming the interior, allowing it to recentlyreopen as a wonderfully varied cultural centre.

The **Djamu Gallery** on level 3 (daily 9.30am–5.30pm; $8 includes admission to the Australian Museum see p.66) is an extension of the Australian Museum, providing the space to finally do justice to its vast collection of indigenous and Pacific Island cultural material. Four rooms show separate themed exhibitions, which last for three to four months, stressing the cultural heritage of the indigenous people of Australia and surrounding regions such as New Zealand and the Torres Strait Islands, and introducing new artists to the public. The shows are provocative, and don't shy away from political and personal issues. The level is shared with **Balarinji Australia**, the indigenous design studio whose work famously enlivens several Qantas and British Airways 747s.

CUSTOMS HOUSE

The Centre for Contemporary Craft has its exhibition gallery **Object Galleries** on level 3 (Tues–Sun 10am–5pm; free), displaying themed groupings and single shows of Australia's best artisans. On the ground floor, the Centre's retail outlet, **Object Stores**, sells beautifully designed glass, ceramics, woodwork and jewellery, all labelled with the artisan and state of origin. On the fourth floor, the **City Exhibition Space** (daily 9am–5pm; free) keeps pace with the sometimes bewildering development of Sydney with a full scale up-to-the-minute model of the city and a multi-media display following Sydney from its inception to the 1930s.

....

The Customs House is well-provided with eateries too: on the fifth floor, a contemporary brasserie *Section 51*, comes with wonderful views; on the ground floor, take a coffee at *Caffe Bianchi*; or eat oysters and have a beer at *Quay Bar*, which has alfresco seating on the newly landscaped Customs House Square out front.

....

JUSTICE AND POLICE MUSEUM

Map 5, D4. Jan Sat–Thurs 10am–5pm, Feb–Dec Sat & Sun 10am–5pm; $6. Circular Quay CityRail or ferry.

A block east of the Customs House, on the corner of Phillip Street, the **Justice and Police Museum** is housed in the former Water Police station, an 1858 sandstone building decorated with some particularly fine ironwork. The crime displays, including some truly macabre death masks, violent weapons and other souvenirs of Sydney's murky past, are all shown within the context of a late nineteenth-century police station and court mock-up. There's also a creative line in themed exhibitions from underworld tattoos to protest movements.

MUSEUM OF CONTEMPORARY ART

Map 5, C3. Daily 10am–6pm; $9 all-day ticket; free tours daily 11am & 2pm. Circular Quay CityRail or ferry.

The **Museum of Contemporary Art** (MCA) on Circular Quay West, with another entrance on George Street (no. 140), is one of the city's most exciting museums. Developing out of a bequest to Sydney University by the art collector John Power in the 1940s, the growing collection finally found a permanent home in 1991 in the former Maritime Services Building. The striking Art-Deco-style 1950s building is now a temple to international twentieth-century art, with an eclectic approach encompassing lithographs, sculpture, film, video, drawings and paintings ranging from Andy Warhol to Aboriginal art. The MCA also has an inventive line in exhibitions, on topics such as contemporary Japanese art, popular culture in the 1950s, or simply television. Its superbly sited, if expensive, café has outdoor tables overlooking the waterfront, and the well-stocked bookshop is worth a browse. A programme of Sunday events range from concerts to readings by leading Australian authors.

The city centre

From Circular Quay to as far south as King Street is Sydney's **Central Business District**, often referred to as the CBD with Martin Place as its commercial nerve centre, and the Museum of Sydney as its most compelling attraction. Stretching south of here to the Town Hall – with George and Pitt streets being the main thoroughfares – is a shopaholics oasis, where you'll find all the department stores and several shopping malls, including the celebrated Queen Victoria Building. The lavish State Theatre and the decorative Town Hall are also worth a peek, and overlooking it all, with supreme views of the city, is the AMP Centrepoint Tower. The short stretch between the Town Hall and Liverpool Street is for the most part teenage territory, a frenetic zone of multiscreen cinemas, pinball halls and fast-food joints. This stretch is trouble-prone on Friday and Saturday nights when there are pleasanter places to choose to catch a film. Things change pace at Liverpool Street, where Sydney's Spanish corner (map 5, B8) consists basically of a clutch of Spanish restaurants and a Spanish Club. George Street becomes increasingly downmarket as it heads to Central Station – but along the way you'll pass Chinatown and Paddy's Market in the area known as Haymarket (see p.75), and just beyond is Darling Harbour (see p.76).

Just east of Martin Place, the southern end of **Macquarie**

Street is lined with the grand edifices that were the result of Governor Macquarie's dreams for a stately city: the State Library, State Parliament House, Sydney Hospital, the former Royal Mint and Hyde Park Barracks. Macquarie Street neatly divides business from pleasure, separating the office towers and cramped streets of the CBD from the open spaces of **The Domain**, directly behind the strip of historic buildings; it runs down alongside the Royal Botanic Gardens (see p.53) to **Mrs Macquaries Point** for sublime views of the harbour; in The Domain you'll also find the **Art Gallery of NSW** and a wonderful outdoor pool. At the southern end of Macquarie Street, **Hyde Park** was fenced off by Governor Macquarie in 1810 to mark the outskirts of his township, and with its war memorials, surrounding churches, and peripheral **Australian Museum**, is still very much a formal city park.

The area covered by this chapter is shown
in detail on colour map 5.

THE CBD

As you stroll from Circular Quay to the open space of Martin Place, the cramped streets of the CBD, overshadowed by high-rise office buildings, have little to offer. However, for some impression of the commerce going on here, stroll past the **Australian Stock Exchange**, opposite Australia Square at 20 Bond St (map 5, C4), and join the throng gazing intently at the computerized display of stocks and shares through the glass of the ground floor. For an idea of how all this wealth might be spent, check out Sydney's most exclusive shopping centre, **Chifley Plaza** (map 5, C5), on the corner of Hunter and Phillip streets; a huge stencil-like sculpture of former Australian Prime Minister

THE CBD

Ben Chifley, by artist Simeon Nelson, was recently installed in the pleasant palm-filled square outside.

Martin Place (map 5, C5), a pedestrian mall stretching five blocks between George and Macquarie streets, with its own underground rail station, is lined with imposing banks and investment companies; check out the splendid marbled interior of the National Australia Bank. The mall has its less serious moments in summer lunchtimes, when street performances are held at the little amphitheatre, and all year round stalls of flower-and-fruit-sellers add some colour. The vast **General Post Office** broods over the George Street end of Martin Place in all its Victorian-era pomp; the upper floors are being developed into yet another luxury hotel; the post office will remain on the ground floor, along with a whole new selection of bars, cafés and restaurants. The other end of Martin Place emerges opposite the old civic buildings on lower Macquarie Street (see p.68).

Museum of Sydney

Map 5, D4. Daily 9.30am–5pm; $6. Circular Quay or Martin Place CityRail.

North of Martin Place, on the corner of Bridge and Phillip streets, is the **Museum of Sydney**. The site itself is the reason for the museum's existence, for here from 1983 a ten-year archeological dig unearthed the foundations of the first Government House built by Governor Phillip in 1788 and home to eight subsequent governors of NSW before it was demolished in 1846. The museum presents history in an interactive manner, through exhibitions, film, photography and multimedia. The permanent exhibition is all very evocative and thought-provoking but you come away from it feeling less well-informed than you expected. A key feature are the special exhibitions, about four each year, which make for a fuller experience; these range in subject from

Sydney's Art Deco architecture to exhibitions of Aboriginal art, and it's worth finding out if the museum is between special shows before you go.

First Government Place, a public square in front of the museum, preserves the site of the original Government House: most of its foundations are marked out on the pavement. The museum itself is built of honey-coloured sandstone blocks, using sandstone tooling representative of the earliest days of the colony right up to modern times – you can trace the stylistic development from bottom to top. Near the entrance, **Edge of the Trees**, an emotive sculptural installation which was a collaboration between a European and an Aboriginal artist, conveys the complexity of a shared history. You can walk among the massive pillars – some inscribed with the names and words of those who arrived with the First Fleet in 1788 or Eora people, others with glass panels through which you can see human hair, ash, feathers or other organic matter suggesting the physical traces of the past – and listen to the haunting, evocative sounds of Eora speech. Entering the museum, you hear a dramatized dialogue between the Eora woman Patyegarang and the First Fleeter Lieutenant Dawes, which gives a strong impression of two cultures meeting and misunderstanding each other. Beneath your feet you can see, through perspex, some of the excavated foundations of Government House.

If you decide to pay to get into the rest of the museum, it's best to go upstairs to the **auditorium** on level 2 and watch the fifteen-minute video on the museum first. Back on level 1 a video screen extends up through all three levels, showing images of the bush, sea and sandstone Sydney as it was before the arrival of Europeans; elsewhere in the museum other exhibits, such as benches with inlays of spotted gum, are evocative of the bush. On level 2, recordings of Sydney Kooris (Aboriginal people) combine with video images to evoke a picture of these people. The **Collectors Chests** allow you to really familiarize yourself with history, as you can slide open the glass and steel drawers to examine various fragments found during the archeological dig here and at various sites in The Rocks, including clay pipes in the shape of skulls, Aboriginal artefacts, bone dominoes, coins and ceramic doll parts. The dark and creepy **Bond Store** on level 3 is the storytelling part of the museum, where holographic "ghosts" relate tales of old Sydney as an ocean port. On the same level, a whole area is devoted to some rather wonderful chronological **panoramas** of Sydney Harbour with views of the harbour itself from the windows.

The museum also contains an excellent **gift shop** with a wide range of photos, artworks and books on Sydney.

....

Near the museum is the expensive, licensed *MOS* café, on First Government Place; usually filled with executives at lunchtime, it's agreeably peaceful for a coffee at other times.

....

KING TO PARK STREET

The rectangle between Elizabeth, King, George and Park streets is Sydney's prime shopping territory, with a number of beautifully restored Victorian arcades and Sydney's two department stores. For more on shopping in this area see p.248.

AMP Centrepoint Tower

Map 5, C6. Daily 9am–10.30pm, Sat until 11.30pm; viewing gallery $10. Town Hall CityRail; Park Plaza Monorail.

The landmark **AMP Centrepoint Tower**, a giant golden

gearstick thrusting up 305m (entrance from **Pitt Street Mall**), is the tallest poppy in the Sydney skyline, recently sponsored by Australian Mutual Providence (AMP), a building society. Its observation level is the highest in the entire southern hemisphere, though management must ruefully admit the tower's height is just beaten by the spire of the Sky Tower in Auckland. The twelve- to sixteen-metre-high steel Olympic sculptures on top of the tower, colourfully lit up at night, were dramatically put in place by helicopter in July 1998 and will remain there until the end of November 2000. Meanwhile a giant clock counts down the days until the big event, while an electronic message panel, facing west in the direction of the Olympic village, Homebush, blats out Olympic info and details of city events. The 360° view from the observation level is especially fine at sunset, and on clear days you can even see the Blue Mountains, 100km away.

....

Another way to enjoy the all-round view of Sydney – without moving, much – is from the revolving restaurants in the AMP. See p.173.

....

State Theatre

Map 5, C6. For tours ✆9373 6655. Town Hall CityRail.
Near the Centrepoint Tower the restored **State Theatre** on Market Street provides a pointed contrast. Step inside and take a look at the ornate and glorious interior of this picture palace opened in 1929 – a lavishly painted, gilded and sculpted corridor leads to the lush, red and wood-panelled foyer. To see more – decorations include crystal chandeliers in the dress circle – you'll need to attend a concert or a play, or even the Sydney Film Festival (see p.224–5) held here in June.

STATE THEATRE

Queen Victoria Building

Map 5, B7. Shopping Mon–Sat 9am–6pm, Thurs until 9pm, Sun 11am–5pm; building open 24hr. Guided tour from the tour desk on the ground floor Mon–Sat 11.30am & 2.30pm, Sun noon & 2.30pm; $5; 1hr; bookings ©9264 9209. Town Hall CityRail.

The stately **Queen Victoria Building** in the block between George and York streets, is another example of Sydney's finest architecture – but this hasn't stopped Sydneysiders, with characteristic disrespect, from abbreviating it to the QVB. Originally built as a market hall in 1898, the restored QVB was reopened as an upmarket shopping arcade in 1986. The interior is magnificent, with its beautiful woodwork, mosaic-tiled floors, elevated walkways and antique lifts; in true republican spirit Charles I is beheaded on the hour, every hour, by figurines on the ground-floor mechanical clock. From Town Hall Station you can walk right through the basement level (mainly bustling food stalls) and continue via the Sydney Central Plaza to Grace Bros department store, emerging on the Pitt Street Mall without having to go outside – very cooling on a hot day. From the basement up, the four levels of the QVB become progressively upmarket.

The Town Hall

Map 5, B7. Town Hall CityRail.

In the realm of architectural excess, however, the **Town Hall** is king – you'll find it next door to the QVB on George Street, at the corner of Druitt Street. It was built during the boom years of the 1870s and 1880s as a homage to Victorian England, and has a huge 8500-pipe organ inside its Centennial Hall, giving it the air of a secular cathedral. Throughout the interior different styles of ornamentation compete for attention in a .riot of colour and detail; the splendidly dignified toilets are a must-see.

Concerts and theatre performances set off the splendid interior perfectly. The Town Hall steps are the traditional place to meet in Sydney, an easy reference point for city outings and romantic trysts, and there's plenty of people-watching opportunities as you sit on the steps and wait for your date.

Tours of the Town Hall are offered by Centrepoint Tours (℗9231 4629). For details of concerts call the City Info line Mon–Fri 9am–6pm on ℗9265 9007.

AROUND HYDE PARK

From the Town Hall, it's a short walk east to **Hyde Park** along Park Street, which divides the park into two sections, with the **Anzac Memorial** in the southern half, and the Sandringham Memorial Gardens and Archibald Fountain in the north, overlooked by St James's Church across the northern boundary, and **St Marys Cathedral** and the **Australian Museum** across College Street.

Hyde Park

Map 5, D7. 24hr access. St James or Museum CityRail.

From Queens Square, **St James's Church** (daily 9am–5pm; map 5, D6) marks the entry to **Hyde Park**; the Anglican church, completed in 1824, is Sydney's oldest place of worship. It was one of Macquarie's schemes built to ex-convict Greenway's design, and the architect originally planned it as a courthouse – you can see how the simple design has been converted into a graceful church. Behind St James Station, the **Archibald Fountain** commemorates the association of Australia and France during World War I and near here, just behind the entrance to St James Station, is a **giant chess set** where you can challenge the locals to a game.

HYDE PARK

Further south the **Sandringham Memorial Gardens** also commemorate Australia's war dead, but the most potent monument is the **Anzac Memorial** (daily 9am–5pm; free daily tours 11.30am & 1.30pm; map 5, D8) across Park Street in the southern end of the park. Fronted by the tree-lined Pool of Remembrance, the thirty-metre-high cenotaph, unveiled in 1934, is classic Art Deco right down to the detail of Raynor Hoff's stylized soldier figures solemnly decorating the exterior. Downstairs, a free, mainly photographic, exhibition looks at Australian wartime experiences.

The Australian Museum

Map 5, D8 Daily 9.30am–5pm; $5, child $2, family $12; special exhibitions extra; 30min orientation tours 10am, 11am, noon, 1pm, 2pm & 3pm. Museum, Town Hall or Kings Cross CityRail.

Facing Hyde Park across College Street, at the junction of William Street as it heads up to Kings Cross, the **Australian Museum** is primarily a museum of natural history, with an interest in human evolution and Aboriginal culture and history. The collection was founded in 1827, but the actual building, a grand sandstone affair with a facade of Corinthian pillars, wasn't fully finished until the 1860s and was extended in the 1980s. The core of the old museum are the three levels of the **Long Gallery**, Australia's first exhibition gallery, opened in 1855 to a Victorian-era public keen to gawk at the colony's curiosities. Many of the classic displays of the following hundred years remain here, Heritage-listed, contrasting with a very modern approach in the rest of the museum.

On the **ground floor**, the impressive **Indigenous Australian** exhibition looks at the history of Australia's Aboriginal people from the Dreaming to contemporary

THE AUSTRALIAN MUSEUM

issues of the "stolen generation", through a diverse range of approaches, from audiovisual personal views to displays of cultural artefacts. The ground-floor level of the Long Gallery houses the **Skeletons** exhibit, where you can see a skeletal human going through the motions of riding a bicycle, for example. **Level 1** is devoted to minerals, but far more exciting are the disparate collections on **level 2** – especially the Long Gallery's **Birds and Insects** exhibit. There are chilling contextual displays of dangerous spiders such as redbacks and funnelwebs, and you can press buttons to illuminate certain specimens of birds and hear the corresponding bird cry.

Pass through the Long Gallery's level 2 to the newer section. The **Biodiversity: life supporting life** exhibition looks at the impact of environmental change on the ecosystems of Australian animals, plants, and micro-organisms, eighty percent of which do not naturally occur elsewhere, giving the country one of the highest levels of biodiversity. **Search and Discover** is aimed at both adults and children, a flora and fauna identification centre with Internet access and books to consult. The **Human Evolution** gallery traces the development of fossil evidence worldwide and ends with an exploration of archeological evidence of Aboriginal occupation of Australia. A separate section deals with fossil skeletons of dinosaurs and giant marsupials: best of all is the model of the largest of Australia's **megafauna**, the wombat-like Diprotodon, which may have roamed the mainland as recently as ten thousand years ago.

St Mary's Cathedral

Map 5, D7. St James or Martin Place CityRail.

North up College Street is Catholic **St Mary's Cathedral**, overlooking the northeast corner of Hyde Park. The huge Gothic-style church opened in 1882, though the foundation stone was laid in 1821. The cathedral will at last gain the twin stone spires originally planned by architect William Wardell in 1865 for the two southern towers, with $8 million of the project funded by State and Federal Governments. The cathedral will also gain an impressive new forecourt –a pedestrianized terrace with fountains and pools – with the $35 million remodelling of the four parcels of traffic-intersected parkland sandwiched between the Cathedral and the Australian Museum. The two parks are being consolidated to create the large **Cook and Phillip Park** (map 7, C5), which will include a recreation centre with a 50m swimming pool and a gym. The remodelling will also create a green link to The Domain.

MACQUARIE STREET

Lachlan Macquarie, reformist governor of New South Wales between 1809 and 1821, gave the early settlement its first imposing public buildings, clustered on the southern half of his namesake **Macquarie Street**. He had a vision of an elegant, prosperous city – although the Imperial Office in London didn't share his enthusiasm for expensive civic projects. Refused both money and expertise, Macquarie was forced to be resourceful: many of the city's finest buildings were designed by the ex-convict **Francis Greenway** – the convicted forger who went on to be appointed civil architect and design forty buildings, eleven of which survive – and paid for with rum-money, the proceeds of a monopoly on liquor sales.

State Library of New South Wales

Map 5, D5. Mon–Fri 9am–9pm, Sat & Sun 11am–5pm; Mitchell Library closed Sun. Martin Place CityRail.

The **State Library of New South Wales** completes the

row of public architecture on the eastern side of Macquarie Street. This complex of old and new buildings includes the 1906 sandstone **Mitchell Library**, its imposing Neoclassical facade gazing across to the Botanic Gardens. Inside, an archive of old maps, illustrations and records relating to the early days of white settlement and exploration in Australia includes the **Tasman Map**, drawn by the Dutch explorer Abel Tasman in the 1640s. Pop into the foyer and look at the floor-mosaic which replicates the map, upon which Australia's shape oddly emerges, still without an East coast and its northern extremity joined to Papua New Guinea. A glass walkway links the Mitchell with the modern building housing the General Reference Library. Free exhibitions relating to Australian history and literature are a regular feature of the Reference Library vestibules while lectures, films and video shows take place regularly in the **Metcalfe Auditorium** (©9273 1414 for details). You can refresh yourself at the recommended café or browse in the library's bookshop, which has the best collection of Australian history books in Sydney.

Sydney Hospital and Parliament House

Map D5 & D6. Martin Place CityRail.

Sandstone **Sydney Hospital**, the so-called "Rum Hospital", funded by liquor-trade profits, was Macquarie's first enterprise, commissioned in 1814; the two remaining convict-built original wings therefore form one of the oldest buildings in Australia. The central section was pulled down in 1879 when it began collapsing; rebuilt by 1894, the sandstone Classical Revival buildings, still functioning as a small general and eye hospital, are also impressive – peep inside at the entrance hall's flower-themed stained glass and the decorative staircase (free guided tours are also available; call ©9382 7400 for details). One of the original

wings of the hospital is now the **NSW Parliament House**
(Mon–Fri 9.30am–4pm; free guided tours Mon & Fri, at
10am, 11am & 2pm; Tues–Thurs, question time at
2.15pm; call ©9230 2111 to check), where as early as 1829
local councils called by the governor started to meet, making it by some way the oldest parliament building in
Australia. Varied exhibitions in the foyer change about
every fortnight – all represent community or public sector
interests and range from painting, art and craft, and sculpture to particularly excellent photographic displays which
often have an overt political content. You can listen in on
question time when the Parliament is sitting. The other
wing was converted into a branch of the **Royal Mint** in
response to the first Australian goldrush. For some time it
served as a museum focusing on gold mining and heritage,
but there are now plans to reopen the wing as a community space.

The Hyde Park Barracks

Map 5, D6. Daily 9.30am–5pm; $6. Martin Place CityRail.

Next door to the old Royal Mint, the **Hyde Park
Barracks**, designed by Francis Greenway, was built in
1819. The barracks were planned to house hundreds of
convicts, mainly orphaned children and single women.
Fittingly, it's now a museum of the social and architectural
history of Sydney, giving an insight into convict life during
the early years of the colony and the lives of nineteenth-
century immigrant women; there are reconstructions of the
convict lodgings, including the very spartan hammocks
which you're welcome to try out, and a computer database
of convicts which lets you trace a chosen subject's career in
the colony, often from strife to success through hard work
and land grants. There are also excellent temporary historical exhibitions.

THE CITY CENTRE

> You can take an interesting short cut through the
> grounds of Sydney Hospital to The Domain and
> across to the Art Gallery of New South Wales.

THE DOMAIN

Map 5, E6. Martin Place or St James CityRail. Bus #441.

The Domain is a large, quite plain, open space that stretches
from behind the historic precinct on Macquarie Street to the
waterfront, divided from the Botanic Gardens by the Cahill
Expressway and Mrs Macquaries Road. It's a popular place for
a stroll from the city across to the Art Gallery of New South
Wales or down to the harbour for wonderful views from Mrs
Macquaries Chair, filled with workers eating sandwiches
under shady Moreton Bay fig trees, playing volleyball, or even
swimming at its outdoor pool. In the early days of the settlement, it was the governor's private park but for many more
years it has been a truly public site, as Sydney's focus for anti-
establishment protests. Since the 1890s, assorted cranks and
soapbox revolutionaries have assembled on Sundays for the
city's version of **Speakers' Corner**, and huge crowds have
registered their disquiet, notably during anti-conscription ral-
lies in 1916 and after the Whitlam Labor government's dis-
missal in 1975. Every January thousands of people gather on
the lawns to enjoy the wonderful free open-air concerts –
Opera in the Park and **Symphony in the Park** – of the
Sydney Festival (see p.266).

Art Gallery of New South Wales

Map 5, F6. Daily 10am–5pm; free except for special exhibitions;
☎9225 1744 for times of free guided tours. Martin Place or St
James CityRail. Bus #441.

THE DOMAIN: ART GALLERY OF NEW SOUTH WALES

Art Gallery Road runs through The Domain to the **Art Gallery of New South Wales** whose collection was established in 1874. The original part of the building (1897), an imposing Neoclassical structure with a facade inscribed with the names of Renaissance artists, principally contains the large collection of European art dating from the eleventh century to the twentieth–extensions were added in 1988 which doubled the gallery space and provided a home for mainly Australian art.

On level 1, the **Yiribana Gallery** is devoted to the art and cultural artefacts of Aboriginal and Torres Strait Islanders; the most striking exhibit is the **Pukumani Grave Posts**, carved by the Tiwi people of Melville Island. At noon (Tues–Sat) a highly recommended half-hour talk and performance of dance and didgeridoo by an indigenous Australian takes place and there's also a free one-hour tour of this gallery (Tues–Fri 11am, Sat & Sun 1pm).

Other highlights include some classic **Australian paintings** on level 4: Tom Roberts' romanticized shearing-shed scene *The Golden Fleece* (1894) and an altogether less idyllic look at rural Australia in Russell Drysdale's *Sofala* (1947), a depressing vision of a drought-stricken town. On level 5, the **photographic collection** includes Max Dupain's iconic *Sunbaker*, an early (1937) study of Australian hedonism. The boldly abstracted image of a sun worshipper lying on a beach looks as if it could have been taken yesterday.

In addition to the galleries, there is also an auditorium used for art lectures, an excellent bookshop, a coffee shop (level 2), and a well-regarded restaurant (level 5).

Mrs Macquaries Chair and "the Boy"

Map 5, G3. Daily Sept–April 6.30am–8pm; $2.50. Martin Place or St James CityRail. Bus #441.

Mrs Macquaries Road, built in 1816 at the urging of the governor's wife, Elizabeth, curves down from Art Gallery Road to Mrs Macquaries Point, which separates idyllic Farm Cove from the grittier Woolloomooloo Bay. At the end is the celebrated lookout point known as **Mrs Macquaries Chair**, a seat fashioned out of the rock, from which Elizabeth could admire her favourite view of the harbour on her daily walk in what was then the governor's private park.

On the route down to Mrs Macquaries Point, the **Andrew "Boy" Charlton Pool** (map 5, G4; see p.282) is an open-air, saltwater swimming pool safely isolated from the harbour waters on the Woolloomooloo side of the promontory, with excellent views across to the engrossingly functional Garden Island Naval Depot.

Around Darling Harbour

I t's only a ten-minute walk to **Darling Harbour** from the Queen Victoria Building down Market Street, along the overhead walkway and across Pyrmont Bridge. Further south there's a pedestrian bridge from Bathurst Street or you can cut through on Liverpool Street to Tumbalong Park. West of the city centre the 1980s redevelopment of the old wharf area around Cockle Bay saw the birth of the Darling Harbour entertainment and retail precinct, with several of the city's major tourist attractions located here and in adjacent areas, including the Aquarium, the National Maritime Museum, and the Fish Markets in adjacent Pyrmont, and the Powerhouse Museum in Ultimo. The neighbouring area of Haymarket, heading towards Central Station, contains Sydney's Chinatown, as well as its oldest market.

The area covered in this chapter is shown in detail on maps 4, 5 & 6 and on the Darling Harbour plan on p.77.

HAYMARKET

Immediately west of Central Station is the area known as **Haymarket** on either side of the downmarket end of George Street. The Light Rail heads through here from Central Station, past Capitol Square where the **Capitol Theatre** was built as a de luxe picture palace in the 1920s, and now hosts big-budget musicals and ballet under a star-studded ceiling representing the southern skies. The area is renowned for its pop culture pleasures, with Her Majesty's Theatre on Quay Street and the ugly concrete bunker of the Sydney Entertainment Centre, the city's mainstream concert venue (see p.209), on the other side of **Chinatown**.

Chinatown

Sydney's **Chinatown** takes over the Haymarket area west of George Street between Liverpool Street and Hay Street, up to the edges of Darling Harbour. It's centred on **Dixon Street Mall** (map 5, A9), entered through Chinese gates, and buzzes day and night as people swarm into numerous restaurants, pubs, cafés, cinemas, food stalls, Asian grocery stores and funky fashion shops. Towards the end of January or in the first weeks of February, Chinese New Year is celebrated here with gusto: dragon and lion dances, food festivals and music compete with the noise and smoke from strings of Chinese crackers. The return of Hong Kong to China in 1997 has resulted in massive investments of Hong Kong money in Chinatown, including Australia's biggest restaurant, the *Kam Fook* (see p.175). Near the edge of Chinatown, on the southern fringes of Darling Harbour is a **Chinese Garden** (see p.78).

Every Friday, Saturday and Sunday frenetic **Paddy's**

Market (map 5, A9), Sydney's oldest (1869), is conducted in its undercover home at the corner of Thomas and Quay streets, selling fresh produce to cheap and cheerful new clothes. Above the old market, the buzzing multilevel **Market City Shopping Centre** (see p.259) has an excellent top-floor Asian food court next to a multiscreen cinema.

DARLING HARBOUR

Darling Harbour is, in some ways, a thoroughly stylish redevelopment of the old wharves around Cockle Bay but most Sydneysiders sneer at it as a soulless, tacky and touristy kind of place, contrasting badly with the authentic vitality of neighbouring Chinatown. Certainly, the 1980s development still puts commercial values foremost and the **Harbourside Shopping Centre**, with its souvenir shops and burger joints, is perhaps the worst offender. Facing Harbourside across the water, the **Cockle Bay wharf development** is a contrastingly upmarket precinct, with a huge nightclub and eight restaurants, all created to drag the CBD kicking and screaming down to the much-maligned Darling Harbour. Behind the development, and accessible from it, is the new **Darling Park**, with paths laid out in the shape of a waratah flower – the state symbol. Meanwhile though the Harbourside Shopping Centre has been given a $60 million refurbishment, its ground floor is still dominated by a noisy video game parlour, tacky souvenir shops and its touristy *Ettamogah* pub serving up Aussie tucker. Persist in trudging through and you'll find its one gem, **Gavala Art** (daily 10am–7pm), an Aboriginal-owned and operated store selling Aboriginal designed art, clothing and accessories plus music.

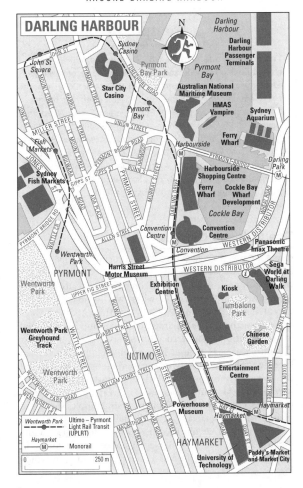

DARLING HARBOUR

N

Darling
Harbour

Darling
Harbour
Passenger
Terminals

Sydney
Casino

John St
Square

Pyrmont
Bay Park

Pyrmont
Bay

Australian National
Maritime Museum

Star City
Casino

HMAS
Vampire

Pyrmont
Bay

Sydney
Aquarium

MILLER STREET

Harbourside

Ferry
Wharf

Fish
Markets

Sydney Fish Markets

Harbourside
Shopping Centre

Darling
Park

Ferry
Wharf

Cockle Bay
Wharf
Development

Cockle Bay

Convention
Centre

Convention
Centre

Panasonic
Imax Theatre

Wentworth
Park

Convention

WESTERN DISTRIBUTOR

Harris Street
Motor Museum

WESTERN DISTRIBUTOR

Sega
World at
Darling
Walk

PYRMONT

Exhibition
Centre

Kiosk

Wentworth
Park

Wentworth Park
Greyhound
Track

Tumbalong
Park

Chinese
Garden

Wentworth
Park

ULTIMO

Entertainment
Centre

Powerhouse
Museum

Haymarket

HAYMARKET

University of
Technology

Paddy's Market
and Market City

| Wentworth Park | Ultimo – Pyrmont Light Rail Transit (UPLRT) |
| Haymarket Ⓜ | Monorail |

0   250 m

DARLING HARBOUR

Transport

The monorail runs from the city centre to one of three stops around Darling Harbour, and has the views to recommend it. State Transit ferries leave from Wharf 5, Circular Quay (about every 45min Mon–Fri 8am–7.30pm, less often Sat & Sun; $3.20), calling at McMahons Point, Darling Street Wharf in Balmain and Sydney Aquarium in Darling Harbour; the privately-run *Matilda Ferry* leaves from the Commissioners Steps, Circular Quay West via the Star City Casino at Pyrmont to the Aquarium Wharf (roughly every 25min, 9am–6.30pm, later Fri–Sun; $3.25 one-way). By bus, fromCircular Quay the #456 goes to Darling Harbour, the casino and the Powerhouse Museum.

The Chinese Garden

Map 5, A8 and p.77. Mon–Fri 9.30am–5.30pm, Sat & Sun 9.30am–6pm; closes 1hr earlier in winter; $4.

In the southeast corner of Darling Harbour, just beyond Chinatown, the **Chinese Garden**, was completed for the Bicentenary Festival in 1988 as a gift from Sydney's sister city Guangzhou. The "Garden of Friendship" is designed in the traditional southern Chinese style. As you wander the miniature landscape, plaques in delightfully formal language tell you how best to experience and understand the various viewpoints. Although not large, it feels remarkably calm and spacious – a great place to retreat from the commercial hubbub to read a book, smell the fragrant flowers that attract birds and listen to the lilting Chinese music that fills the air. The balcony of the traditional tearoom offers a bird's-eye view of the dragon wall, waterfalls, a pagoda on a hill and carp swimming in winding lakes.

> Quite a bit of walking is involved getting around Darling Harbour and if you're exhausted, or just for fun with kids, you might consider hopping on board the dinky People Mover Trains ($2.50; daily: summer 10am–6pm, winter 10am–5pm; full circuit 20min) leaving every fifteen minutes from various points around Darling Harbour.

Darling Walk

Just north of the Chinese Gardens is **Tumbalong Park**, inland between the Exhibition Centre and Darling Walk. Reached from the city via Liverpool Street, the park is the "village green" of Darling Harbour and serves as a venue for open-air concerts and free public entertainment. The tasteful and calm aesthetic of the Chinese Garden contrasts quite violently with the **Darling Walk** retail and entertainment centre on the park's north side. It's Darling Harbour's most frenetic area – at least on weekends during school holidays – as most of the attractions are aimed at children. Dominating the centre is an indoor theme park, **Sega World** (see "Kids Sydney" p.239). During school holidays, events are held on the floating stage on Darling Walk's small lake. West of the lake is a vibrant children's playground area, complete with a merry-go-round. Also in the Darling Walk complex is the new **National Aboriginal Cultural Centre** (daily 9.30am–8pm; free; admission to 45min dance performances at 11am, 1pm, 4pm & 6pm; $14.50). Firmly aimed at tourists, the centre's overt commercialism is a shock if you've visited other excellent Aboriginal cultural centres. Its title is perhaps too grand a claim – the centre is really a commercial art gallery and shop with a performance space attached. No interpretive material is displayed and the overpriced dance performance, amongst shaky sets, is amateurish.

DARLING WALK

79

You can buy the Darling Harbour Super Ticket at the Darling Harbour Visitor Centre (daily 9.30am–5.30pm). The $29.90 ticket includes rides on the monorail, a two-hour cruise with Matilda Cruises, entry to the Aquarium and the Chinese Garden, a meal and discounts at the IMAX Cinema, the Powerhouse Museum and on the People Mover.

The Southern Promenade

Just beyond Darling Walk, the Southern Promenade of Darling Harbour is dominated by the **Panasonic Imax Theatre** (©9281 3300; $13.95) next to the tourist information office. Its giant cinema screen, ten times larger than those showing conventional 35mm films, has a constantly changing programme of four 45-minute films from their 100-film library; the emphasis is on scenic wonders such as Mount Everest. Other Darling Harbour visual onslaughts include **Aquamagic**, a free night-time laser show projected onto a semicircular water screen on Cockle Bay (Wed–Sun: May–Sept 7.10pm & 8.10pm; Oct–April 8.10pm & 9.10pm; 25min). The Cockle Bay wharf development extends along the eastern promenade of Darling Harbour from the Imax cinema to **Pyrmont Bridge**, the world's first electrically operated swing span bridge, and now a pedestrian walkway across Cockle Bay, linking the two sides of the harbour.

Sydney Aquarium

Map 5, A6 and p.77. Daily 9.30am–10pm; $15.90; Aquarium Pass including STA ferry from Circular Quay $19.20; also see Darling Harbour Super Ticket, above.

Beside the eastern side of Pyrmont Bridge is the **Sydney Aquarium**, which has its own wharf: you can also visit the aquarium with Captain Cook Cruises from no. 6 Jetty at Circular Quay (see box p.35). If you're not going to get the chance to explore the Barrier Reef, the aquarium makes a surprisingly passable substitute. Head straight for the underwater walkway where you can wander in complete safety among sharks, wobbegongs, stingrays and eely things. Upstairs are freshwater fish from the Murray–Darling basin, Australia's biggest river system, while another area features exotic species from the warmer waters further north, and the colourful and bizarre world of the Great Barrier Reef.

National Maritime Museum

See map on p.77. Daily 9.30am–5pm; $9; guided tour of ex-destroyer *HMAS Vampire* included or available separately; $6. Pyrmont Bay Light Rail, Harbourside Monorail.

On the western side of **Pyrmont Bridge** the **National Maritime Museum**, with its distinctive modern architecture topped by a wave-shaped roof, highlights the history of Australia as a seafaring nation. However, it goes beyond its remit of maritime interests to look at how the sea has shaped Australia's history, covering everything from immigration to beach culture and Aboriginal fishing methods. Highlights include an exhibition which delves into the culture of Torres Strait Islanders and other Aboriginal groups and another which focuses on the seventeenth century Dutch explorers who first charted the Australian coastline. The museum also hosts excellent temporary exhibitions worth looking out for. Twelve vessels are moored at the museum's own wharfs – from a decommissioned navy destroyer, the *Vampire*, to a Vietnamese refugee boat. There's also a library, auditorium, and pleasant outdoor public access café with views of the boats.

NATIONAL MARITIME MUSEUM |

The Powerhouse Museum

See map on p.77. Daily 9.30am–5pm; $8, free first Sat in month; free orientation and special interest tours daily; ©9217 0100 for tour times. Central Station CityRail, Haymarket Monorail.

From Tumbalong Park in Darling Harbour, a signposted walkway leads to the **Powerhouse Museum** on Harris Street in Ultimo. Located, as the name suggests, in a former power station, this is arguably the best museum in Sydney, a young and exciting place with fresh ideas. The museum was opened here in 1988 but was originally founded in 1880: its main function has always been to collect, care for and interpret "material culture". This notion is open to a wide interpretation and, unusually, the museum combines arts and sciences, design, sociology and technology under the same roof – with the much-anticipated "Fashion of the Year" display featuring Australian fashion every November. Besides this, there's always one or two special exhibitions too, which might range from showcasing cars to fabulous Korean costumes.

The entrance is dominated by the huge **Boulton and Watt Steam Engine**, first put to use in 1875 in a British brewery; still operational, the engine is often loudly demonstrated. The **Kings Cinema** on level 3, with its original Art Deco fittings, shows newsreels and films that a typical Sydneysider would have watched in the 1930s. Judging by the tears at closing time, the **special childrens' areas** have also proved a great success. On level 5, there's a colourfully painted licensed restaurant while downstairs there's a more inexpensive courtyard cafeteria. The souvenir shop is also worth a browse for some unusual gifts.

Motor Museum

See map on p.77. Wed–Sun & public holidays, daily during school holidays, 10am–5pm; $10; Convention Monorail.

Three blocks north of the Powerhouse Museum, at 320 Harris St, the **Motor Museum**, houses around 160 vehicles on three levels. The usual mix of vintage cars and 1950s American-style cruisers, it also has a comprehensive collection of Australian automobilia.

PYRMONT

Frantic redevelopment is taking place at **Pyrmont**, the former industrial suburb jutting out into the water between Darling Harbour and Blackwattle Bay, Sydney's answer to Ellis Island in the 1950s when thousands of immigrants disembarked at Pier 13 – then the city's main overseas passenger terminal. With the NSW government selling $97 million worth of property, this is one of the biggest concentrated sell-offs of land in Australia; from having a population of only nine hundred in 1988, over the coming decade $2 billion worth of investment will see Pyrmont transformed into a residential suburb of twenty thousand. The area has certainly become glitzier, with the Star City Casino, and two TV companies – Channel Ten and Foxtel – now based here. The approach to the spectacularly cabled **Glebe Island Bridge** – Sydney's newest – cuts through Pyrmont.

Star City Casino

Map 4, D3 and p.77. Open 24hr. Bus #443, #888, free Casino Shuttlebus; Casino Light Rail.

Beyond the Maritime Museum, on Pyrmont Bay is **Star City**, the spectacularly tasteless new casino, open 24 hours a day. A lot of taxpayers' money has been spent on the casino, such as the bus and light rail terminal underneath the building, much to the outrage of church groups and charities. A free Casino Shuttlebus attempts to lure punters here from Kings Cross and Circular Quay (free call ☎1800/681 500; every 30min through 24 hours from various locations in Kings Cross; every 30min after 4.15pm from Circular Quay).

As well as the casino, the building houses two theatres, fourteen restaurants and cafés, several theme bars, and a nightclub. It's certainly a place to come for late-night eats, with some good-value joints like the *City Noodle Café*, which stays open until 2am. Add to this ATMs, ice-cream stores, souvenir shops and small supermarkets, and a mini universe is created. The casino interior itself, entered through a sea cave grotto, is a clash of competing themes and patterns – giant palm sculptures, spinning prize cars, Aboriginal painting motifs on the ceiling, a carpet of Australian critters scurrying across a desert-coloured carpet, and an array of flashing pokies beneath what look like Christmas lights.

Sydney Fish Market

Map 4, C5; map 6, 2F and p.77. Daily 7am–4pm. Fish Market Light Rail; bus #443, #501. Ferry from Circular Quay and Balmain weekends only.

The **Sydney Fish Market** is only a five-minute walk from Darling Harbour's Maritime Museum straight down Pyrmont Bridge Road. A popular tourist attraction – second only to Tokyo's fishmarket in terms of variety – it's a frenetic, early-morning, multicultural spectacle, a gathering of the Sydney fishing fleet, cargo boats, fishermen and buyers. You need to visit early to see the high-tech, silent weekday **auctions** (biggest auction floor on Friday with a huge variety of fish; public viewing platform opens 7am), where buyers log onto computer terminals to register their bids. Once a month an early-morning tour of the selling floor and a cookery class – making yourself a fishy breakfast

– is offered by tbe **Sydney Seafood School** based here (2hr; $38 per person includes tour, ingredients, tuition and meal; ©9660 1611).

For a **picnic** you can take away oysters, prawns and cooked seafood from the market, pick up other ingredients from a nearby baker, deli, bottle shop and greengrocer and eat on waterfront tables overlooking Blackwattle Bay, or at nearby Wentworth Park. Alternatively, you can eat in at a cheaper-than-normal branch of Sydney's best-known fish **restaurant**, *Doyles*, an excellent sushi bar, or have dirt-cheap fish and chips at the *Italian Fish Market Café* (Mon–Fri 4am–4pm, Sat & Sun 5am–5pm).

Inner East

To the **east of the city centre**, Surry Hills, Darlinghurst and Paddington were once rather scruffy working-class suburbs, but since the 1970s have been gentrified by the young, arty and upwardly mobile. Kings Cross is home to Sydney's red-light district as well as many of its tourists, and can be reached by a series of steps from Woolloomooloo and the busy naval dockyards, and architecture from Art Deco to colonial, or by walking straight up William Street from Hyde Park past east Sydney. Further east, the "Cross" fades into the more elegant neighbourhoods of Potts Point and Elizabeth Bay, which trade on their harbour views.

The area covered by this chapter can be seen on colour map 7.

SURRY HILLS

Surry Hills, directly east of Central Station from Elizabeth Street, was traditionally the centre of the rag trade, which still finds its focus on **Devonshire Street** (map 7, B10). Rows of tiny terraces once housed its original poor, working-class population, many of them of

Irish background. Considered a slum by the rest of Sydney, the dire and overcrowded conditions were given gritty life in Ruth Park's *The Harp in the South* trilogy, set in the 1940s. The area went on to become something of a cultural melting pot with European postwar immigration, and doubled as a grungy, studenty, muso heartland in the 1980s.

By the mid-1990s, however, the slickly fashionable scene of neighbouring Darlinghurst and Paddington had finally taken over Surry Hills' twin focal points of **Crown Street** (map 7, C10), filled with trendified pubs, cafés, swanky restaurants – like *MG Garage* (see p.182), where you dine alongside classic cars – designer galleries and funky clothes shops, and leafy **Bourke Street** (map 7, C11), where a couple of Sydney's best cafés lurk among the trees. As rents have gone up, only **Cleveland Street** (map 7, B12), running west to **Redfern** (see box overleaf) and east towards Moore Park, retains its ethnically varied population with cheap Lebanese and Turkish restaurants lining its way.

Brett Whitely Studio

Map 7, C11. Sat & Sun 10am–4pm; $6. Central Station CityRail; buses #303, #304, #308, #309.

The artistic side of Surry Hills can be experienced at the **Brett Whitely Studio**, at 2 Raper St, off Davies Street. Whitely was one of Australia's best-known contemporary painters who had gained international recognition by the time he died of a heroin overdose at the age of 53; his work expresses his wild visions of himself and of Sydney Harbour. In the mid-1980s Whitely converted this one-time factory into a studio and living space. Since his death it's become a public gallery showing his paintings and the work of other contemporary artists, as well as Whitely memorabilia.

The Block

Just beyond Surry Hills, and only 2km from the glitter and sparkle of Darling Harbour, **Redfern** is Sydney's squalid under-belly. Around the **Eveleigh Street** area (map 4, D8), Australia's biggest urban Aboriginal community lives in **"the Block"**, a streetscape of derelict terraced houses and rubbish-strewn streets not far from Redfern train station – the closest Sydney has to a no-go zone. The Aboriginal Housing Company, set up as a co-operative in 1973, has been unable to pay for repairs and renovation work, in shocking contrast to Paddington's cutesy restored terraces and the harbourview mansions of Sydney's rich and beautiful. Recent bulldozing of some of these derelict houses and the relocation of the occupants has brought charges of prettifying the area in time for the Olympics.

DARLINGHURST

Oxford Street (map 7, C7), stretching from Hyde Park through **Darlinghurst** to Paddington and beyond, is a major amusement strip. Waiting to be discovered, here and in the side streets, is an array of nightclubs, restaurants, cafés, pubs, bookshops, cinemas and fashion stores.

The Darlinghurst end of Oxford Street is the focus of Sydney's very active **gay and lesbian** movement, and the art college on Burton Street, near the Darlinghurst Courthouse, means there's a new crop of self-conscious young stylemongers every year. Hip and bohemian, Darlinghurst mingles seediness with a certain hedonistic style: some art students and pale, wasted clubbers never leave the district – save for a latte at the Cross or a swim at "the Boy" in The Domain (see p.72, 282).

See "Gay and Lesbian Sydney" p.229–238 for a lowdown on the Oxford Street scene.

DARLINGHURST

There's a concentration of cafés on **Victoria Street** (map 7, E7), north of Oxford Street, a classic pose strip radiating around the legendary *Bar Coluzzi*, with customers nibbling their brioche on milk crates on the pavement and checking out the passing parade; this area also harbours some popular restaurants and bars. More cafés, restaurants and fashion are found on **Liverpool Street** (map 7, C6), heading east and downhill from Oxford towards **East Sydney** near the Australian Museum. Here **Stanley Street** (map 7, C6) has a cluster of cheap Italian cafés and restaurants.

Sydney Jewish Museum

Map 7,E7. Mon–Thurs 10am–4pm, Fri 10am–2pm, Sun 11am–5pm; $6. Kings Cross CityRail.

The **Sydney Jewish Museum** at 148 Darlinghurst Rd, is housed in the old Maccabean Hall, which has been a Jewish meeting point for over seventy years. Sixteen Jews were among the convicts who arrived with the First Fleet, and the high-tech, interactive museum explores over two hundred years of Australian Jewish experience. For coffee and cake or kosher cuisine with a contemporary slant, there's also a café.

You might also like to see the finely wrought Great Synagogue in the city centre, consecrated in 1878; it faces the northern half of Hyde Park at 187 Elizabeth St (map 5,C7; free tours noon Tues & Thurs; Town Hall CityRail).

PADDINGTON & WOOLLAHRA

From the intersection with South Dowling Street in Darlinghurst, Oxford Street strikes southeast through

Paddington and Woollahra to the verdant expanse of Centennial Park. **Paddington**, a slum at the turn of the century, became a popular hangout for hipsters during the late 1960s and 1970s. Since then, yuppies took over and turned Paddington into the smart and fashionable suburb it is today: the Victorian-era terraced houses, with their iron-lace verandahs reminiscent of New Orleans, have been beautifully restored. Many of the terraces were originally built in the 1840s to house the artisans who worked on the graceful sandstone **Victoria Barracks** on the southern side of Oxford Street (map 7, E9), its walls stretching seven blocks, from Greens Road to just before the Paddington Town Hall on Oatley Road. **Shadforth Street** (map 7, F9), opposite the entrance gates, has many examples of the original artisans' homes. Though the barracks are still used by the army, there are free guided tours on Thursday mornings at 10am – complete with army band – while a small **museum** is open to visitors on Sundays (10am–3pm; free; buses #378, #380, #382, #389).

On the northern side of Oxford Street the small, winding, tree-lined streets are a pleasant place for a stroll and offer tantalizing glimpses of the sparkling waters of the harbour – and a chance to wander into the many small **art galleries** (see p.256) or to take some liquid refreshment. Head via Underwood and Heeley streets to **Five Ways** (map 7, F8), where you'll find cafés, speciality shops and a typically gracious old boozer, the *Royal Hotel*. But the main action is on Oxford Street, most lively on Saturday from 10am to around 4pm, when the crowds descend on the fun and fashion-conscious **Paddington Bazaar** (see p.262) in the church grounds at 395 Oxford St.

Woollahra, along Oxford Street from Paddington, is even more moneyed but contrastingly staid, with severely expensive **antique shops** along Queen Street (map 7, I11) replacing the wackier style of Paddington.

Centennial Park

Map 7, I13. Daily 8am–6pm, until 8pm during Daylight Savings.
Buses #378, #380, #382.

South of Oxford Street from Paddington and Woollahra,
lies the green expanse of **Centennial Park** with Bondi
Junction to the east and Randwick to the south. Opened to
the citizens of Sydney at the Centennial Festival in 1888
(the bicentennial version was opened at Homebush in
1988), the park, with its vast lawns, rose gardens and extensive network of ponds resembles an English country park,
but is reclaimed at dawn and dusk by distinctly antipodean
residents, including possums and flying foxes. The park is
crisscrossed by walking paths and tracks for cycling, rollerblading, jogging and horse-riding: you can rent a bike or
rollerblades or hire a horse (see "Sporting Sydney") and
then recover from your exertions in the café or in the finer
months stay on until dark and catch an outdoor film at the
Epson Moonlight Cinema (see p.226).

Adjoining Moore Park, west of Centennial Park, has
facilities for tennis, golf, grass skiing, bowling, cricket
and hockey (see "Sporting Sydney" p.273); it is also
home to the Sydney Cricket Ground (see p.276), the
Sydney Football Stadium (see p.275) and Fox Studios
(see p.228).

KINGS CROSS AND BEYOND

The preserve of Sydney's bohemians in the 1950s, **Kings
Cross** became an R&R spot for American soldiers during
the Vietnam war, and it is now Sydney's red-light district, its
streets prowled by prostitutes, junkies, drunks, strippers and
homeless teenagers. It is also a bustling centre for backpack-

ers and other travellers, especially around leafy and quieter **Victoria Street** (map 7, E5); the two sides of "the Cross" (as locals call it) coexist with little trouble, though some of the tourists seem a little surprised at where they've ended up, and it can be rather intimidating for lone women.

Kings Cross is famed for its backpacker accommodation, see p.154.

The Cross can *seem* threatening but the constant flow of people makes it relatively safe, and it's always lively, with places to eat and drink that stay open all hours. Climbing up **William Street** (map 7, D5) from Hyde Park, Darlinghurst Road beckons with its giant neon Coca Cola sign. At weekends, an endless stream of ice-cream-licking suburban voyeurs, disgorged from the underground Kings Cross train station, trawl along the **Darlinghurst Road** strip (map 7, E5) to the **El Alamein fountain** in the shady **Fitzroy Gardens** (map 7, F4) as touts try their best to haul them into tacky strip-joints and sleazy nightclubs. Kings Cross is much more subdued during the day, with a slightly hung-over feel to it: local residents emerge and it's a good time to hang out in the cafés. There's a small arts and crafts market in the Fitzroy Gardens on Sundays.

Walking tours of the Cross leave from the El Alamein fountain at 10.30am on weekends ($14; 2hr) and explore the celebrity and crime connections of the area; alternatively pop into the Kings Cross library off the gardens and pick up a free *Kings Cross Walking Tour* map.

From the Fitzroy Gardens, the sin strip ends and tree-lined **Macleay Street** (map 7, F4) runs through quieter, upmarket **Potts Point**, with its Art Deco residential apartments, classy hotels, stylish restaurants and occasional harbour glimpses over wealthier **Elizabeth Bay**, just east. Beyond Macleay Street, Wylde Street heads downhill towards grittier **Woolloomooloo**.

Elizabeth Bay House

Map 7, F4. Tues–Sun 10am–4.30pm; $6. Kings Cross CityRail; bus #311.

Barely five minutes' walk northwest of Kings Cross Station, **Elizabeth Bay** is nevertheless a well-heeled residential area, centred around **Elizabeth Bay House**, at 7 Onslow Ave. The grand Greek Revival villa was built between 1835 and 1839 for Alexander Macleay, Colonial Secretary of New South Wales. The large Macleay family, who arrived from Britain in 1826, included two sons and six daughters: all were obsessed with botany or etymology, and the original 54-acre waterfront grounds were said to be a botanist's paradise. The Macleay Museum at Sydney University (see p.96) was formed from the Macleays' natural history collection. The views from the windows of the yachts and water of Elizabeth Bay are pretty stunning.

> Two glorious Woolloomooloo pubs, the *Tilbury* and the *Woolloomooloo Woolshed* are detailed on p.179.

Woolloomooloo

North of William Street just below Kings Cross, **Woolloomooloo** occupies the old harbourside quarter, between The Domain and the grey-painted fleet of the **Garden Island Naval Depot** (map 4, J2). Once a narrow-streeted dockside slum, Woolloomooloo is slowly being spruced up, though luxury housing developments live

ELIZABETH BAY HOUSE, WOOLLOOMOOLOO

uneasily side by side with problematic community housing, and you should still be careful at night in the backstreets. There are some rowdy pubs and some old-fashioned quiet locals, as well as the legendary **Harry's Café de Wheels** on Cowper Wharf Road (map 7, E2), a 24-hour pie-cart operating since 1945. Famous for pea and pie floaters, *Harry's* has become a gathering place for Sydney cabbies and hungry clubbers in the wee small hours. Nearby, the once picturesquely dilapidated **Woolloomooloo Finger Wharf** (map 7, E3), dating from 1917, no longer handles immigrants or cargo. Plans to demolish it were met with fierce protests, but the compromise – its redevelopment as sanitized luxury residential apartments – hasn't pleased many Sydneysiders either. Woolloomooloo is best reached by foot from Kings Cross by taking the **McElhone Stairs** (map 7, E3) or the **Butlers Stairs** (map 7, E4) from Victoria Street – just follow the constant stream of white-clad sailors.

Inner West

West of the centre, immediately beyond Darling Harbour, the inner-city areas of Glebe and Newtown surround Sydney University, their vibrant cultural mix enlivened by large student populations. On a peninsula north of Glebe and west of The Rocks, Balmain comprises a gentrified working-class dock area popular for its village atmosphere, while en route Leichhardt is the focus of Sydney's Italian community.

The areas covered by this chapter are shown in detail on colour map 6.

GLEBE

Glebe, right by Australia's oldest university, and only a fifteen-minute walk up **Broadway** from Central Station, has gradually been evolving from a café-oriented student quarter to more upmarket thirtysomething territory with a New Age slant. Indeed, it's very much the centre of alternative culture in Sydney, with its yoga schools and healing centres offering every kind of therapy, from Chinese massage to homeopathy and float tanks. Saturday is much the best time to come to get a taste of the area, when Glebe Market is in full swing (see p.262). **Glebe Point Road**, the focal point of the area, is filled with an eclectic mix of cafés with trademark leafy courtyards, restaurants, bookshops (check out Gleebooks at no. 49 & no. 191) and secondhand and speciality shops as it runs uphill from Broadway, becoming quietly residential as it slopes down towards the water of **Rozelle Bay**. The side streets are fringed with renovated two-storey terraced houses with white iron-lacework verandahs. Its laid-back villagey feel makes it very popular with travellers: there is a good YHA hostel among others, an Internet café and even a backpackers' travel centre, and the handy, brand-new **Broadway Shopping Centre** (see p.259) linked by an overhead walkway from Glebe Point Road. However, with its twelve-screen movie theatre, it has already impacted on a big slice of Glebe culture.

Sydney University

Map 6, E5. Buses #431, #433 and #434.

Just before the beginning of Glebe Point Road, on Broadway, the recently relandscaped **Victoria Park** has a very pleasant outdoor heated swimming pool (see p.283) complete with a café. Next door to the park, as Broadway turns into **Parramatta Road**, is one of the main gates to **Sydney University**. The university has 35,000 students and its extensive grounds take up a suburb-sized area between Parramatta Road, and City Road running up to King Street, Newtown. Australia's oldest tertiary educational institution, it was inaugurated in 1850; the Main Building, built of stone and complete with gargoyles and a quadrangle, conjures up the architecture of Oxford or Cambridge, especially in its cedar-ceilinged, stained-glass-windowed **Great Hall** which makes a glorious concert venue. Two museums, of antiquities and of natural history, plus an art gallery, can be visited (©9351 2222 for details; free). Famous alumni include

Germaine Greer, Clive James, Jane Campion and the current prime minister John Howard.

Jubilee Park and Blackwattle Studios

Map 6, C2. Buses #431, #434.

A few blocks beyond St Johns Road, the action stops and Glebe Point Road trails off into a more residential area, petering out at **Jubilee Park** with characterful views across the water to boats and Rozelle Bay's container terminal. The pleasantly landscaped waterfront park, complete with huge shady Moreton Bay fig trees and a children's playground, offers an unusual view of far-off Sydney Harbour Bridge framed within Sydney's newest span, the fanciful Glebe Island Bridge.

Across from the park at 465 Glebe Point Rd, it's worth popping into the **Blackwattle Studios** (Mon–Fri 8am–4pm, Sun 9am–4pm). Artists have been operating for over twenty years from this industrial waterside building, formerly a wool warehouse, a lumber- and then a boatyard. Under the rough and ready corrugated iron roof, artists, designers, craftspeople, architects and a film production company have their studios. Some have windows displaying work, while others splurge on a showroom, and after a look you can enjoy the food, coffee and views –across to the Glebe Island Bridge and the boats opposite – at the insouciant café, the *Blackwattle Canteen* (see p.167).

NEWTOWN

Newtown, across Sydney University from Glebe, and easily reached by train to Newtown Station, is another up-and-coming inner-city neighbourhood. What was once a working-class district – a hotchpotch of derelict factories, junkyards and cheap accommodation – has been transformed into a trendy but still offbeat and alternative area with a sense of urban grittiness. Body piercing, shaved heads and weird fashions rule. Newtown is characterized by its large gay and lesbian population, its rich cultural mix, from Africans to Fijians, and a healthy dose of students and lecturers from nearby Sydney University.

The main drag, **King Street** (map 6, D7), is filled with unusual secondhand and speciality shops, funky fashion and home stores and book and record outlets; during the month-long **Newtown Festival** from early October, various shop windows are taken over by young, irreverent and in-your-face art. The street has an enviable number of great cafés – even the newsagents' has an espresso bar attached – and diverse restaurants. A prestige cinema complex, the Dendy (see p.227), with an attached bookshop, excellent record store, and streetfront café, is also open daily and into the night.

King Street becomes quieter on the **St Peters** (map 6, C9) side of Newtown Station, but it's well worth strolling down to look at the furniture shops catering to all budgets and the more unusual speciality shops. You'll also find a couple of theatres and a High School for the Performing Arts, reputed to be one of the top five performing arts schools in the world – Sydney's version of the kids from *Fame*.

So far, **Enmore**, which begins along **Enmore Road** (map 6, B8), stretching west from King Street, opposite Newtown Station, has escaped gentrification, with the result that the migrant population – shops and businesses include Turkish, Chinese, Fijian, Thai, Greek and Italian-run places – hasn't been squeezed out by higher rents and more expensive leases. It's generally much quieter than Newtown, except when a big band is playing at the **Enmore Theatre** (see p.209).

Erskineville Road (map 6, D8), stretching from the eastern side of King Street marks the beginning of the adjoining suburb of **Erskineville**, something of a gay enclave, with its own train station.

The *Imperial Hotel* in Erskineville featured in the film *Priscilla, Queen of the Desert*. See p.233 for details of the Priscilla drag shows – a real riot.

BALMAIN

Balmain, directly north of Glebe (bus #433 or #434), is less than 2km from the Opera House by ferry from Circular Quay to Darling Street Wharf. Stuck out on a spur in the harbour and separated from the centre by Darling Harbour and Johnston's Bay, perhaps it's this degree of separation that has helped Balmain retain its slow, villagey atmosphere and made it the favoured abode of many writers and filmmakers. However, the new Glebe Island Bridge has drastically reduced driving time from the city centre and the #442 can whizz you over from outside the Queen Victoria Building.

Like better-known Paddington, Balmain was once a working-class quarter of terraced houses that has gradually been renovated. The docks at White Bay are still important, though, and Balmain hasn't completely forsaken its roots, with a good mix of old, young and families. **Darling Street** rewards a leisurely stroll, with a bit of browsing in its speciality shops (focused on clothes and gifts), and grazing in its restaurants and cafés. It, and the surrounding backstreets, are also blessed with enough watering holes to warrant a **pub crawl** – two classics are the *London Hotel* on Darling Street (see p.206) and the *Exchange Hotel* on Beattie Street (see p.205). The best time to come is on Saturday, when a lively **market** occupies the grounds of St Andrews Church on the corner opposite the *London Hotel*.

For long light, stunning sunsets and wow-worthy real

BALMAIN

estate, meander down the backstreets towards the spit of land called **Birchgrove**, where Louisa Road leads to **Birchgrove Wharf**. From here you can catch a ferry back to Circular Quay, or stay and relax in the small park on Yurulbin Point. Alternatively, the #441 bus can whisk you back into town.

Leichhardt and Rozelle

It's almost an hour from The Rocks to Balmain by the #440 bus, via **Leichhardt**, Sydney's "Little Italy", where the famous **Norton Street** strip of cafés and restaurants runs off ugly **Parramatta Road**. Leichhardt is very much up-and-coming – new, shiny, trendy Italian cafés keep popping up all along the strip, keeping pace with the development of the street. The focus is on the new upmarket cinema complex, The Palace, with attached record store, bookshop and Internet café; a huge new shopping centre is also being built nearby. But the two most authentic Italian cafés, the low-key *Caffe Sport* at the Parramatta Road end, and the lively and much-loved *Bar Italia* (see p.169), a fifteen-minute walk further down Norton, at the extent of the tempting array of eateries, are still the best.

From Leichhardt, the #440 bus continues to Darling Street, which runs from **Rozelle** right down to Balmain's waterfront. Rozelle, once very much the down at heel, poorer sister to Balmain is now emergently trendy with Sydney College of the Arts and the Sydney Writers' Centre based here in the extensive grounds of the old waterfront hospital. There are also lots of cafés, bookshops, speciality shops, gourmet grocers, restaurants and designer home-goods stores. Its pubs have emerged from their stuporous gloom with glass fronts and breezy decor. Further on towards Balmain, Elkington Park has the quaint **Dawn Fraser Swimming Pool**, an old-fashioned harbour pool named after the famous Australian Olympic swimmer.

Haberfield: a Federation Suburb

Immediately west of Leichhardt, between Parramatta Road and Iron Cove on the Parramatta River, lies the entirely planned suburb of **Haberfield**. "Slum-less, Lane-less, and Pub-less" was the vision of the post-Federation developers; the new nation was to have the ultimate urban environment. The style of the fifteen hundred homes, all designed by the architect J. Spencer-Stanfield, is a classic Australian confection called **Federation Style**, which spread around the country from 1901. Eminently suited to the climate, the houses are a pleasing combination of the functional – wide verandahs that allow cooling breezes to circulate – with the fanciful, such as attics and turrets. Stained glass is an important decorative element, often with very Australian motifs of kookaburras and native flowers or flowing Art Nouveau designs. Elaborate chimneys, fretted woodwork, and gables and eaves are other key features. Every Spencer-Stanfield house in Haberfield is different, so you can easily spend a fascinating afternoon wandering its tranquil, leafy streets. And you still won't find a pub.

To **get there**, take bus #436 from Circular Quay or George Street in the city centre.

Sydney Harbour

Loftily flanking the mouth of Port Jackson, **Sydney Harbour**'s main body of water, are the rugged sandstone cliffs of North Head and South Head, providing spectacular viewing points across the calm water to the city 11km away, where the Harbour Bridge spans the sunken valley at its deepest point. The coves, bays, points and headlands of the harbour, and their parks, bushland and swimmable beaches offer many hours of rewarding exploration. However, harbour beaches are not as clean as ocean ones, and after storms are often closed to swimmers (see p.279 for beach safety and etiquette). Finding your way by ferry is the most pleasurable method: services run to much of the North Shore and to harbourfront areas of the eastern suburbs. The eastern shores are characterized by a certain glitziness and are the haunt of the nouveaux riches, while the leafy North Shore is very much old money. Both sides of the harbour – the North Shore in particular – have pockets of bushland which have been incorporated into Sydney Harbour National Park. The NPWS publishes an excellent free map detailing the areas of the national park and its many walking tracks (℡9337 5511 for general information). Five islands also pepper the harbour with two of them – Goat Island and Fort Denison – visitable on tours; the other three, Shark Island, Clarke Island and Rodd

Island, are bookable for picnics but you must arrange your own transport.

....

The areas covered by this chapter are shown in detail on colour maps 4, 7 & 10.

....

RUSHCUTTERS BAY TO SOUTH HEAD

The suburbs on the hilly southeast shores of the harbour, heading to **Watsons Bay** and **South Head**, are rich and exclusive. An early nineteenth-century mansion, **Vaucluse House**, is open to visitors, giving an insight into the lifestyle of the pioneering upper crust.

Rushcutters Bay

Map 7, G–H5. Bus #324, #325.

Only ten minutes' walk northwest from Kings Cross, **Rushcutters Bay Park** is set against a wonderful backdrop of a yacht- and cruiser-packed marina. Gangs of picnickers book out the **tennis** courts at the popular Rushcutters Bay Tennis Centre (see p.277) feasting in between sets. If you don't have anyone to play with, the friendly managers promise a hitting partner thrown in with the court; there's a nice little coffee bar too if it all seems too much.

Darling Point and Double Bay

Map 10, E7. Ferry from Circular Quay to Darling Point and Double Bay; bus #323, #324, #325, #330 to Double Bay; bus #327 to Darling Point.

Continuing northeast to **Darling Point** from Rushcutters Bay, McKell Park (map 4, M3) provides a wonderful view across to Clarke Island and Bradleys Head, both part of

Harbour Islands

Two harbour islands, Fort Denison and Goat Island, can be regularly visited on NPWS tours. **Fort Denison** (map 4, J1), a small island east of the Opera House and visible from Bennelong Point, was originally used as a special prison for the tough nuts the penal colony couldn't crack: locals still call it "Pinchgut" alluding to the starvation conditions. During the Crimean Wars in the mid-nineteenth century, however, old fears of a Russian invasion were rekindled and the fort was built as part of a defence ring around the harbour. If it's around lunchtime you'll hear the One O'Clock Gun, originally fired so sailors could accurately set their ships' chronometers. Tours are booked from – and meet up at – the NPWS' Cadman's Cottage centre in The Rocks (✆9247 8861). There are daytime tours (Wed 11.30am & 1.30pm, Sat & Sun 11.45am & 1.45pm; $12; 2hr 30min) and longer sunset tours (Thurs & Fri 5.30pm, Sat 6pm; $14; 3hr), where you get some extra time to relax and enjoy the view – you're encouraged to bring some nibbles and a bottle of wine.

Just across the water from Balmain East, **Goat Island** (map 4, D1) is the site of a well-preserved gunpowder magazine complex. The sandstone buildings, including a barracks, were built by two hundred convicts between 1833 and 1839. Treatment of the convicts was harsh: 18-year-old Charles Anderson, a mentally impaired convict with a wild temper who made several attempts to escape, received over twelve hundred lashes in 1835 – and if that wasn't enough, he was sentenced to be chained to a rock for two years in an attempt to break him, with Sydneysiders teasing him as they boated past. Tethered to the rock, which you can still see, his unhealed back crawling with maggots, he slept in a cavity hewn into the sandstone "couch". Eventually Anderson ended up on the penal settlement of

Norfolk Island halfway between Australia and New Zealand, where under the humane prison reform experiments of Alexander Maconochie, the abused Anderson made a startling transformation responsibly managing the island's signal station.

The NPWS runs various **tours** with Sydney Ferries (bookings essential, call ℗9247 5033), making the most of the island's gruesome history and its present use as the shooting location for the popular TV drama series *Water Rats* about the water police. Tours range from a Heritage Tour (Mon, Fri & Sat 1pm; $11), a picnic tour (Sun 11.30am; BYO picnic), to a *Water Rats* tour checking out film sets (Wed noon; $13).

Sydney Harbour National Park. The next port of call is **Double Bay**, dubbed "Double Pay" for obvious reasons. The noise and traffic of New South Head Road are redeemed by several excellent antiquarian and secondhand bookshops, while in the quieter "village" are some of the most exclusive shops in Sydney, full of imported designer labels and expensive jewellery. The Eastern Suburbs socialites meet on Cross Street (map 4, M5), where the swanky pavement cafés are filled with well-groomed women in Armani outfits, their Mercedes and Rolls Royces illegally parked outside. If all this sounds like a turn-off, Double Bay's real delight is **Redleaf Pool** (daily Sept–May dawn–dusk; free; map 4, N5), a peaceful, shady harbour beach, one of the cleanest, enclosed by a wooden pier you can dive off or just laze on; there's also an excellent café famed for its fruit salad and latte.

Rose Bay

Map 10, G7. Ferry from Circular Quay; bus #323, #324, #325.
The ferry to **Rose Bay** gives you a chance to check out the waterfront mansions of **Point Piper** (map 10, F6),

where Dame Joan Sutherland was born, as you skim past. Rose Bay itself is quite a haven of exclusivity, featuring the verdant expanse of the members-only Royal Sydney Golf Course. Directly across New South Head Road from the course, waterfront **Lyne Park** (map 10, F7) has been the base of a **seaplane** service since the 1930s; the planes are a dramatic sight as they lift off and land on the water. There are regular services to Newcastle and planes can be chartered to go to Palm Beach or Berowra Waters, or there are scenic flights (see p.30). Rose Bay is also a popular **windsurfing** spot, and you can rent equipment here if you fancy a dunking (see p.281).

Nielson Park

Map 10, G5. Bus #325.

Sydney Harbour National Park emerges onto the waterfront at Bay View Hill, where the one-and-a-half-kilometre **Hermitage walking track** to Nielson Park begins; the starting point, Bay View Hill Road, is off South Head Road between the Kambala School and the Rose Bay Convent (on bus routes #324 and #325). The walk takes about an hour, with great views of the Opera House and Harbour Bridge, some lovely little coves to dip in and a picnic ground and sandy beach at yacht-filled **Hermit Point**. Extensive, tree-filled **Nielson Park**, on Shark Bay, is one of Sydney's delights (don't worry about the ominous name – it's netted), a great place for a swim, a picnic, or a cappuccino at the popular café. Within the park, the decorative Victorian-era mansion, **Greycliffe House**, built for William Wentworth's daughter in 1852 (see opposite), is now the headquarters of Sydney Harbour National Park; pop in for information on other waterfront walks.

Vaucluse House

Map 10, G7. Tues–Sun & public holiday Mon 10am–4.30pm; $6.
Bus #324.

Beyond Shark Bay, Vaucluse Bay shelters the magnificent Gothic Revival **Vaucluse House** and its 27-acre park-like estate on Wentworth Road. The house dates from the early nineteenth century, but its most famous owner was the influential Australian-born explorer and reformer **William Wentworth**, whose mother was a former convict and father a doctor with a dubious past; a major figure in the colony, he was a member of the first party to cross the Blue Mountains (see p.318). In 1831 he invited four thousand guests to Vaucluse House to celebrate the departure of the hated Governor Darling (1824–31). In his struggle for popular rights in the colony, Wentworth detested Darling's upholding of the king's authority and his favouring of the large landholders. The climax of the evening was a fireworks display which burned "Down with the Tyrant" into the night sky. The house is restored to the middle period of the Wentworths' occupation (1829–1853), and has some of the original furniture.

Buses #324 and #325 go from Circular Quay via Pitt Street, Kings Cross and Edgecliff to Watsons Bay via New South Head Road; the #325 detours at Vaucluse for Nielson Park.

Watsons Bay and South Head

Map 10, G–H5 & G–H4. Ferry from Circular Quay; bus #324, #325.

Narrow **Parsley Bay**, crossed by a pedestrian suspension bridge, follows Vaucluse Bay to **Watsons Bay**, on the finger of land culminating in South Head. Once a fishing village, the suburb has retained a villagey feel with old fishermen's cottages still found on the tight streets. It's an appropriate location for one of Sydney's most famous fish restaurants, *Doyles*, right out on the bay by the old Fishermans Wharf (see p.186). For a less expensive vista, you can settle in at the bayfront beer garden of the adjacent *Watsons Bay Hotel* (see p.204).

Spectacular ocean views are just a two-minute walk away through grassy Robertson Park, across Gap Road to **The Gap** (map 10, 5H), whose high cliffs are notorious as a place to commit suicide. A **walking track** leads to South Head through another chunk of **Sydney Harbour National Park**. The track heads back to the bay side, past **Camp Cove** (map 10, G4), a tiny palm-fronted beach popular with families. If you'd prefer to swim *au naturel*, continue on the track to the next bay just on the harbour side of South Head, to reach Sydney's best-known **nude beach**, Lady Jane (officially "Lady Bay" on maps); unfortunately ogling tour boats cruise past all weekend. From Lady Bay, it's a further fifteen minutes' walk to **South Head** (map 10, H4), the lower jaw of the harbour mouth affording fantastic views of Port Jackson and the city.

THE NORTH SHORE

The **North Shore**, where Sydney's "old money" is mainly found, is generally more affluent than the South. **Neutral Bay** and **Mosman** in particular have some stunning waterfront real estate, priced to match; upmarket **Military Road**, running from Neutral Bay to Mosman, is something of a gourmet strip with a string of excellent, albeit expensive, restaurants, and a number of tempting patisseries and well-stocked delis. Around the water, it's surprising just how much harbourside bushland remains intact here: "leafy" just doesn't do it justice. A ride on any ferry lets you gaze at beaches, bush, yachts and swish harbourfront

Luna Park

Looking across from the Harbour Bridge to the north side of the harbour, you can't miss the huge laughing clown's face that belongs to **Luna Park** (map 10, C5) on Lavender Bay at **Milsons Point**. Built at the height of the amusement park era, it's been a feature of Sydney since the 1930s; it was closed down for several years from the late 1980s until the grand reopening in January 1995 with a new clown's face – the eighth since Luna Park began – closely resembling the 1950s model. Unfortunately, the noise from the state-of-the-art roller coaster upset nearby residents who'd grown used to peace and quiet, and the park promptly closed again, losing developers millions of dollars. If it does reopen, it's well worth checking out the murals in Coney Island, a sort of indoor funfair within a funfair, which were restored by local artists to their 1930s glory.

houses and is one of the chief joys of this area – even if the people who live "on the other side of the bridge" and use the ferry to commute are so inured to the glorious views they keep their eyes firmly glued to their newspapers. Many North Shore office staff don't even need to get to the other side to go to work: **North Sydney** (map 10, C3) itself, just across the bridge, is quite a corporate high-rise centre. At **Crows Nest** (map 10, C3), just north of North Sydney along the Pacific Highway, there's a heavy concentration of restaurants in a very small area.

Kirribilli and Neutral Bay

Map 10. To Kirribilli: ferry to Kirribilli Wharf (Holbrook St); bus #263, #273. To Neutral Bay: ferry to Neutral Bay (Hayes St); bus #263.

Just east of the Harbour Bridge and immediately opposite the Opera House, **Kirribilli** (map 10, D5) on Kirribilli

Bay is a mainly residential area, although it hosts a great antique and bric-a-brac **market** on the last Saturday of the month in Bradfield Park. On Kirribilli Point, the current Prime Minister, native Sydneysider John Howard, lives in an official residence, **Kirribilli House** rather than Canberra. Admiralty House, next door, is the Sydney home of the largely decorative Governor General; it's where the British Royal Family stay when they're in town.

The highlight of North Shore drinking is the shady beer garden at Neutral Bay's *Oaks Hotel* **on Military Road (see p.204).**

Cremorne

Map 10, D–E5 & D4. Ferry to Cremorne Point Wharf; bus #245.

Bush-covered **Cremorne Point**, which juts into the harbour here, is also worth a jaunt. Catch the ferry from Circular Quay and you'll find a quaint open access sea pool to swim in by the wharf; from here, you can walk right around the point to Mosman Bay (just under 2km; see below), or in the other direction, past the pool, there's a very pretty walk along **Shell Cove** (1km).

Mosman Bay

Map 10, D–E5 & D–E4. Ferry from Circular Quay to Mosman South Wharf (Musgrave St) or Mosman Wharf (Avenue St). Bus #230, #236, #247.

Mosman Bay's seclusion was first recognized as a virtue during its early days as a whaling station, since it kept the stench of rotting whale flesh from Sydney Cove. Now the seclusion correlates with wealth. The ferry ride into the narrow, yacht-filled bay is a choice one – get off at Mosman Wharf, not Mosman South – and fittingly finished off with a beer at the unpretentious *Mosman Rowers' Club* (visitors welcome).

> **You can catch a bus from Musgrave St Wharf to upmarket Military Road (see p.108) or to pretty Balmoral Beach on Middle Harbour.**

Taronga Zoo

Map 10, E4–E5. Daily 9am–5pm; $16, child $8.50, family $41: $21 Zoo Pass including return ferry, bus and entry, child pass $10.50. Australian wildlife tours 10.10am, 11.10am & 1.10pm; no booking required. Ferry to Taronga Zoo (Athol) Wharf; bus #227, #238, #247.

What Mosman is most famous for is **Taronga Zoological Park** on Bradleys Head Road, with its superb hilltop position overlooking the city. The zoo houses bounding Australian marsupials, native birds (including kookaburras, galahs and cockatoos), and sea lions and seals from the sub-Antarctic region. You'll also find all the usual exotic beasts from around the world, including a pair of rare snow leopards as well as domestic animals in the form of a farmyard nursery for the little ones. The most scenic form of transport to the zoo, and the best way of reaching it, is the ferry from Circular Quay to the Taronga Zoo Wharf. Though there's a lower entrance near the wharf on Athol Road, it's best to start your zoo visit from the upper entrance so you can wind your way downhill and exit for the ferry: State Transit buses meet the ferries for the trip uphill. When the cable car is repaired you will be able to take it from the base to the top of the zoo for a few extra dollars on top of your entry fee.

TARONGA ZOO

—

Bradleys Head to Chowder Bay

Map 10, E5 & F5. To Bradleys Head, as for Taronga Zoo, then a 4km walk. To Clifton Gardens: bus #228.

Beyond Taronga Zoo, at the termination of Bradleys Head Road, **Bradleys Head**, at the point of a finger extending into the harbour, is marked by an enormous mast that towers over the rocky point. The mast once belonged to *HMS Sydney*, a World War I battleship which sank a German sea-raider, long since gone to the wrecker's yard. It's a peaceful spot with a dinky lighthouse and, of course, a fabulous view back over the south shore. A colony of ringtailed possums nests here, and boisterous flocks of rainbow lorikeets visit. The headland comprises another large chunk of **Sydney Harbour National Park** and you can walk to Bradleys Head via the four-kilometre **Ashton Park walking track** which starts near the Taronga Zoo ferry wharf, and continues beyond the headland to Taylors Bay and Chowder Head, finishing at **Clifton Gardens**, where there's a jetty and sea baths on Chowder Bay. A bus will take you back to the city centre from here. A now defunct military reserve (see opposite) separates Chowder Bay from another chunk of Sydney Harbour National Park on Middle Head.

MIDDLE HARBOUR

Middle Harbour is the largest inlet of Port Jackson, its two sides joined across the narrowest point at **The Spit**. The Spit Bridge opens regularly to let tall-masted yachts through – much the best way to explore its pretty, quiet coves and bays; several cruises pass by (see p.35). Crossing the Spit Bridge (map 10, E1), you can walk all the way to Manly Beach along the ten-kilometre Manly Scenic Walkway (see p.124), while bus #144 runs from Spit Road to Manly Wharf, taking in a scenic route uphill overlooking the Spit marina.

Northbridge and Castlecrag

Map 10, D1 & D2. To Castlecrag: bus #203, #275. To
Northbridge: bus #202.

There are some architectural gems lurking around Middle
Harbour: the 1889 bridge leading to **Northbridge**, which
Jan Morris in *Sydney* describes rather fancifully as "an enormously castellated mock-Gothic bridge, with hefty towers,
arches, crests and arrow-slits, such as might have been
thrown across a river in Saxe-Coburg by some quixotic
nineteenth-century princeling"; and the idyllic enclave of
Castlecrag. The latter was designed in 1924 by **Walter
Burley Griffin**, fresh from planning Canberra and intent
on building an environmentally friendly suburb – free of
the fences and the red-tiled roofs he hated – that would be
"for ever part of the bush".

Middle Head and Cobblers Beach

Map 10, G3. Bus #247.

Between Clifton Gardens in Mosman and Balmoral Beach, a
military reserve and a naval depot block coastal access to both
Georges Head and the more spectacular **Middle Head**,
although they can be reached by road. However, the military
have mostly withdrawn from the site, and plans to build new
housing there have met with fierce protests. On the Hunters
Bay side of Middle Head, tiny **Cobblers Beach** is officially
nude, and is a much more peaceful, secluded option than the
more famous Lady Jane at South Head (see p.108).

Balmoral Beach

Map 10, F3. Ferry from Circular Quay to Taronga Zoo (Athol)
Wharf then bus #238; ferry to Mosman South (Musgrave Street)
Wharf then bus #233, #257.

The bush backdrop provided by Middle Head lends **Balmoral Beach**, on Hunters Bay, the peaceful secluded air that makes it so popular with families (it's netted to keep out sharks, too, which helps). There's something very Edwardian and genteel about palm-filled, grassy Hunters Park and its bandstand, which is still used for Sunday jazz concerts or even Shakespeare recitals in summer. The civilized air is added to by the pretty white-painted **Bathers Pavilion** at the northern end, now converted into a salubrious restaurant/café. There are really two beaches at Balmoral, separated by **Rocky Point**, a noted picnicking spot reached by a decorative footbridge. The low-key esplanade has some takeaway shops, a quiet café, an excellent fish-and-chip shop, and a fine bottle shop. South of Rocky Point, the "baths" – actually a netted bit of beach with a boardwalk and lanes for swimming laps – have been here in one form or another since 1899; you can rent sailboards, catamarans and take lessons from the neighbouring boat shed (see p.280).

The hillside houses overlooking Balmoral have some of the highest price tags in Sydney: for a stroll through some of this, head for **Chinamans Beach**, via Hopetoun Avenue and Rosherville Road.

Ocean beaches

Sydney's beaches are among its great natural joys, key elements in the equation that makes the city special. Its ocean beaches provide surf, but also some more sheltered coves, and there's usually a sea pool where you can swim laps away from the waves. With the harbour splitting the city in half, the two stretches of ocean beaches on either side are deemed the Northern Beaches – which continue beyond Manly for 30km up to Barrenjoey Heads and Palm Beach – and the Eastern Beaches – from Bondi stretching south to Maroubra. For a full rundown on beach safety and etiquette, and surfing tips and lessons, see p.279.

The areas covered in this chapter are shown on map 2, and in detail on maps 8 and 9.

BONDI BEACH

Map 8. Bondi Junction CityRail then bus #361, #365, #380, #382, #389. Airport Express bus #351.

Bondi Beach is synonymous with Australian beach culture, and indeed the mile-long curve of golden sand must be one of the best-known beaches in the world. Big, brash and action-packed, it's certainly not the best place for a quiet sunbathe and swim, but the sprawling sandy crescent really is a spectacular sight when you first see it as you swoop down the hill of Bondi Road. Red-tiled houses and apartment buildings crowd in to catch the view, many of them erected in the 1920s when Bondi was a working-class suburb. Although still residential, it has long since become a popular gathering place for backpackers from around the world who turn Christmas Day into a big beach event (see "Festivals and Events" p.265), though the charm has begun to wear off and many have headed south to Coogee or north to Manly, especially as Bondi is now a favourite with rampaging teens on Friday and Saturday nights.

Beachfront **Campbell Parade** (map 8, E–F1) is both cosmopolitan and highly commercialized, lined with cafés and shops. Much money has recently been spent improving the congested parade, widening the footpaths and landscaping, so that sidewalk dining is now the norm.

Between Campbell Parade and the beach, **Bondi Park**, always full of sprawling bodies in fine weather, slopes down to the promenade where there are two board ramps for rollerblading and skateboarding. The focus of the promenade is the arcaded, Spanish-style **Bondi Pavilion** (map 8, F1), built in 1928 as a de luxe changing-room complex and now converted to a **community centre** hosting an array of workshops, classes and events, from drama and comedy to day-time dance parties and outdoor film festivals (programme details on ©9130 3325 Mon–Fri, ©9368 1253 Sat & Sun). Downstairs in the foyer, photos of Bondi's past are worth checking out, with some classic beach images of men in 1930s bathing suits, and the adjoining **souvenir shop** (daily 9.30am–5.30pm) is a haven of old-fashioned Bondi imagery. There's also an **art gallery** (daily 10am–5pm) exhibiting local artists.

On Sunday the **Bondi Beach markets** (10am–5pm) in the grounds of the primary school on the corner of

Bondi's Surf Lifesavers

Surf lifesavers are what made Bondi famous and there's a bronze sculpture of one outside the Bondi Pavilion. The surf lifesaving movement began in 1906 with the founding of the Bondi Surf Life Bathers' Lifesaving Club in response to the drownings that accompanied the increasing popularity of swimming. From the beginning of the colony, swimming was harshly discouraged as an unsuitable bare-fleshed activity. However, by the 1890s swimming in the ocean had become the latest fad, and a Pacific Islander introduced the concept of catching waves or **bodysurfing** that was to become an enduring national craze. Although "wowsers" (teetotal puritanical types) attempted to put a stop to it, by 1903 all-day swimming was every Sydneysider's natural right.

The bronzed and muscled surf lifesavers – of both sexes – in their distinctive red and yellow caps are a highly photographed, world-famous Australian image. **Surf lifesavers** (members of what are now called Surf Life Saving Clubs, abbreviated to SLSC) are volunteers working the beach at weekends, so come then to watch their exploits such as whizzing out in the rescue boats for some practise manoeuvres – or look out for a surf carnival; **lifeguards**, on the other hand, are employed by the council and work all week during swimming season (year-round at Bondi).

Campbell Parade and Warners Avenue facing the northern end of the beach, sells some groovy fashion and jewellery.

Beached at Bondi, below the lifeguard lookout tower, rents out everything from umbrellas, wetsuits, cozzies and towels to surfboards and body-boards. They also sell hats and sun block and have lockers for valuables.

The beach

Surfing is part of the Bondi legend, the big waves ensuring that there's always a pack of damp young things hanging around, bristling with surfboards. However, the beach is carefully delineated, with surfers using the southern end. There are two sets of flags for swimmers and boogie-boarders, with families congregating at the northern end near the sheltered saltwater pool (free), and everybody else using the middle flags. The beach is netted and there hasn't been a shark attack for over forty years. If the sea is too rough, or if you want to swim laps, a seawater swimming pool at the southern end of the beach under the Bondi Icebergs Club building on Notts Avenue costs $1.

Topless bathing is allowed at Bondi – a long way from conditions right up to the late 1960s when stern beach inspectors were constantly on the lookout for indecent exposure. In fact, so blasé are the attitudes now that every January an irreverent sunset **nude surfing competition** is held, watched by TV cameras and a huge crowd offering a wry commentary.

THE EASTERN BEACHES

Many people find the beaches to the **south of Bondi** more enticing, and it's a popular walk or jog right around the oceanfront and clifftop **walking track** (with a fitness circuit) to Bondi's smaller, less brazen but very lively cousin **Coogee** (about 2hr 30min). En route you'll pass through gay favourite **Tamarama**, family-focused, café-cultured **Bronte**, narrow **Clovelly**, and **Gordons Bay** with its underwater nature trail. Randwick Council has designed the "Eastern Beaches Coast Walk" beyond Coogee to more downmarket Maroubra Beach; stretches of boardwalk and interpretive boards detailing environmental features which include some impressive rock pools brimming with sealife. The council provides a free guide-map detailing the Coogee to Maroubra walk, which can be picked up from the Customer Service Office, 30 Francis St, Randwick (©9399 0999), or from Coogee at the beachfront Coogee Kiosk, on Arden Street opposite *McDonald's*.

Tamarama

Map 8, E3. Bus #360, #361, #380.

From Bondi Beach, walk past the Bondi Icebergs Club on Notts Avenue, round Mackenzies Point, through Marks Park, until you reach the modest and secluded **Mackenzies Bay**, with convenient large slabs of rock on which to leave your towel. Next is **Tamarama Bay** (a 15min walk from Bondi), a deep, narrow beach favoured by the smart set and a hedonistic gay crowd ("Glamarama" to the locals), as well as surfers (who stay further out). Topless bathing is the norm here.

Apart from the small Surf Life Saving Club, where you can even take in a drop-in yoga class, the intimate beach has a popular café. However, if you don't feel like stretching, or getting up at all, a Riviera-style service (bookings on free call ©1800/232 242) offers chaise longues, umbrellas, fluffy white towels, and rather handsome attendants bringing drinks and snacks from the café, all for $10 an hour.

Bronte

Map 8, D4. Bus #378.

Walking through Tamarama's park you can follow the oceanfront road for five minutes to the next beach around, **Bronte Beach** on Nelson Bay, more of a family affair than Tamarama. The valley-like **park** beyond the beach is extensive and shady; there's a **mini-train ride** for small children

TAMARAMA, BRONTE

and an imaginative children's playground. At the **southern end** of the beach, palm trees give a suitably holiday feel against blue water views as you relax at one of the outside tables of Bronte Road's wonderful café strip. A natural rock enclosure makes a calm area to swim in, and there are rock ledges to lie on around the enclosed sea swimming pool known as **Bronte Baths** (open access; free).

It's a pleasant five-minute walk past the baths to **Waverly Cemetery** (map 8, D5), a fantastic spot to spend eternity. Established in 1877, it contains the graves of many famous Australians, with the bush poet contingent well represented by Henry Lawson.

Clovelly and Gordons Bay

Map 8, C–D7. Bus #X39, #329, #339, #340.

Beyond Waverly Cemetery – another five-minute walk – on the other side of the ominously named Shark Point, is the channel-like **Clovelly Bay**, with concrete platforms on either side and several sets of steps leading into the very deep water; the sheltered bay is a popular place for lap-swimming. On Sunday afternoons, the nearby **Clovelly Hotel** is a popular spot with locals and travellers, offering free live music.

From Clovelly you can rock-hop around to equally narrow **Gordons Bay**, though this can be a little tricky – backed by high sandstone cliffs with some rocky tunnels to pass through – you might be better off sticking to the road route along Cliffbrook Parade (map 8, C7). The rocks are a peaceful fishing spot, or locals choose secluded rocks to sunbathe on. The bay is a popular diving/snorkelling area with its protected **underwater nature trail**, a sort of underwater bush walk showing typical Sydney shore life. From here, a walkway leads around the waterfront to Major Street and then onto **Dunningham Reserve** (map 8, B8) overlooking the northern end of Coogee Beach; the walk to Coogee proper takes about fifteen minutes in all.

Coogee

Map 8, A–B7 to A–B9. Bus #314, #315, #372, #373.

Coogee is another long-popular seaside resort, almost on a par with Manly and Bondi. Dominated by the extensive *Coogee Bay Hotel*, which sits on the centre of beachfront **Arden Street** and is one of Sydney's best-known music venues, Coogee has had a reputation for entertaining Sydneysiders since Victorian times. At the northern end of the beach, the dome you can see over the *Beach Palace Hotel* is an 1980s restoration of the 1887 Coogee Palace Aquarium; in its heyday a gigantic dance floor surrounded by tanks of exotic fish that could accommodate 3000 pleasure-seekers; you can now eat *yum cha* and some pretty good Chinese-styleseafood under the roof (see p.188). If the Coogee Palace wasn't extreme enough, a vast entertainment pier opened inthe 1920s with a 1400-seat theatre as its centrepiece, but it wasn't a match for the strong surf and lasted less than ten years.

With its hilly streets of California-style apartment blocks looking onto a compact pretty beach enclosed by two cliffy green-covered headlands, Coogee has a snugness and a friendly local feel that its cousin Bondi just can't match. Everything is close to hand: Arden Street has a down-to-earth strip of cafés that compete with each other to sell the cheapest cooked breakfast, while the main shopping street, **Coogee Bay Road** (map 8, A8), running uphill from the beach has a choice selection of coffee spots and eateries, plus a big super-market. The imaginatively modernized promenade is a great place to stroll and hang out; between it and the beach a grassy park has free electric barbecues, picnic tables and shelters.

One of Coogee's chief pleasures are its baths, beyond the

COOGEE

southern end of the beach. The first, McIvers Baths, for women and children only, is known by locals as **Coogee Women's Pool** (noon–5pm; 20¢; map 8, B9); it's suitably secluded, with plenty of hidden rocks, for nude sunbathing if you prefer. Just south of women's pool, **Wylie's Baths**, a saltwater pool on the edge of the sea, is at the end of Neptune Street (7am–7pm; $2; map 8, B9) with big decks to lie on, and solar-heated showers. Immediately south of Wylie's, **Trenerry Reserve**'s spread of big flat rocks offer tremendous views and make a great place to chill out.

MANLY

Manly, just above **North Head** at the northern mouth of the harbour, is doubly blessed with both ocean and harbour beaches, plus bushwalking in the nearby stretch of Sydney Harbour National Park, and a cycling track heading in the other direction.

When Captain Arthur Phillip, the commander of the First Fleet, was exploring Sydney Harbour in 1788, he saw a group of well-built Aboriginal men onshore, proclaimed them to be **"manly"** and named the cove in the process. During the Edwardian era it became fashionable as a recreational retreat from the city, and the cheesy slogan of the time "Manly – seven miles from Sydney, but a thousand miles from care" still rings true today. The area has become quite a travellers' centre in recent years, with some of Sydney's best backpackers' hostels. An excellent time to visit is over the long weekend **Jazz Festival** in early October.

....

Ferries leave wharves 2 and 3 at Circular Quay for Manly twice an hour ($4; 30min); they operate until 11.30pm, after which, night bus #150 runs from Wynyard Station. The JetCat catamaran ($5.20) goes

twice as fast but isn't as interesting.

A day-trip to Manly, rounded off with a dinner of fish and chips, offers a classic taste of Sydney life. The ferry trip out here has always been half the fun: the legendary Manly Ferry service has been running from Circular Quay since 1854, and the service comes complete with a kiosk dispensing the ubiquitous Aussie meat pie. Ferries terminate at Manly Wharf in **Manly Cove** (map 9, B5), near a small section of harbour beach with a netted-off swimming area popular with families. Like a typical English seaside resort, **Manly Wharf** (map 9, B5) has always had a **funfair**: although it has now been modernized into a sort of two-storey shopping mall, a colourful Ferris wheel and merry-go-round still light up the waterfront.

The Manly Visitor Information Centre (daily 10am–4pm; ©9977 1088; map 9, 4B) is by South Steyne where a six-kilometre-long cycle path (shared with pedestrians and rollerbladers) runs north to Seaforth, past North Steyne Beach and Queenscliff. You can rent bikes from the Australian Travel Specialists at Manly Wharf (half-day $15, full day $25), though their rates are expensive.

Many first-time visitors mistake Manly Cove for the ocean beach, which is called **South Steyne** (shading into North Steyne) and is recognizable by the stands of Norfolk pine which line the shore; it in fact lies on the other side of the isthmus, 500m down **The Corso** (map 9, B4), Manly's busy pedestrianized main drag, lined with shops, cafés, pubs and fish-and-chip shops. The waterfront **Esplanade** has a host of more upmarket cafés, while **Belgrave Street** (map 9, B4), running north from Manly Wharf, is Manly's alternative strip, where you'll find some

MANLY

good cafés, interesting shops to browse and the Manly Environment Centre.

For a more idyllic beach than the long stretch of South Steyne, follow the footpath from the southern end of the beach around the headland to Cabbage Tree Bay, with two very pretty, green-backed beaches at either end – **Fairy Bower** to the west (map 9, C5) and **Shelley Beach** (map 9, D5) to the east.

Oceanworld

Map 9, A4. Daily 10am–5.30pm; $14.50, child $7.50, family $25–39; Ocean Pass including return ferry to Manly, adult $20.50, child $10, family $54.

From the wharf, the West Esplanade leads to **Oceanworld**, where clear acrylic walls hold back the water so you can saunter along the harbour floor, gazing at sharks and stingrays, and an impressive coral reef display. Seals are fed at 11.45am and 2pm.

Manly Scenic Walkway

Map 9, A4 & map 10, F–H1 & F–G2.

A wonderful long-distance seaside walk starts at Manly Cove. The **Manly Scenic Walkway** follows the harbour shore inland west from Manly Cove all the way back to Spit Bridge on Middle Harbour, where you can catch bus #180 back to Wynyard Station in the city centre (20min). The eight-kilometre walk takes you through a section of **Sydney Harbour National Park**, past a number of small beaches and swimmable coves, Aboriginal middens and some subtropical rainforest. The entire walk takes three to four hours but is broken up into six sections with obvious exit/entry points if you're not up to doing the whole thing; pick up a map from the Manly Visitor Information Centre (overleaf) or NPWS offices (p.28).

North Head

Map 9, E9. Bus #135.

You can take in more of the Sydney Harbour National Park south of Manly: catch the #135 bus from Manly Wharf to **North Head**, the harbour mouth's upper jaw, and follow the short circuitous Fairfax Walking Track to three lookout points including the **Fairfax Lookout** for splendid views. If you have your own car, there's a fee for parking ($3 hour, $5 day), but you can drop in en route to the NPWS office (daily 9am–4.30pm), 1km before the lookouts, to pick up free information leaflets. Smack bang in the middle of all this is National Park, a military reserve with its own **National Artillery Museum** (Wed, Sat & Sun noon–4pm; $4) sited in the historic **North Fort** (map 9, D8), which consists of a curious system of tunnels built into the headland.

There's more history at the old **Quarantine Station** (map 9, B–C8), on the harbour side of North Head, used from 1828 until 1984: arriving passengers and crew on ships where anyone had a contagious disease were set down at Spring Cove to serve a spell of isolation, all at the shipping companies' expense. Sydney residents, too, were forced here, most memorably during the plague which broke out in The Rocks in 1900, when 1832 people were quarantined (104 plague victims are buried in the grounds). The site, its buildings still intact, is looked after by the NPWS which offers **guided history tours** (Mon–Fri 10.40am, tour 1hr 30min, Sat & Sun 11.40am, tour 2hr; $10; booking essential ℡9977 6522), giving an insight not only into Sydney's immigration history but the evolution of medical science, often in gory detail. The tours (co-ordinating with the #135 bus) provide the only opportunity to get out to this beautiful isolated harbour spot. Night-time **ghost tours** (Wed & Fri–Sun at 7.30pm; 3hr; $20, including billy tea and damper; over 12 years only; see p.30 for Kids' Ghost Tour) are very popular but there's no public transport in the evening.

THE NORTHERN BEACHES

Map 2, E6.

The **northern beaches**, stretching from Manly to Palm Beach, can be reached by regular **bus** from Wynyard in the city in about 45 minutes on an express service and there are also buses from Manly. Bus #190 and #L90 runs from Wynyard to Avalon, continuing to Palm Beach via the Pittwater side of the Barrenjoey Peninsula.

Freshwater to Newport

Immediately on from the long stretch of North Steyne Beach at Manly, **Freshwater**, sitting snugly between two rocky headlands on Queenscliff Bay, is one of the most picturesque of the northern beaches. There's plenty of surf culture around the headland at **Curl Curl** and a walking track at its northern end, commencing from Huston Parade, which will take you above the rocky coastline to the curve of **Dee Why Beach** (bus #136 from Manly Wharf). Dee Why provides consistently good surf, while its sheltered lagoon makes it popular with families. Beyond the lagoon, windsurfers gather around **Long Reef**, where the point is surrounded by a wide rock shelf creviced with rock pools and protected as an aquatic reserve – well worth a wander to peek at the creatures within. The long, beautiful sweep of **Collaroy Beach** (bus #151, #155 or #157 from Manly Wharf or #151, #183 or #187–190 from

Carrington Street, Wynyard), now with a popular new YHA (see p.157), shades into **Narrabeen Beach** (bus #183 from Wynyard). Narrabeen is an idyllic spot backed by the extensive, swimmable and fishable **Narrabeen Lakes** popular with anglers and families; there's a good campsite by the lakes. Beyond Narrabeen, **Mona Vale** is a long, straight stretch of beach with a large park behind and a sea pool dividing it from sheltered **Bongin Bongin Bay** whose headland reserve and rocks to clamber on make it ideal for children. After Bongin Bongin Bay the Barrenjoey Peninsula begins, with calm Pittwater (see p.295) on its western side and ocean beaches running up its eastern side until it spears into Broken Bay. **Newport** (bus #187 from Milsons Point), boasts a fine stretch of ocean beach between two rocky headlands; on Sunday crowds gather to listen to live jazz in the beer garden of the *Newport Arms* (see p.204) on Kalinya Street, overlooking Heron Cove on Pittwater. Unassuming **Bilgola Beach**, next door to Newport, is one of the prettiest of the northern beaches.

Avalon, Whale and Palm beaches

#190 and #L90 to Avalon and Palm Beach, bus #193 from Avalon to Whale Beach.

From Newport, a trio of Sydney's best beaches, for both surf and scenery, runs up the eastern fringe of the mushroom-shaped peninsula: **Avalon** and **Whale Beach** – popular surfie territory – are less fashionable than Palm Beach. The good people of Avalon controversially said a loud no in early 1999 to the filming of American babe-fest *Baywatch* at their beach, after experiencing the shooting of the tacky *Australia* special there the year before. Disappointed potential cast members are already back to waitressing in Bondi.

However, **Palm Beach**, has long let the cameras roll: the

beach leads a double life as "Summer Bay" in the famous Aussie soap *Home and Away*, with the Barrenjoey Lighthouse and headland regularly in shot; for $8 you can go on a popular location tour with the *YHA* (see p.157). Not that you could accuse Palm Beach of being tacky: living up to its name, it's a hangout for the rich and famous – you can even get here by Hollywood-style seaplane from Rose Bay (see p.105). The bush-covered headland is actually an outpost of Ku-Ring-Gai Chase National Park, the bulk of which is across Pittwater and visitable with Palm Beach Ferries (©9918 2747; cruise $25; 4hr 30min; Pittwater and Patonga hourly 9am–5pm, Sun 9am–6pm, $7 one-way).

The outskirts

ydney's mostly unattractive western suburbs cover the flat plains heading to the Blue Mountains, most westward travellers ultimate destination. The city's first successful farming area, Parramatta, has a cluster of historic buildings not swallowed up by development, and at the foothills of the mountains, Penrith offers river cruises on the Nepean River. The southern suburbs of Sydney have pockets of beauty and interest at La Perouse and Botany Bay National Park, and a superb surf beach at Cronulla.

The area covered in this chapter is shown on colour maps 2 & 3.

SOUTH

The southern suburbs of Sydney, arranged around huge **Botany Bay**, are seen as the heartland of red-tiled-roof suburbia, a terracotta sea spied from above as the planes land at **Mascot** airport. Clive James, the area's most famous son, describes it as a 1950s suburban wasteland in his tongue-in-cheek *Unreliable Memoirs* (see p.351). The popular perception of Botany Bay is coloured by its proximity to an airport, a high-security prison (Long Bay), an oil refinery, a container terminal and a sewerage outlet. Yet the surprisingly clean-looking water (pollution levels are high, however) is fringed by quiet, sandy beaches and the marshlands shelter a profusion of birdlife. Whole areas of the waterfront on either side at **La Perouse**, with its associations with eighteenth-century French exploration, and on the **Kurnell Peninsula** where Captain Cook first put anchor, are designated as part of **Botany Bay National Park**.

La Perouse

La Perouse (map 3, G7), tucked into the northern shore of Botany Bay, contains Sydney's oldest Aboriginal settlement, the legacy of a mission. The suburb took its name from **Laperouse**, the eighteenth-century French explorer, who set up camp here for six weeks, briefly and cordially meeting Captain Arthur Phillip, who was making his historic decision to forgo swampy Botany Bay and move on to Port Jackson. After leaving Botany Bay, the Laperouse expedition was never seen again. A monument erected in 1825 and an excellent museum between them tell the whole fascinating story.

The surrounding headlands and foreshore have been incorporated into the northern half of **Botany Bay National Park**, with a **visitor centre** (no park fee; ©9311 3379) sitting on a grassy headland between the pretty beaches of Congwong Bay and Frenchmans Bay in the same building as the Laperouse Museum (see opposite) where details of potential walks are available – there's a fine one past Congwong Bay Beach to Henry Head and its lighthouse (5km return). Nearby, the *Boatshed Cafe* is an idyllic spot for a cappuccino sitting right over the water with pelicans floating below. La Perouse is at its most lively on **Sunday** (and public holidays) when, following a tradition established at the turn of the century, Aboriginal people come down to sell boomerangs and other crafts, and demonstrate boomerang throwing; snake-handling skills are on display from 1.30pm. There are also tours of the nineteenth-century fortifications on **Bare Island** (Sat, Sun & public holidays 12.30pm, 1.30pm, 2.30pm & 3.30pm; $7; no booking required, wait at the gate to the island), joined to La Perouse by a walkway.

The Laperouse Museum

Map 3, G7. Tues–Sun 10am–4pm; $5. Bus #393, #394, #L94.

The **Laperouse Museum**, run by the NPWS, traces Laperouse's voyage in great detail, the displays enlivened by relics from the wrecks, exhibits of antique French maps and copies of etchings by the naturalists on board. The voyage was commissioned by the French king Louis XVI in 1785 as a purely scientific exploration of the Pacific to rival Cook's voyages, and strict instructions were given for Laperouse to "act with great gentleness and humanity towards the different people whom he will visit". After an astonishing three-and-a-half-year journey through South America, the Easter Islands, Hawaii, the northwest coast of America, and past China and Japan to Russia, the *Astrolabe* and the *Boussole* struck disaster – first encountering hostility in the Solomon Islands and then in their doomed sailing from Botany Bay, on March 10, 1788. (Even as he was about to be guillotined Louis XVI asked "At least, is there any news of Monsieur de Laperouse?") Their disappearance remained a mystery until 1828, when relics were discovered on Vanikoro in the Solomon Islands; the wrecks themselves were found only in 1958 and 1964.

A recent addition to the museum is an exhibition which looks at Aboriginal history and local culture.

THE LAPEROUSE MUSEUM |

The Kurnell Peninsula

Map 2, E9.

From La Perouse, you can see across Botany Bay to the **Kurnell Peninsula** and the red buoy marking the spot where Captain James Cook and the crew of the *Endeavour* anchored on April 29, 1770 for an eight-day exploration. Back in England, many refused to believe that the uniquely Australian plants and animals they had recorded actually existed – the kangaroo in particular was thought to be a hoax. **Captain Cook's Landing Place** is now the south head of **Botany Bay National Park**, where the interesting Discovery Centre (Mon–Fri 10am–4pm, Sat & Sun 9.30am–4.30pm; $7.50 fee per car; ©9668 9111) looks at the wetlands ecology of the park and tells the story of Cook's visit and its implications for Aboriginal people. Indeed the political sensitivity of the park has led to a search for an Aboriginal replacement name. One suggestion has been "Gillingarie" (land that belongs to us all) from the language of the original Dharawal people of the area. Set aside as a public recreation area in 1899, the heath and woodland is unspoilt and there are some secluded beaches for swimming; you may even spot parrots and honeyeaters if you keep your eyes peeled. To get here by **public transport**, take the train to Cronulla then Kurnell Bus Services #987 (©9524 8977 for times).

On the ocean side of the **Kurnell Peninsula** is Sydney's longest beach: the 10km stretch begins at **Cronulla** (map 2, E7) and continues as deserted, dune-backed **Wanda Beach**. This is prime surfing territory – and the only Sydney beach accessible by train (Cronulla CityRail). From Cronulla, you can catch a ferry to Bundeena in the Royal National Park (see p.334).

WEST

For fifty years, Sydney has been sliding ever west in a

monotonous sprawl of shopping centres, brick-veneer homes and fast-food chains, in the process swallowing up towns and villages, some of which date back to colonial times. The first settlers to explore inland found well-watered, fertile river flats, and quickly established agricultural outposts to support the fledgling colony. **Parramatta** and **Penrith**, once separate communities, have become satellite towns inside Sydney's commuter belt, but the beauty of the **Blue Mountains** (see p.318), are the eventual destination for most tourists heading west.

Three of Sydney's racecourses are in the western suburbs, see p.278 for details.

Parramatta

Map 3, A1

Situated on the Parramatta River, a little over 20km upstream from the harbour mouth, **Parramatta** was the first of Sydney's rural satellites – the first farm settlement in Australia, in fact. The fertile soil of "Rosehill", as it was originally called, saved the fledgling colony from starvation with its first wheat crop of 1789. It's hard to believe today, but dotted here and there among the malls and busy roads are a few remnants from that time – eighteenth-century public buildings and original settlers' dwellings that warrant a visit if you're interested in Australian history.

You can call in to Parramatta on your way out of Sydney to the Blue Mountains – a rather depressing drive along the ugly and congested Parramatta Road – or endure the dreary thirty-minute suburban train ride from Central Station. But much the most enjoyable way to get here is on the sleek RiverCat ferry from Circular Quay up the Parramatta River (1hr; $5 one-way). The wharf at Parramatta is on

Phillip Street, a couple of blocks away from the helpful **Parramatta Visitors Centre** on the corner of Church and Market streets (Mon–Fri 10am–4pm, Sat 9am–1pm, Sun 10.30am–3.30pm; ©9630 3703), which hands out free walking maps.

Historic Houses

Parramatta's most important historic feature is the National Trust-owned **Old Government House** Tues–Fri 10am–4pm, Sat & Sun 11am–4pm; last admission 3.30pm; $5) in **Parramatta Park** by the river. Turn left onto Marsden Street from the visitors centre, cross the river, then go right onto George Street. Entered through the 1885 gatehouse on O'Connell Street, the park – filled with native trees – rises up to the gracious old Georgian-style building, the oldest remaining public edifice in Australia. It was built between 1799 and 1816 and used as the viceregal residence until 1855; one wing has been converted into a pleasant tea-house. The three other main historic attractions are close together: from Parramatta Park, follow Macquarie Street and turn right at its end onto Harris Street. Running off here is Ruse Street, where the aptly named **Experiment Farm Cottage** Tues–Thurs 10am–4pm, Sun 11am–4pm; $5, free for National Trust members), at no. 9, was built on the site of the first land grant, given in 1790 to reformed convict James Ruse, a former Cornwall farmer who successfully raised wheat at a time when the colony was starving. Governor Phillip's "experiment" in giving land grants to convicts proved to be both an agricultural and social success. On parallel Alice Street, at no. 70, **Elizabeth Farm** (daily 10am–5pm; $6) dates from 1793 and claims to be the oldest surviving home in the country. The farm was built and run by the Macarthurs, who bred the first of the merino sheep that made Australian wealth "ride on a sheep's back"; a small café serves refreshments. Nearby **Hambledon Cottage** on

Lane Cove River

Some of Sydney's prettiest suburbs lie on the **Lane Cove River** (map 2, E1–E2) which runs into the Parramatta River. Exclusive Hunters Hill and Woolwich, are found on a peninsula which looks something like a map of Italy – with the Parramatta River on its southern side and the Lane Cove River on its northern side. The impressive houses, with beautiful gardens and views over both rivers, provide the setting for an elegant stroll. The peninsula can be reached via ferry from Circular Quay to the Valentia Street Wharf in **Woolwich** (map 10, A4) near its tip. A great way to explore it is to take a bus (North And Western Buses; ©9808 1000) up the hill to **Hunters Hill** (map 10, A4) and then wander back down Woolwich Road. Turn right off Woolwich Road at Elgin Street and follow it down into Clarke Road for Clarke Point Reserve with its lookout. On the first Sunday of the month, you might also like to drop in to look at an example of early Sydney domestic architecture, the tiny four-room Vienna Cottage, 38 Alexandra St, Hunters Hill (10am–4pm; $4), built in 1871 with an adjoining park and orchard.

As Lane Cove River meanders north from Hunters Hill, a valley of bushland between North Ryde and Chatswood is the **Lane Cove National Park** (©9412 1811) offering riverside walking tracks, a wildlife shelter and boat rental. You can camp or stay in en-suite cabins at an adjoining caravan park. To reach the park by public transport, take the train to Chatswood then bus #550 or #551; if you're driving, the park is accessed by Delhi Road, Lane Cove Road or Lady Game Drive.

Hassel Street (Wed, Thurs, Sat & Sun 11am–4pm; $3), built in 1824, was part of the Macarthur estate.

Featherdale Wildlife Park

Map 2, D6. Daily 9am–5pm; $12, children 4–14 $6, under 4s free, family $30. Blacktown CityRail and then bus #725.

About 10km northwest of Parramatta, at 217 Kildare Rd, Doonside, you can meet native animals at **Featherdale Wildlife Park**: cuddly koalas are the special attraction. Featherdale is 30km west of the city centre off the Western Highway between Parramatta and Penrith.

Penrith

Map 2, C6.

Penrith is the most westerly of Sydney's satellite towns, in a curve of the Nepean River at the foot of the Blue Mountains. It has an old-fashioned Aussie feel about it – a tight community that is immensely proud of the Panthers, its boisterous rugby league team (see p.274). From Penrith Station, you can't miss the huge lettering announcing the **Museum of Fire** on Castlereagh Road (Mon–Sat 10am–3pm, Sun 10am–5pm; $5), a very appropriate museum for the hot plains which head west to the bushfire-prone Blue Mountains: you can see simulations of fire and exhibits relating to bushfires, and, naturally, old fire engines. From town you can take in the spectacular **Nepean Gorge** from the decks of the paddle steamer *Nepean Belle* (bookings ℂ4733 1274; range of cruises from $12 for 1hr 30min) or head 24km south to the **Warragamba Dam**. The dam has created the huge reservoir of **Lake Burragorang**, a popular picnic spot with barbecues and a kiosk, and some easy bushwalking trails.

LISTINGS

Accommodation

There are a tremendous number of places to stay in Sydney, and fierce competition helps keep prices down. Finding somewhere to stay is only a problem from Christmas to the end of January, and during Mardi Gras in late February/early March: at these times you'll definitely need to **book ahead**. And needless to say, all accommodation will be scarce and expensive during the Olympics in September 2000.

Accommodation Prices

Rates are highest in December and January and during school holidays. Our listings for hotels, motels and B&Bs feature a code (eg ③) for the least expensive double room available outside peak holiday periods. Hostel rates are given in figures.

① Under $45	⑤ $90–115
② $45–60	⑥ $115–150
③ $60–75	⑦ $150–200
④ $75–90	⑧ $200–250

These prices do not include a ten percent **bed tax**, which applies to city centre (including Kings Cross) and North Sydney hotels; hostels are exempt from the tax.

Many places offer a discount for **weekly bookings**, and may also reduce prices considerably during the **low season** (roughly May–October, school holidays excepted; see box p.139).

HOTELS

The term "hotel" does not necessarily mean the same in Australia as it does elsewhere in the world – traditionally, an Australian hotel was a pub, a place to drink. Today, plenty of **pubs** have cleaned up their act and offer pleasant rooms (see listing p.151). Some budget places use the name **private hotel**, to distinguish themselves from licensed establishments. The city's larger **international hotels** are concentrated in The Rocks and the CBD, and charge around $150–220 for a double room. Rates in Kings Cross and nearby Potts Point, Elizabeth Bay and Woolloomooloo are much less expensive, with budget hotels charging from $50–60, and three- or four-star hotels around $130. **Serviced holiday apartments** (see box p.153) can be very good value for a group, but are generally heavily booked.

THE ROCKS

Old Sydney Park Royal
Map 5, C2. 55 George St ℗9252 0524, fax 9251 0393. Circular Quay CityRail/ferry. Airport Express #300.
Four-star right in the heart of The Rocks, with a central atrium that creates a remarkable feeling of space. The best rooms have harbour views, as does the rooftop swimming pool (plus spa and sauna). ⑦–⑧.

The Regent
Map 5, B4. 199 George St ℗9238 0000, fax 9251 2851. Circular Quay CityRail/ferry. Airport Express #300.

One of Australia's best hotels, this modern five-star has views of the Harbour Bridge and the Opera House. While there are certainly other more luxurious hotels in Sydney, *The Regent* has a well-earned reputation for personal service. ⑧.

CITY CENTRE

Hotel Intercontinental
Map 5, D4. 117 Macquarie St ⓒ9230 0200, fax 9240 1240. Circular Quay CityRail/ferry. Airport Express #300.

The old sandstone Treasury building forms the entry and lower floors of this 31-storey five-star property, with stunning views of the Botanic Gardens, Opera House and harbour. The vaulted arches of the old building rise up for three levels above the foyer's marble floor. There are four restaurants, a swimming pool on the top floor and a gym. ⑧.

Wynyard Vista Hotel
Map 5, B4. 7–9 York St ⓒ9274 1222, fax 9274 1274. Wynyard CityRail. Airport Express #300.

Handy for both the CBD and The Rocks. The best rooms in this recently refurbished 22-storey are the spacious studios; each has a kitchen, voicemail facility and a CD player. Pleasant café-brasserie. ⑦.

HAYMARKET

Aarons Hotel
Map 4, E6. 37 Ultimo Rd ⓒ9281 5555, fax 9281 2666. Central CityRail.

Recently renovated hotel in a lively area, with its own modern café where the light breakfast is served. Rooms may be charmless and cheaply furnished, but they're comfortable en-suites, all with TV, ceiling fan or air-con. Pricier courtyard rooms have air-con; all rates include breakfast. 24-hour reception and room service. ④–⑦.

HOTELS: CITY CENTRE, HAYMARKET

Carlton Crest

Map 4, E6. 169–179 Thomas St ©9281 6888, fax 9281 6688.
Central CityRail. Airport Express #300, #350, #352.
A modern, eighteen-storey tower fronted by an old hospital
facade in a quiet street near Chinatown. The hotel has a
relaxed atmosphere, and modern decor plain enough to suit all
tastes. Heated outdoor swimming pool and spa; terrace garden
with BBQ area. ⑦.

Goldspear Hotel

Map 5, B9. Capitol Square, Campbell and George streets ©9211
8633, fax 9211 8733. Central CityRail. Airport Express #300.
One of the centre's most affordable four-stars – doesn't cater to
tour groups, and is small enough to feel personal. In an excellent location right next to a number of cafés, it also has its own
restaurant serving Asian and European food. Price includes
buffet breakfast and free access to a gym. ⑥.

Westend Hotel

Map 4, F6. 412 Pitt St ©9211 4822, fax 9281 9570. Central CityRail.
Airport Express #350.
Old-style hotel with tastefully decorated, air-conditioned en-
suite rooms. Nearby traffic can be noisy. There's a bar and bottle shop, and the management are helpful. ⑤.

KINGS CROSS

De Vere Hotel

Map 7, F4. 44–46 Macleay St, Potts Point ©9358 1211, fax 9358
4685. Kings Cross CityRail or Bus #311. Airport Express #350.
Comfortable three-star hotel in a great position, close to cafés
and restaurants. Third- and fourth-floor rooms have stunning
views of Elizabeth Bay; studios with kitchenette are also available. ⑤–⑥.

Gazebo Hotel

Map 7, F4. 2 Elizabeth Bay Rd, Elizabeth Bay ©9358 1999, fax 9356 2951. Kings Cross CityRail. Airport Express #350.

Right next to Kings Cross' Fitzroy Gardens, with views over the city and harbour from most rooms and the top floor bar. Has a rooftop restaurant and bar, swimming pool and sauna, and parking is free. ⑥.

Highfield Private Hotel

Map 7, E5. 166 Victoria St, Kings Cross ©9326 9539, fax 9358 1552. Kings Cross CityRail. Airport Express #350.

Run by Scandinavians this is a very clean, modern, safe place. Rooms are well-equipped with fans, heating and sinks. Also three-bed dorms. Tiny kitchen/common room with TV. Rooms ①–②, dorms $19.

Macleay Lodge

Map 7, F4. 71 Macleay St, Potts Point ©9368 0660, fax 9357 4742. Kings Cross CityRail or Bus #311. Airport Express #350.

Don't expect anything fancy from this budget option on four floors, but it's fine and in a fab spot in the midst of Potts Point's café and restaurant scene. All rooms (bar one) share bathroom and come with sink, plates, cutlery, kettle, fridge and wonky colour TV; furniture is cheap and rooms are salmon pink. Best rooms have access to the balcony area. ②.

Manhattan Park Inn

Map 7, F4. 8 Greeknowe Ave, Elizabeth Bay ©9358 1288, fax 9357 3696. Kings Cross CityRail or Bus #311. Airport Express #350.

The foyer and restaurant are Art Deco and the decorative ceiling mouldings, and windows you can actually open, are a civilized touch. Bathrooms are colourful, and have tubs you can soak in. "Superior" rooms are large, with views over Elizabeth Bay. ⑥–⑦.

HOTELS: KINGS CROSS

Montpelier Central Hotel

Map 7, G4. 39a Elizabeth Bay Rd, Elizabeth Bay ℭ & fax 9358 6960.
Kings Cross CityRail or Bus #311. Airport Express #350.
Long-established budget hotel on four floors (no lift) in a central, scenic location; simple and clean, with friendly British management. Rooms come with TV, fridge and kettle; shower and toilets down the hall. Small kitchen and a laundry on the rooftop, with views over Rushcutters Bay. Lockers available. ①–②.

Sebel of Sydney

Map 7, F4. 23 Elizabeth Bay Rd, Elizabeth Bay ℭ9358 3244, fax 9357 1926. Kings Cross CityRail or Bus #311. Airport Express #350.
When the *Sebel* opened as Sydney's first five-star in the 1960s, it quickly became the entertainment industry's choice. Signed celebrity portraits cover the walls of the foyer and the tiny bar, but there's not a hint of snobbery or grandeur. Warmly furnished rooms, some with views of Rushcutters Bay Marina. Rooftop pool and sun deck, gym and sauna. ⑦–⑧.

DARLINGHURST & SURRY HILLS

City Crown Lodge

Map 7, C8. 289 Crown St (cnr Reservoir St), Surry Hills ℭ9331 2433, fax 9360 7760. Central CityRail.
A standard motel, but well located, offering en-suite units with heating, fan and small kitchenette. Free in-house movies. Some parking space; enter on Reservoir St. ⑤.

Kirketon Hotel

Map 7, E6. 229–231 Darlinghurst Rd, Darlinghurst ℭ9332 2011, fax 9332 2499. Kings Cross CityRail.
This renovated hotel is top in the fashion stakes, thanks to the big name Australian designers who created the swish interiors. On the ground level, stylish bars and a restaurant beckon, while

the forty rooms boast luxuries such as toiletries by Aveda, mohair throw rugs and CD players. You may feel less beautiful than the staff, but service is slick and 24-hour. ⑦–⑧.

L'Otel

Map 7, E6. 114 Darlinghurst Rd, Darlinghurst ☎9360 6868, fax 9331 4536. Kings Cross CityRail.

Stylish hotel with sixteen rooms, all en suite with TV, video, mini-bar and ceiling fans. Trendy bar and brasserie downstairs, befitting its location on a prime café strip. ⑥–⑦.

Oxford Koala Hotel

Map 7, C7. Cnr Oxford and Pelican streets, Darlinghurst ☎9269 0645, fax 9283 2741. Town Hall or Museum CityRail.

Multistoreyed hotel overlooking Hyde Park. The fully equipped apartments are ideal for families, and the complex has a swimming pool. Room service. ⑤–⑥.

GLEBE

Rooftop Motel

Map 6, E4. 146 Glebe Point Rd ☎9660 7777, fax 9660 7155. Bus #431, #433, #434. Airport Express #352.

Reasonably priced motel with 24-hour reception, right in the heart of Glebe; barbecue, swimming pool. Parking included. ⑤.

Hotel Unilodge

Map 6, A4. Cnr Broadway and Bay streets ☎9338 5000, fax 9338 5111. Bus #431–434, #438, #440.

Converted from a former department store, this hotel has a luxury feel but reasonable rates. Some of the self-catering rooms sleep up to five – excellent value for a small group. There's a tiny gym, lap pool, spa and sauna and a BBQ; 24-hour convenience store and food court in the foyer. Parking $5 per day. ⑥.

HOTELS: GLEBE

Gay & lesbian accommodation

Gay and lesbian couples are unlikely to experience problems booking in to a Sydney hotel; however, we've listed several places that are notably gay-friendly, and/or are close to Oxford St.

Helen's Hideaway ℭ9360 1678, fax 9360 4865 (address and rates provided on enquiry). Lesbian-owned B&B, catering for women only, in a peaceful, leafy street close to Oxford St. Bedrooms are individually designed, there's a sunny atrium, elegant dining room, balcony, and a sitting room with TV. ③.

Pelican Private Hotel 411 Bourke St ℭ & fax 9331 5344. *www.rainbow.net.au/pelican* Comfortable budget accommodation in one of Sydney's oldest gay guesthouses. Rooms have TV and fridge, but share facilities. Communal kitchen and courtyard; rate includes continental breakfast. ②.

Sydney Manor House Boutique Hotel 86 Flinders St ℭ9380 6633, fax 9380 5016; *manor@rainbow.net.au* This was the residence of Sydney's first Lord Mayor, now gay-owned and run mostly for men. Rooms have decks overlooking the courtyard, where there's a heated pool and a spa. Licensed restaurant and bar. Continental breakfast included. ⑤.

Wattle Private Hotel 108 Oxford St ℭ9332 4118, fax 9331 2074. Gay-friendly hotel in the heart of the pink strip, and although the rooms aren't flash, they're clean. Ask for the room on the roof, which opens out to the garden and spectacular views. Continental breakfast included. ④.

BONDI

Bondi Beachside Inn

Map 8, E1. 152 Campbell Parade ℭ9130 5311, fax 9365 2646. Bus #380, #382. Airport Express #351.

Multistoreyed motel opposite the beach: all the rooms – clean and modern with air-con – have balconies, and half have ocean views. Some have kitchenettes, and there's a two-bedroom apartment. Free security parking; 24-hour reception. ④–⑥.

MANLY

Manly Pacific Park Royal
Map 9, B4. 55 North Steyne, Manly ⊘9977 7666, fax 9977 7822. Manly wharf.

Beachfront, multistoreyed four-star hotel with 24-hour reception, room service, spa, sauna, gym and heated rooftop pool. Rooms with an ocean view are pricier. ⑦–⑧.

B&BS AND GUESTHOUSES

We have included places which label themselves **boutique hotels** in this section. Generally small and upmarket, they offer more personal service; you'll pay around $95–100 for a double en-suite room. **Guesthouses** and **B&Bs**, which are generally cheaper, are often pleasant, renovated old houses; some have share bathrooms (and possibly kitchen facilities), with prices from around $60 per room up to about $120.

THE ROCKS

The Russell
Map 5, C3. 143a George St ⊘9241 3543, fax 9252 1652. Circular Quay CityRail/ferry.

Charming, small heritage-listed hotel with Colonial-style decor. some are en suite but the small shared bathroom options are very popular – and a great price for the area. The best rooms have views of the Quay. Sunny central courtyard and a rooftop garden, sitting-room and bar, and downstairs restaurant for the continental breakfast. B&B ⑤–⑦.

Challis Lodge

Map 7, F3. 21–23 Challis Ave, Potts Point ©9358 5422, fax 8356 9047. Kings Cross CityRail or Bus #311. Airport Express #350.
Wonderful old mansion, recently refurbished, with polished timber floors throughout. In a great location on a quiet, tree-filled street that has three good cafés. Best rooms open off the extensive balcony frontage (these all en suite). All rooms have TV, fridge and sink; laundry but no kitchen. ①–③.

Regents Court Hotel

Map 7, E5. 18 Springfield Ave ©9358 1533, fax 9358 1833. Kings Cross CityRail. Airport Express #350.
Small hotel raved about by international style mags, from *Wallpaper* to *British Vogue* – yet despite lots of arty guests, the place is very friendly and homey. Classic designer furniture, and each room has a sleek kitchen area. Instead of a bar down-stairs, you'll find a well-chosen wine-list (at bottleshop prices), and you can help yourself to coffee and *biscotti*. A small kitchen and BBQ area is located on the rooftop, amongst citrus trees growing in pots. A breakfast of fresh, baked goodies and just-squeezed juice costs extra. ⑧.

Simpsons of Potts Point

Map 7, F3. 8 Challis Ave, Potts Point ©9356 2199, fax 9356 4476. Kings Cross CityRail or Bus #311. Airport Express #350.
Small personal hotel, designed in 1892 for a parliamentarian, and beautifully restored. Carpeted and quiet, the three floors of comfortable rooms, all en suite, are furnished with antiques (the guest sitting-room even has a piano); breakfast is served in a sunny conservatory. ⑦.

Victoria Court Sydney

Map 7, E4. 122 Victoria St ©9357 3200, fax 9357 7606. Kings Cross

CityRail. Airport Express #350.

Boutique hotel in two interlinked Victorian terrace houses; very tasteful and quiet. En-suite rooms with all mod cons, some with balconies; buffet breakfast included and served in the conservatory. Security parking a bonus. ⑤–⑥.

DARLINGHURST

Medusa

Map 7, E6. 267 Darlinghurst Rd ©9331 1000, fax 9380 6901. Kings Cross CityRail.

A Victorian-era terrace, which houses one of Sydney's swankiest boutique hotels. Interiors were designed by architect Scott Western, known for his innovative use of colour, and the furnishings are well funky. Luxurious marble bathrooms, sleek kitchenettes, and stereos and VCRs in the rooms (with plenty of CDs and videos to choose from). Smoking in the interior courtyard only. ⑧.

GLEBE & NEWTOWN

Alishan International Guesthouse

Map 6, F4. 100 Glebe Point Rd, Glebe ©9566 4048, fax 9525 4686. Bus #431, #433, #434. Airport Express #352.

Japanese-owned, beautifully restored villa offering chintzy double en-suite rooms (two furnished in Japanese fashion), as well as spotless four-bed dorms. Guest kitchen, spa, airy common room with barbecue area. Rooms ⑤, dorms ①.

Australian Sunrise Lodge

Map 9, C9. 485 King St, Newtown ©9550 4999, fax 9550 4457. Newtown CityRail.

Inexpensive, tastefully furnished and well-managed small, private hotel. Sunny rooms, all with TV, fridge and toaster, most with bath and balcony; family rooms available. Guest kitchen. ②.

B&BS AND GUESTHOUSES: DARLINGHURST, GLEBE & NEWTOWN

Tricketts Bed and Breakfast

Map 6, A2. 270 Glebe Point Rd, Glebe ℂ9552 1141, fax 9692 9462.
Bus #431, #433, #434. Airport Express #352.

Luxury B&B accommodation in an 1880 mansion; en-suite
rooms furnished with antiques and Persian rugs. The lounge,
complete with a billiard table and leather armchairs, was originally a small ballroom. The price for all this is very reasonable,
especially as it includes a generous breakfast. ⑥.

BONDI

Ravesi's

Map 8, E1. Cnr Campbell Parade and Hall St ℂ9365 4422, fax 9365
1481. Bus #380, #382. Airport Express #351.

Swanky boutique hotel: most rooms (all en suite) have sea
views and small balconies. There are standard rooms, split-level
suites with their own private terrace, and a top-floor penthouse. The well-regarded restaurant has glorious sea views
from its balcony. ⑤–⑧.

Thelellen Lodge

Map 8, E1. 11a Consett Ave ℂ9130 1521, fax 9365 6427. Bus #380,
#382. Airport Express #351.

Budget accommodation in a big two-storey house in a quiet
tree-filled street but close to the action. Rooms (share bathrooms), have TV, air-con, fridge, toaster. Guest kitchen and
laundry, small sunny courtyard outside, big sun deck upstairs. ②.

MANLY & NORTHERN BEACHES

Jonah's

Map 2, E9. 69 Byna Rd, Palm Beach ℂ9974 5599, fax 9974 1212.
Bus #190, #L90.

Indulge yourself by staying at this small 1920s resort, with its
period decor and tropical gardens. Wonderful ocean views to

enjoy while eating breakfast on the terrace. Its restaurant has a
fine reputation; dinner and B&B packages available. Room
only ⑧.

Periwinkle Guesthouse
Map 9, B5. 18–19 East Esplanade (cnr Ashburner St), Manly ✆9977
4668, fax 9977 6308. Manly ferry.
Pleasant B&B in a turn-of-the-century homestead near Manly
Cove. Rooms, furnished in Colonial style, have fridge and
fans. Several en-suites, with big bathtubs to soak in; larger
rooms suitable for families. Guest kitchen, BBQ and parking.
⑤–⑥.

PUBS

Plenty of pubs have cleaned up their act and offer pleasant
old-fashioned rooms, usually sharing bathrooms. The main
drawback can be the noise from the bar; ask for a room
well away from the action.

THE ROCKS

Glasgow Arms Hotel
Map 4, D6. 527 Harris St, Ultimo (opposite the Powerhouse
Museum) ✆9211 2354, fax 9281 9439. Haymarket Monorail.
Handy to Darling Harbour, with rooms – nicely decorated,
all air-con and en suite plus TV and radio – situated
above a pleasant pub with courtyard dining. Bar shuts
around 10pm so noise levels aren't a worry. Breakfast included.
⑥.

Lord Nelson Brewery Hotel
Map 5, A2. Cnr Argyle and Kent streets ✆9251 4044, fax 9251 1532.
Circular Quay CityRail/ferry.
B&B in a historic pub with an upmarket brasserie. The ten

PUBS: THE ROCKS

very smart, Colonial-style rooms, recently renovated, are most-ly en suite. Price varies according to size and position: best is the corner room with views of Argyle St. ⑦.

Mercantile Hotel

Map 5, C2. 25 George St ℗9247 3570, fax 9247 7047. Circular Quay CityRail/ferry.

Sydney's best-known Irish pub (see p.195), right on the edge of The Rocks near the Harbour Bridge; has a stash of fab rooms upstairs. Original features include huge fireplaces in several rooms, which are all furnished in Colonial style. Several have bathrooms complete with spa baths. Full breakfast included. ⑤.

Palisade Hotel

Map 5, A2. 35 Bettington St, Millers Point ℗9247 2272. Circular Quay CityRail/ferry or Bus #431–434.

Magnificent tiled pub standing like an observatory over Millers Point; plenty of old-world charm about its bar (no pokies) and its simple rooms. Clean, cute and bright rooms share bath-room; some have fantastic views over the inner harbour and Harbour Bridge. Also has a stylish, contemporary restaurant. ④.

HOSTELS

All hostels have a laundry, kitchen, and common room with TV unless stated otherwise. Most include linen but some-times not blankets, so it's a good idea to travel with a sleep-ing bag. There's usually a key deposit of about $10. Office hours are generally restricted, typically 8am–noon and 4.30–6pm, so it's best to call and arrange an arrival time; we have indicated where places have longer reception hours. The **Kings Cross** area – which includes Potts Point, Woolloomooloo and Elizabeth Bay – has a heavy concen-

Self-catering

Enochs Holiday Flats ©9388 1477, fax 9388 1353. One- and two-bedroom apartments sleeping four to six people, all close to Bondi Beach. $400–820 weekly.

Manly National 22 Central Ave, Manly, NSW 2095 ©9977 6469, fax 9977 3760. Manly ferry apartment complex with swimming pool. One-bedroom $450–585 weekly, two-bedroom $550–695; linen not supplied.

Medina Executive Apartments Head office, Level 1, 355 Crown St, Surry Hills, NSW 2010 ©9360 1699, fax 9360 7769. Central CityRail. Upmarket, serviced apartments with resident managers, in various locations across Sydney. Their flagship is *Medina on Crown* (**Map 7, C9**; 359 Crown St, Surry Hills); stylish apartments with air-con, lounge, dining area, TV, video and telephone, and a café, gym, sauna and swimming pool downstairs. 24-hour reception and free undercover parking; $205 per night.

Plage Bondi Map 8, C2. 212 Bondi Rd ©9387 1122, fax 9389 1266. Bus #380, #382. Serviced, air-con, studio apartments with modern furniture, TV, telephone, kitchen, and balconies with sea view. Best of all is the rooftop pool. Parking included. Nightly rates $95; Cheaper rates if you stay a week or more.

Sydney City Centre Serviced Apartments Map 5, C5. 7 Elizabeth St, Martin Place ©9223 6677, fax 9235 3432. Martin Place CityRail. Apartments with kitchenette, TV, video, fans; basic, but in an excellent location. No weekly rate; $75 per night.

Woolloomooloo Waters Map 7, E4. 88 Dowling St, Woolloomooloo ©9358 3100, fax 9356 4839. Kings Cross CityRail. Studio apartments with balcony views over Woolloomooloo Bay or the city. Pool, spa and restaurant. Light breakfast included; $155.

tration of hostels. It's best to avoid the dodgy places that spring up overnight on Darlinghurst Road; nearby, leafy Victoria St and the backstreets of Potts Point offer a more pleasant atmosphere. **Glebe** is a laid-back, inner-city locale, and the beachside hostels at **Bondi**, **Coogee** and **Manly** are popular. (Some hotels and guesthouses also offer a few dorm beds, so check these listings too.)

CITY CENTRE

Sydney Central YHA

Map 7, A8. Cnr Pitt St and Rawson Pl ©9281 9111, fax 9281 9199. Central CityRail. Airport Express #300, #350.

Centrally-located building, refurbished and transformed into a snazzy hostel; over 500 beds – spacious four-share dorms or en-suite twins and doubles. There's a rooftop swimming pool, sauna, BBQ area, video and TV lounges, kitchens, dining and lounge areas. 24-hour reception. Licensed bistro plus a bar. Some parking available. Rooms $58–66, dorms $20–23.

YWCA

Map 7, B6. 5–11 Wentworth Ave ©9264 2451, fax 9283 2485. Town Hall or Museum CityRail.

Great location just off Oxford St. Double or twin rooms with en-suite or shared bathrooms, plus $60 singles sharing bathrooms and four-bed dorms. En-suite rooms come with a TV, or there are TV lounges. No kitchen, but facilities include a café (open 7am–8pm), and a laundry. En-suite rooms $80–110, dorms $24.

KINGS CROSS

Eva's Backpackers

Map 7, E4. 6–8 Orwell St ©9358 2185, fax 9358 3259. Kings Cross CityRail. Airport Express #350.

Family-run hostel with clean, colourfully painted rooms, some of them en suite. Rooftop garden with barbecue area – and fantastic views over the city. 24-hour reception; rooms $45, dorms $18.

Funk House

Map 7, E5. 23 Darlinghurst Rd ℂ9358 6455, fax 9358 3506. Kings Cross CityRail. Airport Express #350.

With colourful murals on every door – acid art, Aboriginal and cartoons – and upbeat music playing in the corridors, this place has a groovy vibe. Not too squeezy either, with three- and four-bed dorms. Doubles and twins come with fridge and TV. Free lifts to Bondi in the summer. Rooms $40–48, dorms $16–19.

Original Backpackers

Map 7, E5. 160–162 Victoria St ℂ9356 3232, fax 9368 1435. Kings Cross CityRail. Airport Express #350.

The first backpackers' hostel in the Cross, in an 1887 mansion. Offers a choice of simple, well-maintained rooms and three- to ten-bed dorms. Pleasant outdoor courtyard, cable TV – and happy to cater for families. Rooms $48, dorms $18.

The Pink House

Map 7, F5. 6–8 Barncleuth Square ℂ & fax 9358 1689; Kings Cross CityRail. Airport Express #350.

Attractive Art Deco mansion with big dorms and a few doubles, and all the expected amenities plus cable TV in the common room and a café. Friendly, very peaceful place, but close to the action. (YHA-associated). Rooms $42, dorms $18.

GLEBE & NEWTOWN

Billabong Gardens

Map 6, D7. 5–11 Egan St, Newtown ℂ9550 3236, fax 9550 4352. Newtown CityRail.

In a quiet street but close to the action, and run by a friendly team, this purpose-built hostel is arranged around a peaceful

HOSTELS: GLEBE & NEWTOWN

inner courtyard and has a swimming pool. Clean dorms (up to 6-bed), rooms, and motel-style en-suites. Communal facilities include a gym, pool table and Internet access. Undercover car park ($5 night). Rooms $45, en-suite $65, dorms $18.

Glebe Point YHA

Map 6, D2. 262 Glebe Point Rd, Glebe ©9692 8418. Bus #431, #433, #434. Airport Express #352.

Reliable YHA with helpful, patient staff. Private rooms as well as four-bed dorms. Facilities include a sunroof, pool table, TV and video lounge, and luggage storage. Activities organized. Reception 7am–11pm. Rooms $50, dorms $19–21.

Glebe Village Backpackers

Map 6, D2. 256 Glebe Point Rd, Glebe ©9660 8133, fax 9552 3707. Bus #431, #433, #434. Airport Express #352.

Three large old houses, staffed by young locals who know what's going on around town. Double and twin rooms as well as dorms. Relaxing alfresco café overlooking the street, shady courtyard and a travel agency. Rooms $50, dorms $18.

BONDI & COOGEE

Coogee Beach Backpackers

Map 8, B7. 94 Beach St, Coogee ©9315 8000, fax 9664 1258. Bus #372, #373, #374. Airport Express #351.

Clean, attractive rooms and dorms in four characterful neighbouring houses, with balconies overlooking the ocean. Each house has a well-equipped kitchen and common room, and there are several gardens. Congenial and well managed, it's the best of the bunch. Rooms $45, dorms $18–20.

Indy's at Bondi

Map 8, E1. 35a Hall Street, Bondi ©9365 4900, mobile 0413/836 681, fax 9365 4994. Bus #380, #382, #389. Airport Express #351.

HOSTELS: BONDI & COOGEE

Justifiably popular, this spacious hostel feels like a friendly student share house – except it's well organized. Every amenity, including pool table, voicemail, excellent security and free use of surfboards and bikes. Travel bookings, social events and trips organized. Dorms only (4- to 8-bed) – couples and families can stay at their beachfront annexe, *Couples on the Beach*, at North Bondi (all rooms have TV, and there's a small kitchen and rooftop seating area; dorms $16–20, rooms $36–42).

Indy's Beachside Backpackers

Map 8, A9. 302 Arden St, Coogee ℂ9315 7644, fax 9365 4994. Bus #372, #373, #374. Airport Express #351.

Small hostel with a laid-back atmosphere; feels more like a share house. Mostly 4-bed dorms; no doubles. Cheap day-trips to the countryside. Rate includes a light breakfast. $20.

MANLY & NORTHERN BEACHES

Avalon Beach Hostel

Map 2, E6. 59 Avalon Parade, Avalon ℂ9918 9709, fax 9973 1322. Bus #190, #L90.

Located at one of Sydney's best – and most beautiful – surf beaches, this purpose-built hostel is certainly conducive to year-round relaxation, with its fireplaces, balconies and green surrounds. 4- to 6-bed dorms and private rooms. Surfboard rental available. Rooms $44, dorms $18–20.

Sydney Beachhouse YHA

Map 2, E6. 4 Collaroy St, Collaroy Beach ℂ9981 1177, fax 9981 1114. Bus #151, #155, #157, #183, #187–190.

Sydney's new beachside YHA hostel. Boasts a heated swimming pool, open fireplaces, video lounge and games rooms. 4- to 6-bed dorms, plus several doubles and family rooms. Free bikes, surfboards and surfing lessons. Trips include the popular jaunt to the *Home and Away* filming location ($8). A shuttle bus runs up here from *Sydney Central YHA*. Rooms $50–56, dorms $18–19.

Wharf Backpackers

Map 9, B5. 48 East Esplanade, Manly ©9977 2800, fax 9977 2820. Manly ferry.

Wonderfully quirky but well-run hostel, directly opposite the ferry terminal – really gets into the concept of outdoor living. The big back garden (where pet rabbits roam) has a kitchen, TV, tables, and oversized chess set. There's room for 100 guests, but with several kitchens and TV rooms, the place never feels too crowded. Colourful dorms (4-, 6- and 8-bed) have ceiling fans and heaters; doubles have a TV. Free bikes, body boards and wet suits; surfboards for rent. Rooms $40, dorms $15–$18.

Eating

Sydney has blossomed into one of the great restaurant capitals of the world, and offers a fantastic range of cosmopolitan eateries, covering every imaginable cuisine. Quality is uniformly high, with the freshest produce, meat and seafood always on hand, and a culinary culture of discerning, well-informed diners. The places we've listed below barely scratch the surface of what's available; for a comprehensive guide, consider investing in the latest edition of *Cheap Eats in Sydney,* or the *Sydney Morning Herald Good Food Guide*, both of which try to keep track of the best places in town.

Sydney has several great eat streets, each with a glut of cafés and restaurants: **Victoria Street** and **Oxford Street** in Darlinghurst, **Macleay Street** in Potts Point, **Crown Street** in Surry Hills, **King Street** in Newtown, and the **Darling Street strip** running from Rozelle to Balmain. By the sea, **Bondi Beach**, **Coogee** and **Manly** all have countless café and dining options. The standout ethnic restaurant areas are: Italian on **Stanley Street** in East Sydney and **Norton Street** in Leichhardt; Turkish, Lebanese and Indian restaurants on **Elizabeth Street** and **Cleveland Street** in Surry Hills; Eastern European and Jewish around Bondi; and Chinese in the **Chinatown** section of Haymarket. Sydney's Vietnamese community is concentrated in **Cabramatta**, west of the CBD (fourteen stops from Central CityRail); there are some superb restaurants clustered along Park Road and John Street, just west of Cabramatta Station.

CAFÉS

Sydney has a thriving café scene, and a selection of the best can be found along **Victoria Street** in Darlinghurst; **Challis Avenue** in Potts Point; **Glebe Point Road** in Glebe; **King Street** in Newtown; and in the beachside neighbourhoods of **Bondi**, **Bronte** and **Coogee**. Sydney can thank its sizeable Italian population for having elevated **coffee-drinking** to the status of a serious pastime: in the local coffee lingo, a flat white is a cappuccino without the froth; a cafe latte is a milkier version served in a glass; a long black is a regular black coffee; and a short black is an espresso (transformed by a splash of milk into a *macchiato*). Any of these will cost $2–2.50 Most cafés are open for breakfast, particularly those in the beach areas, and some stay open until the small hours. All those listed are in the cheap or inexpensive category, most serving main courses for $10 or less.

Meal prices

All eating section listings are price-coded into five categories, going on the price of a typical main course:

Cheap	under $10
Inexpensive	$10–15
Moderate	$15–20
Expensive	$20–30
Very expensive	$30 plus

Food Courts

The Southeast Asian style food courts of Chinatown offer some of the best cheap eats in Sydney, with hot dishes for $5–7, and not only Chinese but often Vietnamese, Thai, Japanese, Korean and Indian food for sale. All have a licensed bar.

Dixon House Food Court Map 5, A9. Basement level, cnr Little Hay and Dixon streets. Daily 10.30am–8.30pm.

Market City Food Court Map 5, A9. Level 3, Market City Shopping Centre, cnr Quay and Thomas streets. Daily 8am–10pm.

Sussex Centre Map 5, B9. First floor, 401 Sussex St. Daily 10am–9pm.

CITY

Glasshouse Café

Map 5, C5. State Library, Macquarie St. Martin Place CityRail.
Mon–Fri 10am–4.30pm, Sat & Sun 11am–3.30pm.
Airy and with masses of plants, this glass-roofed space on the 7th floor of the State Library is a relaxing spot for lunch, or just coffee and cake. The inexpensive menu changes often.

Paradiso

Map 5, C4. Shop 1, 7 Macquarie Pl. Circular Quay CityRail.
Mon–Fri 7am–4.30pm.
Stylish outdoor café, close to Circular Quay. Fab spot, on an historic square with big shady trees; or sit inside on stools and listen to jazzy music on a wet day. Plunge in for great coffee, *pizzetta* and focaccia.

Roma Caffe

Map 7, A7. 191 Hay St, Haymarket. Central CityRail.
Mon–Sat 8am–6pm.

CAFÉS: CITY

City coffee hits

Italian **espresso bars** have popped up all over the CBD, many with outside seating for sunny days, and braziers for the winter. We've listed four of the best below.

Bar Milazzo Map 5, C8. 379 Pitt St. Museum or Town Hall CityRail. Mon–Fri 7am–6pm.

Bambini Espresso Map 5, C8. 299 Elizabeth St. Museum or Town Hall CityRail. Mon–Fri 7am–6pm.

Caffe Corto Map 5, B5. 10 Barrack St. Martin Place CityRail. Mon–Fri 7am–4.30pm.

Jet Map 5, B7. Cnr York and Druitt streets (QVB). Town Hall CityRail. Mon–Fri 8am–6pm, Sat 9am–5pm.

The *Roma* has been in the area for over 35 years, dispensing fabulous coffee, great breakfasts, and a huge display of wicked Italian desserts, plus delicious focaccia and fresh pasta – try the home-made pumpkin tortellini.

Rossini
Map 5, D3. Between wharves 5 & 6, Circular Quay. Circular Quay CityRail/ferry.
Daily 7am–11pm. Licensed.
Quality Italian fast-food alfresco, perfect for while you're waiting for a ferry or just watching the Quay. *Panzerotto* – big, cinnamon-flavoured and ricotta-filled doughnuts – are a speciality.

KINGS CROSS

Cafe Hernandez
Map 7, G6. 60 Kings Cross Rd. Kings Cross CityRail.
24-hour.

CAFÉS: KINGS CROSS

Argentinian-run, with walls covered in oil paintings. Spanish food (*hurros*, tortillas, *empanadas*) and good pastries are available, but the coffee is the highlight. Relaxed, friendly and comfortable.

Dean's Cafe
Map 7, F5. 5 Kellett St. Kings Cross CityRail.
Mon–Thurs 7pm–3am, Sat & Sun 7pm–6am. Licensed and BYO.
A haven after a night out in the Cross; toasted sandwiches plus other favourites like pumpkin soup, nachos and cakes.

Macleay's Pizza Bar
Map 7, F4. 101 Macleay St. Kings Cross CityRail.
Daily noon–2.30am except Fri & Sat until 4.30am.
Unassuming pizza bar; great prices and pizzas.

Spring Espresso Bar
Map 7, F3. Challis Ave (near cnr Macleay St). Kings Cross CityRail or Bus #311.
Mon–Sat 7am–7pm, Sun 8am–7pm. BYO.
Recently nominated by *Wallpaper* magazine as serving just about the best breakfast in the world, this always crowded, sunny bolt-hole with street seating, also serves some of the best coffee in Sydney and some great pastries and *panini*.

DARLINGHURST

Bar Coluzzi
Map 7, E6. 322 Victoria St. Kings Cross CityRail.
Daily 5am–7.30pm.
Famous Italian café, run by a genial former boxer. Tiny place, always packed, with a crew of regular customers spilling out to the tables on the pavement; occasional, impromptu opera-singing from the patron. (You can watch the carryings-on from a safe distance at the trendier, though equally tiny *Parmalat* next door).

CAFÉS: DARLINGHURST

Eating around the clock

Loads of places in Sydney cater to hungry night owls, or those in need of a late-night caffeine fix. Of the ones open late (or even 24-hour), there are several in Chinatown, the most famous being *BBQ King* (p.174) and *Lam's* (p.176). In Kings Cross, many cafés have extended trading hours, including *Café Hernandez* (p.162) and *Deans* (p.163); you can grab an early-morning pizza at *Macleay's Pizza Bar*, or a 4am grill at the *Bourbon and Beef Steak* (p.197). In the inner-west, there's *George's Café* (p.168), and on the North Shore you'll find *Maisys Cafe* (p.170) open 24-hours.

Betty's Soup Kitchen

Map 7, C7. 84 Oxford St. Bus #378, #380, #382.
Daily noon–10.45pm (Fri & Sat until 11.45pm). BYO.
Soup is the speciality ($5.50), served with damper. Salads, pies, nachos and desserts too. Nothing over $9.

Le Petit Crème

Map 7, E6. 118 Darlinghurst Rd. Kings Cross CityRail.
Mon–Sat 7am–3pm, Sun 8am–3pm.
Popular French café serving huge, filled baguettes, steak and *frites*, omelettes, *pain au chocolat* and big bowls of *café au lait*; the bread and pastries are baked on the premises.

Tropicana

Map 7, E6. 227b Victoria St. Kings Cross CityRail.
Daily 5am–11pm (Fri & Sat until midnight). BYO.
The birthplace of the Tropfest film festival (see p.225). The coffee's average, but it's still one of *the* places to hang out, on weekends especially. For $6, the Trop salad is fuel for a whole day.

Café Niki
Map 7, C11. 544 Bourke St. Bus #301–303.
Mon–Fri 7am–10pm, Sat 8am–10pm, Sun 8am–6pm.
Corner café which manages to be groovy but not pretentious;
buzzes with the young staff. Cheap, delicious food – best are
their soups and focaccia.

La Passion du Fruit
Map 7, C11. 633 Bourke St. Bus #301–303.
Mon–Sat 8am–5pm.
The best brunch in town is served at this bright and friendly
place; interesting salads, sandwiches and light meals, and some
of the freshest fruit-drinks and frappés in town.

Burgerman
Map 8, D2. 249 Bondi Rd. Bus #380, #382.
Daily noon–10pm. BYO.
Their gourmet burgers will have you drooling. Busy takeaway
service and a small, eat-in area. (Darlinghurst branch also, at
116 Surrey St.)

Gelato Bar
Map 8, E1. 140 Campbell Parade. Bus #380, #382.
Daily 8am–midnight.
Hungarian-run place that's been serving up Eastern European
dishes and cakes for over thirty years – and ice cream too.
Gleaming coffee-lounge decor.

Lamrock Café
Map 8, E1. 72 Campbell Parade (cnr Lamrock Ave). Bus #380, #382.
Daily 7am–midnight. Licensed.

CAFÉS: SURRY HILLS, BONDI

Stalwart Bondi café with fab ocean views. An unpretentious crowd work through the straightforward menu, which includes *panini* sandwiches, salads, pasta, burgers and fish and chips. Breakfast is popular, and you can even have a cocktail along with it – try a "Shark Attack", their version of a Bloody Mary.

Le Paris Go Café

Map 8, E1. 38 Hall St (cnr Consett Ave). Bus #380, #382, #389.
Mon–Sat 7am–5pm, Sun 8am–5pm.
French-run café in a sunny spot, with cushioned benches out front. Inside, jazzy music plays as patrons soak up the congenial ambience and play chess. Try the excellent croissants, teamed with steaming bowls of coffee; other French snacks include *croque monsieur* and *salad niçoise*.

The Red Kite

Map 8, E1. 95 Roscoe St ✆9365 0432. Bus #380, #382.
Daily 8am–6pm.
Funky vegetarian café, just back from Campbell Parade – attracts a young crowd. Imaginative food and freshly squeezed juices.

The One That Got Away

Map 8, C2. 163 Bondi Rd. Bus #380, #382.
Daily 10am–9pm.
Award-winning fish shop, which sells kosher fish and sushi; grills or fries up fish and chips, and has a small eat-in section with some tasty accompaniments like salads and yam chips.

COOGEE & BRONTE

Globe

Map 8, A8. 203 Coogee Bay Rd, Coogee. Bus #372, #373.
Mon–Sat 8am–6pm, Sun 9am–6pm.
This relaxed, daytime hangout has vivid paintings on the walls,

fold-back windows to let in the sights and sounds of the street, plus really good coffee. Healthy food also available, from gourmet sandwiches to Mediterranean mains.

Sejuiced

Map 8, D4. 487 Bronte Rd, Bronte. Bus #378.

Daily 6.30am–6pm.

Delicious fresh juices, smoothies and frappés, combined with ocean and palm tree views, make this place a beauty to kick-start a summer's day. The "Morning Energiser" (beetroot, apple, ginger and carrot juice) ought to get you going, and there's all manner of breakfast foods. Salads, soups and pasta are terrific too.

GLEBE & NEWTOWN

Badde Manors

Map 6, F5. 37 Glebe Point Rd, Glebe ©9660 1835. Bus #431, #433, #434.

Mon–Fri 8am–midnight, Sat & Sun 9am–1am.

Vegetarian corner café with a light-and-airy ambience and laid-back staff; always packed, especially for weekend brunch.

Blackwattle Canteen

Map 6, C1. Blackwattle Studios, 465 Glebe Point Rd, Glebe. Bus #431, #434.

Mon–Fri 8am–4pm, Sat & Sun 9am–4pm. BYO.

Stunning views from this artists' cafe right at Glebe Point; big windows look out to the Glebe Island Bridge. Expect great coffee, and generous servings from the simple menu, which includes home-made cakes and lots of breakfasty stuff.

El Bahsa Sweets

Map 6, D7. 233 King St, Newtown. Newtown CityRail.

Mon–Thurs & Sun 8am–10.30pm, Fri & Sat 8am–11.30pm.

CAFÉS: GLEBE & NEWTOWN

Lebanese coffee lounge selling Lebanese sweets, all home-made, as well as snacks and meals.

Feel Cafe

Map 6, D7. 165 King St, Newtown. Newtown CityRail.
Daily 8am–midnight. BYO.
The multicoloured walls of this chatty café are covered with art for sale. As well as coffee and cake, you can get tasty meals like scallop risotto, or a plain sirloin steak. Garden courtyard outside.

George's Café

Map 6, D7. 222 King St, Newtown. Newtown CityRail.
Sun–Thurs 10am–midnight, Fri & Sat 24-hour.
Late-night cake heaven, with delights including mango-and-passionfruit coconut cake. Lots of cheesecakes, and they serve light meals too. Comfy booths to sink into.

Iku

Map 6, F4. 25a Glebe Point Rd, Glebe ⓒ9692 8720. Bus #431, #433, #434.
Daily 11am–8pm.
Healthy and delicious macrobiotic meals – vegetarian or vegan. Meditative interior, and outdoor dining area – both non-smoking. (Also at The Grove shopping centre, 168 Military Rd, Neutral Bay ⓒ9953 1964, and 279 Bronte Rd, Waverley ⓒ9369 5022).

Lolita's

Map 6, F4. 29 Glebe Point Rd, Glebe. Bus #431, #433, #434.
Mon–Fri 10am–10pm, Sat & Sun 9am–10pm.
The place for a big weekend breakfast (9am–1pm), with a great deck to soak up the sun and an upstairs balcony too.

The Old Fish Shop

Map 6, D7. 239 King St, Newtown. Newtown CityRail.

Daily 6am–11pm.

This little corner place, decorated with strands of dried garlic and chilli, is pure Newtown: lots of shaven heads, body piercings, tattoos and bizarre King Street fashions. Food is simple – mainly focaccia and mini pizzas – and the excellent raisin loaf goes well with the coffee.

Well Connected Café

Map 6, F4. 35 Glebe Point Rd, Glebe. Bus #431, #433, #434.
Mon–Fri 8am–11pm, Sat & Sun 10am–11pm.

Glebe's Internet café ($12 per hour, or 5min blocks); the best place to eat and work is upstairs on the huge front verandah. The menu features tasty sandwiches made with Turkish bread.

BALMAIN & LEICHHARDT

Bar Italia

Map 3, E3. 169 Norton St, Leichhardt. Bus #438, #440.
Sun & Mon 10am–midnight, Tues–Thurs 9am–midnight, Fri 9am–1am, Sat 10am–1am. BYO.

Like a community centre, with the day-long comings and goings of Leichhardt locals – and it's packed at night. The lunchtime focaccia comes big and tasty, but it runs out early. Coffee is spot-on and the *gelato* is the best in Sydney; pasta from $6.50. Try to squeeze into the shady courtyard out back on a fine day.

Canteen

Map 10, A5. 332 Darling St, Balmain. Balmain ferry; bus #432, #441, #445, #446.
Mon–Sat 7am–5pm, Sun 8am–5pm.

Airy, simply styled café with whitewashed walls; gourmet food on the blackboard suggests a Tuscan influence. Eggy breakfasts are popular, particularly on weekends when customers spill out onto streetside stools.

Maisys Cafe
Map 10, D3. 164 Military Rd, Neutral Bay. Bus #228–230, #247.
24-hour. BYO.
All metal, mirrors and sunny yellow tiles plus funky music,
smiling staff – and smoking is allowed! Good for breakfast or
delicious Maltese *pastizzi*, soups, burgers, pasta and cakes.

RESTAURANTS

You're likely to come across the term "contemporary
Australian" or "modern Australian" in various restaurant
descriptions. This refers to an adventurous blend of influences
from around the world – mostly Asian and Mediterranean –
combined with fresh local produce (including kangaroo, emu
and crocodile); the result is a dynamic, eclectic and very
healthy cuisine, also sometimes called "Pacific Rim cuisine",
in common with Californian cookery. An average Sydney
restaurant main is about $14; top dollar at the city's finest is
around $38. Many places allow you to **BYO** (Bring Your
Own) wine or beer, but will probably add a corkage charge
($1–2 per person). Several **pubs** have well-regarded restau-
rants; pub meals rarely cost more than $15 in their bistro sec-
tions and a huge steak is likely to be at the top of the menu.

All restaurants listed below are open daily for lunch
and dinner, unless otherwise stated (actual hours vary,
so it's advisable to phone and check).

CITY CENTRE

Edna's Table
Map 5, B7. 204 Clarence St ℘9267 3933. Wynyard CityRail.

Closed Sat lunch and all Sun. Licensed. Expensive.

A chance to sample some expensive *haute cuisine* bushtucker among upmarket kitsch Australian decor. The chargrilled kangaroo fillet served with a warm salad of wild yams with a curried dressing is ever popular.

Kables

Map 5, B4. Regent Hotel, 199 George St ℗9255 0266. Circular Quay CityRail/ferry.

Lunch Tues–Fri, dinner Tues–Sat. Licensed. Very expensive.

World-class hotel restaurant; wonderful service and elegant surroundings. Chef Serge Dansereau places an emphasis on fresh local produce, sourcing from the growers themselves. The $42.50 two-course set lunch, including coffee and parking, is a good deal; the 5-course *dégustation* menu is $100.

THE ROCKS

bel mondo

Map 5, B3. Level 3, Argyle Department Store, 12–24 Argyle St ℗9241 3700. Circular Quay CityRail/ferry.

Closed Sat & Sun lunch. Licensed. Very expensive.

Impressive views over The Rocks and the harbour, and North Italian food – the best of its kind in Sydney – from chef Steve Manfredi. A sophisticated crowd eats here, but for less cash you can get views and similar food at its fashionable *Anti-Bar.*

Bennelong

Map 5, E2. Sydney Opera House ℗9250 7548. Circular Quay CityRail/ferry.

Closed Sun night. Licensed. Very expensive.

UK import Michael Moore is head chef at the Opera House's restaurant. One of Sydney's most fabulous locations, with views of the city skyline; if you can't afford a meal here, try a drink at the stylish cocktail bar, or a few pricey oysters from the adjoining *Crustacea Bar*.

Doyles on the Quay

Map 5, C3. Overseas Passenger Terminal, Circular Quay West ℗9252 3400. Circular Quay CityRail/ferry.
Licensed. Expensive.

Downtown branch of the Watson's Bay seafood institution (see p.186); pricey but excellent, with great harbour views from the outdoor waterfront tables. You'll probably need to book.

Quay

Map 5, C3. Overseas Passenger Terminal ℗9251 5600. Circular Quay CityRail/ferry.
Closed Sat & Sun lunch. Licensed. Very expensive.

The cruise ships still pull in here, but the observation tower has been given over to this restaurant. Views are fabulous, and the French chef, Guillaume Brahimi, is one of Sydney's best. Posh and very pricey. Bookings essential.

Rockpool

Map 5, C3. 109 George St ℗9252 1888. Circular Quay CityRail/ferry.
Closed Sun & lunch Sat. Expensive.

One of Sydney's most glamorous dining spots, run by chef Neil Perry, with celebrities filing in to eat the raved-about seafood and contemporary creations, surrounded by funky, colourful decor.

Sydney Cove Oyster Bar

Map 5, D3. 1 Circular Quay East. Circular Quay CityRail/ferry.
Mon–Wed 11am–10.30pm, Thurs–Sat 11am–midnight, Sun 11am–8pm. Licensed. Expensive.

It's not hard to be lured into this place, via a stroll to the Opera House. The waterfront tables are just the place to sample some Sydney rock oysters (around $17.50 a dozen). There's other seafood as well, or just come for coffee, or a beer, and the view.

Sydney's Top Chefs

You'll find some of Sydney's top chefs at the restaurants cross-referenced below, including the legendary Tetsuya Wakuda at *Tetsuya's* in Rozelle. Interiors are straight out of the latest style mag; all are licensed and in the very expensive category; expect to pay $30–35 for a main course.

Ampersand	(p.174)	*MG Garage*	(p.182)
bel mondo	(p.171)	*Paramount*	(p.178)
Bennelong	(p.171)	*Quay*	(p.172)
Cicada	(p.177)	*Rockpool*	(p.172)
Darley Street Thai	(p.178)	*Tetsuya's*	(p.186)
Kable's	(p.171)	*Watermark*	(p.190)

Wharf Restaurant

Map 5, B1. Pier 4, Hickson Rd (next to the Wharf Theatre) ℡9250 1761. Circular Quay CityRail/ferry.
Closed Sun. Licensed. Moderate to expensive.
Enterprising modern food (at least one vegetarian dish), in an old docks building with heaps of raw charm and a harbour vista; bag an outside table for the best views. Coffee and drinks from the cocktail bar from noon, until end of evening performance.

There are two revolving restaurants at the top of AMP Centrepoint Tower (see p.62) that provide a 360-degree view of the harbour, though the food and service don't live up to the vistas. Level 2 is an all-you-can-eat buffet (lunch $34, dinner $40); a three-course meal in the à la carte restaurant on Level 1 costs about $52. Bookings ℡8223 3800.

HAYMARKET & DARLING HARBOUR

Ampersand

Map 5, A7. Cockle Bay Wharf, Darling Harbour ✆9264 6666. Town Hall CityRail or Darling Park Monorail.

Closed Sat lunch & Sun dinner. Expensive.

On the roof terrace of the new Cockle Bay restaurant precinct, chef Tony Bilson's *Ampersand* offers wonderful views and French-style dining with Japanese influences.

BBQ King

Map 5, B9. 18–20 Goulburn St, Haymarket ✆9267 2433. Central CityRail or Haymarket Monorail.

Daily 11.30am–2am. Licensed. Cheap to inexpensive.

Unprepossessing but perpetually crowded Chinese restaurant, specializing in barbecued meat; but there is also, surprisingly, a big vegetarian list on the menu. Quick service, takeaways.

Blackbird

Map 5, A7. Cockle Bay Wharf, Darling Harbour ✆9283 7835. Town Hall CityRail or Darling Park Monorail.

Daily 7am–1am. Licensed. Inexpensive.

This place has the feel of a funky American diner; sit on stools at the bar, the couches out the back, or enjoy the water views from the terrace. Generous meals – from *dahl* to spaghetti, steak, noodles, salads, pizzas from a hot-stone oven, and breakfast until 4pm.

Bodhidharma

Map 7, A7. Capitol Square, 730–742 George St, Haymarket ✆9211 8966. Central CityRail.

Cheap to inexpensive.

In a modern "Eat Street" arcade attached to the Capitol Theatre; organic and biodynamic produce is used, with a menu embracing Mediterranean, Asian and bushtucker influences. (The same company runs the *Bodhi Vegetarian*

Restaurant at 187 Hay St, Haymarket ©9212 2828, which offers vegan versions of *yum cha)*; both are open daily for lunch and dinner.

Capitan Torres

Map 5, B8. 73 Liverpool St, Haymarket ©9264 5574. Town Hall CityRail.

Closed Sun lunch. Licensed. Moderate.

Atmospheric Spanish place, which specializes in seafood; they also do paella, and there's tapas available at the bar.

Doyle's Fish Market Bistro

Map 6, F2. Sydney Fish Markets, Pyrmont ©9552 4339. Fish Market Light Rail or bus #443, #501.

Mon–Thurs 11am–3pm, Fri & Sat 11am–9pm, Sun 11am–5pm. Inexpensive to moderate.

A very casual and more affordable version of the famous *Doyles* fish restaurant in Watsons Bay (p.186). Plastic tables; order at the counter. Daily specials of the best fish market offers.

Ippon Sushi

Map 5, B9. 404 Sussex St, Haymarket ©9212 7669. Central CityRail or World Square Monorail.

Daily 11am–10.30pm. Licensed and BYO. Cheap.

Fun, inexpensive Japanese sushi train downstairs, with a revolving choice of delectables from $1–4.

Kam Fook Sharks Fin Seafood Restaurant

Map 5, A9. Market City, cnr Quay and Haymarket streets, Haymarket ©9211 8988. Central CityRail or Haymarket Monorail.

Yum cha Mon–Fri 10am–5.30pm, Sat & Sun 9am–5.30pm, dinner nightly. Licensed. Moderate.

The name matches the size of this 800-seater Cantonese establishment, officially Australia's largest restaurant; serves the best *yum cha* in Sydney. Despite the size, bookings are advised.

RESTAURANTS: HAYMARKET & DARLING HARBOUR |

La Grand Taverna

Map 5, B8. *Sir John Young Hotel*, 557 George St (cnr Liverpool St), Haymarket ☎9267 3608. Town Hall CityRail.
Closed Sun. Licensed. Inexpensive.
Spanish food, including tapas; lively, authentic atmosphere, and a no-frills setting for some of the best paella and sangria in town.

Lam's Seafood Restaurant

Map 5, A9. 35 Goulburn St, Haymarket ☎9281 2881. Central CityRail or Haymarket Monorail.
Daily noon–4am. Licensed and BYO. Inexpensive.
A Chinatown institution that's a great place for seafood steamboats as dawn approaches.

The Malaya

Map 4, E7. 761 George St, Haymarket ☎9211 0946. Central CityRail.
Closed Sun. Licensed. Inexpensive to moderate.
Popular, veteran Chinese–Malaysian place, serving some of the best, most authentic and spicy laksa in town.

Pho Pasteur

Map 5, B9. 709 George St, Haymarket ☎9212 5622. Central CityRail.
Daily 10am–9pm. Cheap.
Very popular, casual Vietnamese eatery: food comes quick, fresh and authentic. Great noodle soups for $5.

Tai Pei

Map 4, E6. Prince Centre, 8 Quay St, Haymarket ☎9281 4508. Central CityRail or Haymarket Monorail.
Daily 11am–9pm. Cheap.
Tiny, congenial and cheap Taiwanese eatery, offering generous servings; good dumplings from $4–6, and a tasty version of the Taiwanese speciality Mama Po's Tofu.

Wokpool

Map 5, A7. Darling Harbour (next to the Imax Theatre) ℭ9211 9888.
Town Hall CityRail or Darling Park Monorail.
Licensed. Moderate to expensive.

Stylish combination of upmarket noodle bar, and swish Asian
seafood restaurant. Owned by Neil Perry (who also runs the
glamorous *Rockpool*, p.172), it's undoubtedly classy, but in a
rather tacky location.

KINGS CROSS

A Touch of Thai

Map 7, E5. 230 William St ℭ9326 9343. Kings Cross CityRail.
BYO. Cheap to inexpensive.

Tiny, frenetic Thai café – friendly young staff cook in the open
kitchen to the strains of Thai pop music. Dishes are generous,
delicious, and the daily specials are inventive.

Bayswater Brasserie

Map 7, F5. 32 Bayswater Rd ℭ9357 2177. Kings Cross CityRail.
Mon–Sat noon–midnight; closed Sun. Licensed. Moderate to
expensive.

Lively, upmarket brasserie consistently rated for its interesting
modern food (plus the fact that Sydney celebs and high profil-
ers can often be spotted here). Constantly changing seasonal
menu.

Cicada

Map 7, F3. 29 Challis Ave ℭ9358 1255. Kings Cross CityRail.
Lunch Wed–Fri, dinner Mon–Sat. Licensed. Very expensive.
Peter Doyle dishes up French-style food – with the odd cross-
cultural reference creeping in – in very civilized surrounds.
You can eat on the glassed-in balcony of the pretty Victorian
building.

RESTAURANTS: KINGS CROSS

Darley Street Thai

Map 7, F5. 28–30 Bayswater Rd ©9358 6530. Kings Cross CityRail.
Dinner nightly. Licensed. Very expensive.

Chef David Thompson does wonders with the flavours and textures of Thai food: try the set menu at $80. Minimalist interior with a vibrant colour wall. Attached takeaway, *DST Tuckshop* (closed Sun; $10–12).

Lime and Lemongrass

Map 7, F5. 42 Kellet St ©9358 5577. Kings Cross CityRail.
Dinner nightly. Licensed. Inexpensive to moderate.

Shady Kellet Street's high-ceilinged, terrace houses are home to several good value eateries. This Thai restaurant is a knockout, both for food and ambience, but the prices are very reasonable.

Minami

Map 7, F4. 87c Macleay St ©9357 2481. Kings Cross CityRail.
Mon–Sat noon–1am, Sun noon–midnight. BYO. Cheap.

Tiny, authentic Japanese noodle bar, where you'll find both Japanese residents and visitors squeezed around one large counter; popular choices like *ramen*, *yakisoba* and *kushikatsu*.

Paramount

Map 7, F4. 73 Macleay St ©9358 1652. Kings Cross CityRail.
Dinner nightly. Licensed. Very expensive.

Another of Sydney's top chefs, Christine Manfield, co-owns this glamorous restaurant. Her delectable, imaginative dishes, with influences from France through to China, have been featured in all the gourmet mags; she even has her own cookbook, *Spice*. Choice of menu: $100 6-course, $85 3-course, $65 2-course.

The Pig and The Olive

Map 7, F4. 71a Macleay St ©9357 3745. Kings Cross CityRail.
Mon–Sat 6–11pm, Sun 6–10pm. Licensed & BYO. Moderate.

Gourmet pizza bar with wild toppings like marinated lamb with feta. Also check out the small menu of contemporary-style dishes, which includes grilled polenta, spicy rack of lamb, and a few pasta options.

Star Bar and Grill

Map 7, E4. 155 Victoria St ✆9356 2911. Kings Cross CityRail.
Tues–Wed 6–11pm, Thurs–Sat 6pm–1am (bar closes 2am).
Inexpensive to moderate.

Fashionable bar and brasserie on several levels, offers fantastic city views from the window at the back. The most expensive thing on the bar menu is $10, and you can slurp oysters for $2.50 a go. Choose from grills and Moroccan *tagines* on the sit-down menu.

Venice Beach Restaurant

Map 7, F5. 2 Kellet St ✆9326 9928. Kings Cross CityRail.
Daily 5.30pm–midnight. Licensed. Cheap.

In a big, Victorian terrace house with a courtyard and a cushion room, this is a seriously stylish, cheap eatery. All entrees are $4.90, and the mains (all under $10) range from pasta to steak. A giant, chargrilled seafood platter for two costs $30.

WOOLLOOMOOLOO

Tilbury Hotel

Map 7, D3. Cnr Forbes and Nicholson streets ✆9368 1955. Bus #311.
Moderate.

Great pub with traditional pub grub – lots of steaks – plus more exotic dishes, accompanied by a varied programme of cabaret-style entertainment.

The Woolloomooloo Woodshed

Map 7, 5D. 132 Forbes St ✆9357 1978. Bus #311.

Closed lunch Sat & Sun. Licensed. Moderate.
All-Australian restaurant – grilled lamb chops or juicy steaks with chips and salad, served amongst woolshed memorabilia.

For vegetarian eats, try *Bodhidharma* **(p.174),**
***Badde Manors* (p.167),** *Govinda's* **(p.228),** *Iku* **(p.168),**
Harvest **(p.185), and** *The Red Kite* **(p.166).**

DARLINGHURST

Balkan Seafood Restaurant

Map 7, D8. 215 Oxford St ☎9331 7670. Bus #378, #380, #382.
Dinner Tues–Sun. BYO. Moderate.
Hearty Croatian/Italian cuisine: fish and seafood is the best choice, but you can also get huge schnitzels and other continental meat dishes. A bustling Darlinghurst institution, with a steaming, open kitchen at the front.

Bill and Toni

Map 7, C6. 72–74 Stanley St ☎9360 4702. Bus #324, #325.
Daily 7am–midnight. BYO. Cheap.
Cheap and cheerful Italian restaurant upstairs, with balcony tables; queue to get in. The café downstairs is a popular meeting spot, and serves tasty Italian sandwiches.

Chu Bay

Map 7, D8. 312a Bourke St ☎9331 3386. Bus #377, #390–392.
Dinner nightly. BYO. Cheap.
Tiny Vietnamese restaurant that's authentic and very popular.

Fez

Map 7, E7. 247 Victoria St (cnr Liverpool St) ☎9360 9581. Kings Cross CityRail.
Daily 7am–10.30pm (Sat & Sun from 8am). Licensed and BYO. Inexpensive.

With its corner position and cushioned window seats, this Middle Eastern and North African café is a favoured Darlinghurst locale. You can start the day with a breakfast of sweet couscous, and end it with a spicy lamb *tagine*.

Fishface
Map 7, E7. 132 Darlinghurst Rd ©9332 4803. Kings Cross CityRail.
Dinner nightly, lunch Sun only. BYO. Moderate.
Best market buys of fish, and a chance to taste some unusual varieties, served at stool-height tables and benches.

fu-manchu
Map 7, E7. 249 Victoria St ©9360 9424. Kings Cross CityRail.
BYO. Cheap.
Chinese and Malaysian noodles, served up at stainless-steel counters. Non-smoking.

Una's Cafe Restaurant
Map 7, E6. 340 Victoria St ©9360 6885. Kings Cross CityRail.
Daily 6.30am–11pm (Sun from 8am). BYO. Cheap to inexpensive.
Bustling café that's been dishing up cheap, tasty schnitzel and other German dishes for years. The big breakfasts, complete with potato, are very popular.

SURRY HILLS

Abdul's
Map 7, A11. 563 Elizabeth St (cnr Cleveland St) ©9698 1275. Bus #301–303.
Daily 10am–midnight (Thurs–Sat until 2am). BYO. Cheap.
This good-value Lebanese place is a late-night, post-pub institution. Eat-in or takeaway; belly-dancing Fri & Sat nights.

Dhaba House
Map 7, C12. 466 Cleveland St ©9319 6260. Bus #301–303.
Lunch Wed–Sun, dinner nightly. BYO. Cheap.

RESTAURANTS: SURRY HILLS

Downmarket decor matches the prices at this crowded Indian place, but the food is better than average.

Erciyes

Map 7, C12. 409 Cleveland St ℗9319 1309. Bus #301–303.
11am–midnight. Closed Mon. BYO. Cheap.
Among the offerings at this busy Turkish restaurant is *pide* (a bit like pizza) with a range of toppings, many vegetarian. Belly-dancing Fri & Sat nights.

MG Garage

Map 7, C10. 488 Crown St ℗9383 9383. Bus #301–303.
Closed Sun & lunch Sat. Licensed. Expensive.
Flash restaurant doubles as a car showroom, with MG sports cars sharing the dining space. Janni Kyritsis' modern Australian fare is superb, and if you can afford it, this makes a fun night out. There's a cheaper bistro version, *Fuel*, next door.

Nepalese Kitchen

Map 7, C11. 481 Crown St ℗9319 4264. Bus #301–303.
Dinner nightly. BYO. Cheap to inexpensive.
The speciality here is goat curry, served with *achars*, freshly cooked relishes which traditionally accompany Nepalese dishes; wide range of vegetarian options, too. Cosy, calming atmosphere, with traditional music playing.

Prasit's Northside Take-away

Map 7, C9. 395 Crown St ℗9319 0748. Bus #301–303.
Tues–Sun noon–3pm & 5–10pm. BYO. Inexpensive to moderate.
Be prepared for taste sensations as bold as the purple colour scheme. Entrees are available by the piece, so you can work your way through the delicious repertoire. Diners are squeezed onto stools downstairs, with a few more places upstairs. There's also a sit-down BYO restaurant further along

at 415 Crown St ©9319 0748 (lunch Thurs & Fri, dinner Mon–Sat).

Sushi-Suma
Map 7, C12. 419 Cleveland St ©9698 8873. Bus #301–303.
Closed Mon; dinner only Sat & Sun. BYO. Inexpensive.
That this small, noisy Japanese restaurant is so popular with Japanese locals and visitors says it all; booking is recommended.

PADDINGTON

Grand National Hotel
Map 7, H10. 161 Underwood St (cnr Elizabeth St) ©9963 4557. Bus #378, #380, #382.
Lunch Wed–Sun, dinner nightly. Licensed. Expensive.
One of the best pub restaurants in Sydney. Dishes up imaginative mod Oz fare, but with old-fashioned, attentive service. Booking essential at weekends.

Royal Bar & Grill
Map 7, G8. *Royal Hotel*, 237 Glenmore Rd ©9331 2604. Bus #389.
Licensed. Moderate.
Pub-restaurant, serving generous portions of meaty modern Australian fare. Smart interior and staff. Eating on the verandah is a real treat, but places fill fast – and they don't take bookings. However, you can wait in the top floor Elephant Bar, with great views of the city, until they call you.

GLEBE & NEWTOWN

Borobudur
Map 6, E4. 123–125 Glebe Point Rd, Glebe ©9660 5611. Bus #431, #433, #434.
Dinner only Mon–Sat. Licensed and BYO. Inexpensive.
Value-for-money Indonesian with an outdoor courtyard and courteous service.

Dakhni

Map 6, F4. 65 Glebe Point Rd, Glebe ☏9660 4887. Bus #431, #433, #434.

Closed Mon–Wed lunch. BYO. Inexpensive.

A range of Indian dishes from tandoori through to delicious vegetarian *masala dosai* (filled pancakes). Tasteful blue and coral decor but not as expensive as it looks, with a meat or vegetarian thali around $12. A popular spot, so book ahead.

Darling Mills

Map 6, E4. 134 Glebe Point Rd, Glebe ☏9660 5666. Bus #431, #433, #434.

Licensed and BYO. Very expensive.

Innovative modern Australian cuisine with fresh herbs and floral ingredients grown on the premises, served in an old sandstone building in a leafy garden. Very posh – an expensive treat.

Le Kilimanjaro

Map 6, C8. 280 King St, Newtown ☏9557 4565. Newtown CityRail.

BYO. Cheap to inexpensive.

Senegalese-run place, but the authentic menu travels from West African marinated chicken all the way to North African couscous. Casual and friendly atmosphere.

Old Saigon

Map 6, D7. 107 King St, Newtown ☏9519 5931. Newtown CityRail.

Lunch Wed–Fri, dinner Tues–Sun. Licensed and BYO. Inexpensive to moderate.

Vietnamese food with French, Thai and Japanese influences. Saigon memorabilia covers the walls of this cosy restaurant, which is run by a former war correspondent and his Vietnamese wife.

Steki Taverna

Map 6, D7. 2 O'Connell St, Newtown ☏9516 2191. Newtown CityRail.

Dinner Wed–Sun. Licensed. Inexpensive.
Atmospheric Greek taverna, with live music and dancing at
weekends (when you'll need to book).

Sumalee
Map 6, C8. *Bank Hotel*, 324 King St, Newtown ℂ9565 1730.
Newtown CityRail.
Closed Mon. Licensed. Moderate.
Superb Thai restaurant, in the courtyard of a popular pub next
to the train station. Best spot to dine is the leafy beer garden.

Thai Potong
Map 6, C8. 294 King St, Newtown ℂ9550 6277. Newtown CityRail.
Closed Mon lunch. Licensed and BYO. Inexpensive to moderate.
King Street's best Thai; excellent service and moderate prices.
Essential to book on the weekend.

Thanh Binh
Map 6, D7. 111 King St, Newtown ℂ9557 1175. Newtown CityRail.
Closed lunch Mon–Wed. Licensed and BYO. Inexpensive.
Newtown's celebrated Vietnamese eatery, with a huge range of
noodles to choose from.

LEICHHARDT & ROZELLE

Frattini
Map 3, E3. 122 Marion St, Leichhardt ℂ9569 2997. Bus #438, #440.
Closed Sat lunch. BYO. Moderate.
One of the best Italian restaurants in Little Italy, run by a genial
family. Modern airy space, but white tablecloths and old-fashioned service. The fish, with daily specials, is recommended
here, especially the whitebait fritters.

Harvest
Map 10, A6. 71 Evans St, Rozelle ℂ9818 4201. Bus #440, #445.

Dinner only; closed Sun. Licensed & BYO. Moderate.

Upmarket vegan and vegetarian restaurant – leans on Vietnamese, Japanese and Italian styles. Food is delicious, desserts decadent, coffee gets the thumbs up, and there's even a cocktail bar. (Also at 152 Jersey Rd, Woollahra ℂ9328 1939.)

Tetsuya's

Map 10, A6. 729 Darling St (cnr Cambridge St), Rozelle ℂ9555 1017. Bus #440, #445, #446.

Closed Sat dinner, Sun & Mon. Licensed and BYO. Very expensive.

Internationally renowned Tetsuya Wakuda, creatively presents exquisite Japanese/French-style fare; you'll need to book weeks in advance – they recently had to turn down members of the Japanese royal family. Six-course *dégustation* dinner menu at $100, or a $70, five-course lunch.

WATSONS BAY

Doyles on the Beach

Map 10, G7. 11 Marine Parade, Watsons Bay ℂ9337 1350. Watsons Bay Wharf; bus #324, #325.

Licensed. Expensive.

The seafood is good, but the views of the city across the water are among Sydney's best; *Doyles Wharf Restaurant*, which simply offers more of the same, is right next door (ℂ9337 1572). A fun way to get here is by water taxi from Circular Quay.

BONDI

Bondi Tratt

Map 8, E1. 34b Campbell Parade ℂ9365 4303. Bus #380, #382.

Daily 7am–11pm. Licensed and BYO. Moderate.

Modern Italian food, in a great setting overlooking the beach, and there's an outdoor terrace. Invariably buzzing.

Hugo's

Map 8, E1. 70 Campbell Parade ℗9300 0900. Bus #380, #382.

Brunch Sat & Sun 9am–4pm, dinner nightly. Licensed. Expensive.

There's ocean views, but also grittier ones of the bus stop outside and the raucous passing parade; inside it's all white tablecloths, table-lamps softly glowing, obliging waiters, a light-hearted noisy atmosphere, and towering plates of modern Australian food.

Sean's Panorama

Map 8, G1. 270 Campbell Parade ℗9365 4924. Bus #380, #382.

Closed Sun night. BYO. Moderate to expensive.

Sean Moran's food is among the most inventive in Sydney. Breakfast on weekends runs from 7am–3pm (and can easily meander into the Mediterranean-inspired lunch); the two- or three-course set dinner menus are $35–40.

The Sports Bard

Map 8, E2. 32 Campbell Parade ℗9130 4582. Bus #380, #382.

Mon–Fri 5pm–midnight, Sat & Sun 10am–midnight. Licensed and BYO. Moderate.

Cheerful brasserie, decorated with sporting memorabilia and with a pool table out back. Refreshingly simple food – fish, meat and roast chicken.

COOGEE

Barzura Cafe Ristorante

Map 8, B9. 62 Carr St ℗9665 5546. Bus #372, #373.

Daily 7am–11pm. Licensed and BYO. Inexpensive.

Fantastic spot with up-close ocean views. Breakfast (options include banana porridge and free-range eggs) is available until 1pm; snacks Turkish bread sandwiches are served until 7pm. Main meals (dishes such as seafood spaghetti and kangaroo fillets) are available for lunch and dinner. Unpretentious service encourages a local crowd.

RESTAURANTS: COOGEE

The Beach Pit

Map 8, A8. 211 Coogee Bay Rd ℘9665 0068. Bus #372, #373.
Noon–10pm, Sun 10am–9pm. Closed Tues & Wed. BYO.
Inexpensive to moderate.

Café restaurant, with Coogee's trademark informality and friendliness. Small but succulent menu: modern Australian, with plenty of fish and seafood. Servings are generous and well-presented. Bookings essential on weekends.

Coogee Bay Hotel Beach Brasserie

Map 8, A8. 212 Arden St ℘9665 0000. Bus #372, #373.
Daily 7am–10pm. Licensed. Inexpensive.

Very reasonably priced pub food, with an interesting menu that features dishes like roasted Moroccan chicken breast. Traditionalists can cook their own steak on the barbie.

Regal Pearl Seafood Restaurant

Map 8, B8. *Coogee Palace*, 169 Dolphin St ℘9665 3308. Bus #372, #373.
Licensed. Inexpensive.

Better and cheaper seafood than in Chinatown – plus ocean views. A great spot for *yum cha*.

Sari Rasa

Map 8, A8.186 Arden St (above *McDonald's*) ℘9665 5649. Bus #372, #373.
Daily noon–3pm & 6pm–late. BYO. Inexpensive.

A mostly Indonesian menu, plus some delicious Malaysian and Indian specialities, accompanied by ocean views (some tables outside on the balcony). Servings are generous.

MANLY

Brazil Café

Map 9, B3. 46 North Steyne ℘9977 3825. Manly ferry.

Daily 8am–midnight. Licensed and BYO. Expensive.
A classy, surf-front café that's more Italian/eclectic than
Brazilian; transforms into a pricey restaurant in the evening. A
popular local hangout, particularly for breakfast and Sunday
brunch.

Café Tunis

Map 9, B4. 30 South Steyne ℗9976 2805. Manly ferry.
Daily 7am–9pm. Licensed and BYO. Inexpensive to moderate.
Beachfront restaurant, airy and cool, with tiled floors. The
Cous Cous Royale is the signature dish, or you could opt for a
tasty *pide* sandwich – extremely filling. Some unusual drinks,
like lime and rosewater, go very well with the food.

Le Kiosk

Map 9, C5. 1 Marine Parade, Shelly Beach ℗9977 4122. Manly ferry.
Licensed. Expensive.
The coastal walk from Manly wharf to secluded Shelly Beach is
a delight in itself, and *Le Kiosk* has just the right laid-back
beach-house feel. If you can't afford the generous but pricey
contemporary fare, some fish and chips from the attached kiosk
is an excellent option.

Somi's

Map 9, C4. 48 Victoria Parade (cnr South Steyne) ℗9977 7511.
Manly ferry.
Licensed and BYO. Inexpensive.
Thai restaurant across from the beach, with a fresh and deli-
cious range of spicy seafood dishes on the menu.

Twocan

Map 9, B4. 27 Belgrave St ℗9977 1558. Manly ferry.
Closed Sun, Mon & lunch Sat. BYO. Moderate.
Colourful, Latin American decor on the walls, and yummy
modern Australian food on the menu. The desserts are divine.

RESTAURANTS: MANLY

Bathers Pavilion

Map 10, F3. The Esplanade, Balmoral Beach ©9968 1133. Mosman South ferry then bus #233, or Taronga Zoo ferry then bus #238.

Licensed. Expensive.

Indulge in some delicious seafood in this slickly renovated, beachside former dressing-shed. Weekend breakfast here (with champagne, of course) is a chic-but-casual North Shore ritual. The café is less expensive, and offers soothing natural light, water views and excellent coffee.

Indian Empire

Map 10, C4. 5 Walker St, North Sydney ©9923 2909. North Sydney CityRail.

Closed Sat & Sun lunch. BYO. Inexpensive.

Spectacular view of the city across Lavender Bay, plus everything you'd expect from a good Indian restaurant.

....

Also in North Sydney, the highly recommended
Prasit's **(p.182) have** *Prasit Northside Thai***, 77 Mount St**
*©***9957 2271; there's also a branch of the** *Malaya*
Restaurant **(p.176) at 86 Walker St** *©***9955 4306.**

....

Just Hooked

Map 10, D3. 236 Military Rd, Neutral Bay ©9904 0428. Bus #228–230, #247.

Dinner nightly, lunch Fri only. BYO. Inexpensive to moderate.

A small range of delicious fresh fish (just five starters, and five main courses) in a classy version of a classic fish shop, with white-tiled walls and high stools.

Watermark

Map 10, F3. 2a The Esplanade, Balmoral Beach ©9968 3433. Bus

#257, or Mosman South ferry then bus #233.

Licensed. Very expensive.

For a memorable Sydney meal, both for location and food, you can't go wrong here. Chef Kenneth Leung is well-known for his fusion of Eastern and Western cooking styles and ingredients. There are views across the water, a terrace on which to dine under the sun (or stars), and the service is fabulous.

There's a wonderful outdoor noodle market on Sunday afternoons at 234 Miller St, North Sydney (11.30am–4.30pm; map 10, C4).

RESTAURANTS: NORTH SHORE

Drinking

ustralians have a reputation for enjoying a drink, and **hotels** – more commonly known as **pubs** – are where this mostly takes place. Typically, a pub will have at least a public bar (traditionally rowdier) and a lounge bar (more sedate), a pool table, and in some cases a beer garden. Many offer meals, either in a restaurant or bistro setting, or served up informally at the bar. Ten percent of the world's **poker machines** are found in NSW, and the noisy, money-eating things have taken over many Sydney pubs. We have chosen places where these monsters are absent, or at the least, few and unobtrusive. Sydney doesn't have a huge **bar scene** (most of the those listed are attached to big hotels), but a recent relaxing of licensing laws means restaurants are now able to serve drinks to non-diners, which may liven things up.

Some pubs and bars have 24-hour licenses, though few actually stay open continuously (we have indicated those that have them, and their normal hours of operation). Standard opening hours are Mon–Sat 11am–midnight and Sun 11am–10pm, but many places stay open until at least 2am, particularly on Friday and Saturday nights.

The standard, ten-ounce (half-pint) glass of draught **beer** is known as a **middy** (around $2), and the larger one is the fifteen-ounce **schooner** (around $3). Imports such as

Guinness and Stella cost a bit more. Three local beers readily available on tap are: Toohey's New, a pretty standard lager; Toohey's Old, a darker, more bitter brew; and Reschs, a tastier, Pilsner-style beer. Upmarket places may only serve beer in bottles, starting from about $4. Wine by the glass is available at many places, usually from $4 – and a glass of local champagne is often the cheapest choice. Cocktails bars are very popular, and happy hour (times given in reviews) at one of these can be a great chance to catch the sunset over cheap drinks; outside of these times a cocktail will set you back $8–11.

Some pubs serve such good food that we have listed them separately in the "Eating" chapter. Likewise, some pubs listed in the "Live Music and Clubs" chapter are among the city's best watering holes.

We have divided our drinking account into areas, starting from The Rocks and ending with Balmain. Some **CBD** bars are closed on the weekend (the big nights out downtown are Thursday and Friday). **The Rocks**, with its huge range of lively watering holes, is a fair option on any night, though it does attract a pretty boisterous, beery crowd. A better choice for a cool, gay, or arty scene is **Darlinghurst,** or nearby **Paddington** and **Surry Hills**. One rewarding bar-crawl takes you from the bottom of Oxford Street to Paddington, with a detour along Darlinghurst Road to favourites the *Green Park* (p.199) and the *Darlo Bar*, (p.199). Otherwise, a stroll south from Oxford Street takes you into **Surry Hills**, and through the door of the *Cricketers Arms* (p.201). You can get a drink any time, day or night, in **Kings Cross**; there's a burgeoning gay/lesbian pub scene in inner-city **Newtown**, and the old neighbourhood pubs of **Balmain** make for a great pub crawl. The best seaside drinking spots are **Bondi,**

DRINKING

Watsons Bay and **Newport,** and we've also included three **international hotel bars** where you can catch breathtaking harbour and city views.

Australian Hotel
Map 5, C2. 100 Cumberland St. Circular Quay CityRail/ferry.
Mon–Sat 11am–midnight, Sun 11am–10pm.
Convivial corner hotel with crowded outside tables. Inside, original fittings give a lovely old-pub feel. Known for its local Bavarian-style draught beer, plus gourmet pizzas.

Glenmore Hotel
Map 5, C2. 96 Cumberland St. Circular Quay CityRail/ferry.
Mon–Sat 11am–11pm/midnight, Sun noon–10pm.
Breezy pub with great views from large windows in the public bar and from the rooftop beer garden. Opposite the entrance to the Harbour Bridge pedestrian walkway, it's a good refresher before or after the bridge walk. Serves up reasonably priced pub grub.

Hero of Waterloo
Map 5, B2. 81 Lower Fort St, Millers Point. Circular Quay CityRail.
Mon–Sat 10am–11pm, Sun 10am–10pm.
One of Sydney's oldest pubs, built in 1843, this place has plenty of atmosphere. Open fireplaces make it a good choice for a winter drink, and it serves simple meals.

Lord Nelson Brewery Hotel
Map 5, A2. Cnr Argyle and Kent streets, Millers Point. Circular Quay CityRail; bus #431–434.
Mon–Sat 11am–11pm, Sun noon–3.30pm & 5–8.30pm.
Licensed in 1841, this very old pub serves beer brewed on the premises, plus bar food daily and upmarket meals from

its first floor brasserie (see p.151). Ask for a tour of the brewery.

Mercantile Hotel

Map 5, C2. 25 George St. Circular Quay CityRail/ferry.
Mon–Wed & Sun 10am–midnight, Thurs–Sat 10am–1am.
High-spirited Irish pub where you can get Sydney's best Guinness; free folk music nightly 8–11pm, bistro meals and a weekend outdoor café.

Million dollar views

Horizons Bar Map 5, B4. 36th floor, *ANA Hotel*, 176 Cumberland St, The Rocks. Circular Quay CityRail/ferry. Daily noon–1am (Sun until midnight). This top floor bar has a 270-degree view – taking in the Opera House, Darling Harbour, Middle Harbour, and Homebush Bay to the Blue Mountains. Smart dress essential. Expensive bar snacks include smoked salmon and oysters. Beer $6.50, cocktails from $12.

International Bar Map 7, E6. 14th floor, 227 Victoria St, Darlinghurst. Kings Cross CityRail. Daily 5.30pm–midnight. Try to come for just one drink, to admire the fantastic view of the Sydney skyline. Get dressed up in your most stylish gear, and hope that the door gorillas don't turn you away from this beautiful people's bar. Local beer $7, cocktails $12-plus. Pricey bar snacks include Russian caviar.

Penthouse Bar Map 7, F5. 17th Floor, *Gazebo Hotel*, 2 Elizabeth Bay Rd, Elizabeth Bay. Kings Cross CityRail. Tues–Sat 6–11.30pm. Crescent shaped, intimate bar on the top floor of this circular high-rise hotel, with city and harbour vistas. Fresh air and good views from the standing-room-only balcony. Cocktails from $8, bottled beer from $5.

Bar Luca
Map 5, D4. 52 Phillip St. Circular Quay CityRail.
Mon–Fri 7am–10.30pm, closed Sat & Sun.
Trendy city bar – all natural woods and fresh flowers. It doubles
as an Italian café, with breakfast from 7am and main meals
through the day; or you can just come in for a coffee.

Customs House Bar
Map 5, C4. Macquarie Pl, Bridge St. Circular Quay CityRail/ferry.
Mon–Fri 11am–10pm; closed Sat & Sun.
An attractive building (circa 1826) which backs onto a city
square; a city/suit crowd spills out the doors and schmoozes
amongst the palm trees and statues. Cheap lunches
$3.50–9.50.

Dendy Bar and Bistro
Map 5, C5. Dendy Cinema, 19 Martin Pl. Martin Place CityRail.
24-hour license: Mon–Fri 8am–late, Sat & Sun 11am–late.
This basement bar, separate from the Dendy cinema, makes a
cool downtown meeting spot, especially as neither the dread-
ed poker machines nor city suits are found here. There's
cushioned seating along the wall, a big screen where short
films are shown on Sun nights, and a pool room. Happy
hour Mon–Thurs 5–7pm. Occasional live music and club
nights.

Forbes Hotel
Map 5, B6. Cnr King and York streets. Wynyard CityRail.
Mon–Thurs to midnight, Fri & Sat to 3am, Sun to 8pm.
Turn-of-the-century hotel with a lively, ground-level bar.
Upstairs has a pool table and plenty of window seating – the
best spot is the tiny, cast-iron balcony, with just enough room
for two.

The Marble Bar

Map 5, C7. *Hilton Hotel*, 259 Pitt St. Town Hall CityRail.
Mon–Thurs noon–11.30pm, Fri noon–2am, Sat 5pm–2am; closed Sun.

A sightseeing stop as much as a good place for a drink, amongst Victorian decor which features Italian marble. This was the original 1893 basement bar of the *Tattersalls Hotel*. Pricey drinks, happy hour 5–7pm. Free jazz or blues Tues–Sat nights.

Scruffy Murphy's

Map 5, B9. 43 Goulburn St. Central CityRail.
24-hour license: Daily 11am–3.30/4.30am.

Rowdy, late-opening Irish pub with Guinness on tap, of course; phenomenally popular.

Slip Inn

Map 5, A6. 111 Sussex St. Darling Park Monorail; Wynyard CityRail.
Mon–Thurs noon–midnight, Fri noon–2am, Sat noon–4am. Closed Sun.

On three levels overlooking Darling Harbour, this place has several bars, a bistro, and a nightclub, *The Chinese Laundry* (Fri & Sat night; $10–15). It attracts a young, style-conscious, after-work crowd. The front bar has a pool room, while downstairs a boisterous beer garden fills up on sultry nights; there's a quieter bar beside it with candle-lit tables. Expensive pub food and gourmet pizzas by day, tasty contemporary fare in the bistro by night. Live jazz Thurs night, DJs Fri night.

KINGS CROSS

Bourbon and Beefsteak Bar

Map 7, F5. 24 Darlinghurst Rd. Kings Cross CityRail.
24-hour.

Infamous – and outrageously tacky – Kings Cross watering hole, which opened in 1968 to attract US soldiers on

KINGS CROSS

R&R. Come here for a steak breakfast and a Bloody
Mary after a night out. $5 cover charge Fri & Sat 10pm–5am.
Live music – jazz, rock'n'roll – all week (Fri & Sat until
5.30am).

Piccadilly Hotel

Map 7, E5. 171 Victoria St. Kings Cross CityRail.

24-hour license: *Soho Bar* Mon–Thurs & Sun 11am–2am, Fri & Sat
11am–4/5am. *Lounge Bar* Thurs 7pm–2am, Fri & Sat
7pm–4.30am.

This trendy, Art Deco pub is a good place for a chat.
Popular with travellers is the downstairs *Soho Bar*; most
locals head for the *Lounge Bar* upstairs, to hang out on the
back balcony and play pool. Attached nightclub and gaming
lounge.

**See the *Tilbury Hotel* (p.179) and the *Woolloomooloo
Woolshed* (p.179), two Woolloomooloo pubs reviewed
in the Eating chapter.**

DARLINGHURST

Burdekin Hotel

Map 7, C6. 2 Oxford St. Museum or Town Hall CityRail; bus #378,
#380, #382.

24-hour license: Mon–Thurs noon–1am, Fri noon–4/5am, Sat
3.30pm–4/5am. *Dug Out Bar* Tues–Thurs 5pm–midnight, Fri
5pm–2am, Sat 6pm–3am. Closed Sun.

This well-preserved, Art Deco pub has several trendy bars on
four levels. The basement *Dug Out Bar* is tiny and beautifully
tiled, and has table service and generous cocktails; the spacious,
ground-level *Main Bar* sports dramatic columns and a huge
round bar; *Cherry Blue*, on the first floor, has poker machines
and pool tables, and DJs Fri & Sat from 9pm (free), The beau-

tiful third floor *Lava Bar*, with its luscious pink interior, is usually only open for functions but sometimes lets punters in weekends, from 9pm until late.

Darlo Bar

Map 7, E7. *Royal Sovereign Hotel*, cnr Darlinghurst Rd and Liverpool St. Kings Cross CityRail.
Mon–Sat 10am–midnight, Sun noon–10pm.

Popular Darlinghurst meeting place, with a lounge room atmosphere – the comfy chairs, sofas and lamps have a 1950s feel, and look great against the burnished walls. Drinks are fairly cheap, (house wines from $3.20 glass), the crowd mixed and unpretentious. You can order from the menu of nearby *Fishface* at night (see p.181), and from *Eca Bar* during the day, and they'll fetch the food for you.

Green Park Hotel

Map 7, E7. 360 Victoria St. Kings Cross CityRail.
Mon–Sat 10am–1am, Sun noon–midnight.

Great for a daytime drink; always lively, packed and cruisey at night with a crowd of young regulars. The pool tables out back are a big attraction.

Judgement Bar

Map 7, D8. *Courthouse Hotel*, 189 Oxford St. Bus #378, #380, #382.
24-hour license: Mon–Thurs 11am–3am, Fri & Sat 24-hour, Sun 11am–midnight.

Overlooking Taylor Square, this is *the* late-opener of choice; your *Courthouse* punishment may be to find yourself here in the wee hours, among an assortment of young clubbers and old drunks. Totally undiscriminating and drinks aren't pricey. Wakes up around 1am.

DARLINGHURST

....

**Another legendary, late-night Darlinghurst haunt is
the *Taxi Club* – see Gay Sydney (p.236).**

....

Lizard Lounge

Map 7, C7. *Exchange Hotel*, 34 Oxford St. Bus #378, #380, #382.
Daily 5pm until late.

Stylish, straight bar in a gay strip – spacious interior, wooden
floorboards, changing art exhibition on the walls and comfy
leather couches in the corner (bag one of these early). Happy
hour (5–8pm) gets them in, and as the crowd gathers and the
music cranks up, posing/staring becomes the main game.

L'Otel

Map 7, E6.114 Darlinghurst Rd. Kings Cross CityRail.
Daily 6pm–3am.

Chic, intimate, café-style bar with table service, attached to a
fashionable boutique hotel. Cocktails $8. DJs Sun nights.

Palace Hotel

Map 7, D9. Cnr Flinders and South Dowling streets. Bus #372,
#373, #397–399.
Mon–Wed 4pm–midnight, Thurs–Sat 4pm–1am, Sun 4–11pm.

Classic Art Deco tiled pub, fashionably done-up. Noisy smart-
set hang out downstairs, and a tiny eating area services a kitchen
of good repute. Star attraction is the several rooms of pool tables
upstairs, where crimson-red drapes create a very baroque feel.

SURRY HILLS

Bar Cleveland

Map 7, C12. Cnr Cleveland and Bourke streets. Bus #393–399.
24-hour license: Mon–Wed 11am–2am, Thurs–Sat 11am–4am, Sun
noon–midnight.

Huge, plate-glass windows have opened this pub onto the busy, gritty street of Turkish takeaways and secondhand clothes shops, and punters have packed it ever since for an authentic urban brew. DJs Fri & Sat nights. Cocktail bar upstairs.

Bentley Bar

Map 7, C7. 320 Crown St. Bus #378, #380, #382.
24-hour license: Mon–Thurs 2pm–3am, Fri & Sat noon–5am, Sun 10am–midnight.

Perennially popular, pre- and post-clubbing venue. Dark, noisy and packed. DJs Mon, Wed, Thurs & Sun nights.

Clock Hotel

Map 7, C10. 470 Crown St. Central CityRail.
Mon–Sat 11am–midnight, Sun noon–10pm.

This huge hotel has expanded out of all touch with its 1840s roots, emblematic of the new Surry Hills. (The landmark clock tower was only added in the 1960s.) Upstairs, a swish restaurant and cocktail bar runs off the huge balcony – a great place to hang out. Booths in the front bar have clocks telling you what time it is elsewhere in the world, and there's a popular pool-hall and basement gaming room.

Cricketers Arms

Map 7, C9. 106 Fitzroy St. Central CityRail.
Mon–Sat noon–midnight, Sun noon–10pm.

Just down the road from the live music scene at the *Hopetoun* (p.212), the *Cricketers* has an equally dedicated clientele. A young, offbeat crowd – plenty of piercings and shaved heads – cram in and fall about the bar, pool room, and tiny beer garden, and yell at each other over a funky soundtrack. Hearty bar snacks (Tues–Sun 3–10pm; under $9) and, in surprising contrast, a posh restaurant.

SURRY HILLS

Dolphin Hotel

Map 7, C9. 412 Crown St. Central CityRail.

Mon–Sat 10am–midnight, Sun noon–10pm.

Fashionably renovated pub; the lounge bar doubles as a café, while the public bar is as down-to-earth as ever. Upstairs, a tiny bar which overlooks the stunning architecture of the *Dolphin's* restaurant, is a good spot for a chat and a glass of wine.

O'Bar

Map 7, B10. *Clarendon Hotel*, cnr Devonshire and Waterloo streets. Central CityRail.

Mon–Sat noon–midnight, closed Sun.

The name comes from the perfectly round bar of this upmarket pub. A complete absence of poker machines makes this is a good place for a chat over a glass of wine from the well-considered list. A lovely, early evening light suffuses the pale wood interior, making it a particularly attractive stop before dinner on nearby Crown Street – or try the well-regarded restaurant right here.

PADDINGTON AND WOOLLAHRA

Elephant Bar

Map 7, G8. *Royal Hotel*, 237 Glenmore Rd, Paddington. Bus #389.

Mon–Fri 5pm–midnight, Sat 4.30pm–midnight, Sun 4.30–10pm.

The top-floor bar of this beautifully renovated, Victorian-era hotel has knockout views of the city, best appreciated at sunset (happy hour 6–7pm; cocktails $7). The small interior is swell too, with its fireplaces, paintings and elephant prints. As it gets crowded later on, people cram onto the stairwell and it feels like a party.

Lord Dudley

Map 7, I9. 236 Jersey Rd, Woollahra. Bus #330, #389.

Mon–Sat 10am–midnight, Sun 10am–10pm.

Sydney's most British pub, complete wtih fireplaces, fox-hunting pictures, dark wood furniture – and a dartboard. Thirty-six beers on tap, many imported, including Newcastle Brown Ale. The bistro serves up hearty British fare.

Paddington Inn

Map 7, G10. 338 Oxford St, Paddington. Bus #378, #380, #382.
Mon–Fri & Sun 11.30am–midnight/1am, Sat 10am–1am.

The recently renovated *Paddington Inn* is full of interior design statements: textured glass, cushioned booths, polished concrete floors and fabric-lined walls. You can eat (or just drink) anywhere on the two levels; the affordable menu falls somewhere between pub and restaurant food, but there's no table service. Packed on Saturdays, as it's opposite the market.

BONDI

Bondi Hotel

Map 8, F1. 178 Campbell Parade. Bus #380, #382.
Mon–Sat 10am–4am, Sun 10am–midnight.

Huge pub dating from the 1920s, with many of its original features intact in its several bars. Sedate during the day, it turns into a rowdy, late-night backpackers' hangout.

Bondi Icebergs Club

Map 8, E2. 1 Notts Ave. Bus #380, #382.
Mon–Thurs 11am–9/10pm, Fri–Sun 11am–10/11pm.

Unassuming place with cheap beer – and the most stunning views in Bondi, right over the southern end of the beach. For entry as a non-member, bring a passport or other ID (to prove you're from out of town). Live music Sunday afternoons, 4–8pm.

Other Bondi watering holes are *BB's* and the *Beach Road Hotel*, detailed in Live Music and Clubs (p.210).

BONDI

Legendary beer gardens

Many Sydney pubs have an outdoor drinking area, perfect for enjoying the sunny weather – the three listed below, however, are outright legends.

Newport Arms Hotel Map 2, E6. 2 Kalinya St, Newport. Bus #187–190. Daily 10am–midnight (Sun until 9.30pm). Overlooking Pittwater; Sunday is the big day, with free jazz outside (1–5pm), and the bistro serving food from noon right through until closing time.

The Oaks Hotel Map 10, D3. 118 Military Rd, Neutral Bay. Bus #143, #243. Daily 10am–midnight (Fri & Sat until 1am). The North Shore's most popular pub, takes its name from the huge oak that shades the entire beer garden. Make use of the BBQ and cook your own (expensive) steak, or if you're feeling lazy, there's a gourmet pizza restaurant inside.

Watsons Bay Hotel Map 10, H5. 10 Marine Parade, Watsons Bay. Bus #324, #325. Daily 10am–10pm (Fri & Sat until midnight). Relaxing beer garden with views over Watsons Bay, crowded on weekends with people enjoying a beer with their fish and chips (good-value bistro meals).

GLEBE & NEWTOWN

Bank Hotel

Map 6, C8. 324 King St, Newtown. Newtown CityRail. 24-hour license: Mon & Tues noon–12.30am, Wed & Thurs noon–1.30/2am, Fri & Sat noon–4am, Sun noon–midnight. Stylish pub – always packed and open late. Pool table out front, cocktail bar out back (happy hour nightly 6–9pm), and a big beer garden with a recommended Thai restaurant, *Sumalee* (see p.185).

Marlborough Hotel

Map 6, D7. 145 King St, Newtown. Newtown CityRail.

24-hour license: Mon–Sat 10am–2/3am, Sun noon–midnight.

A spacious pub with several bars, it's a favourite with students from nearby Sydney University (bands Fri and Sat nights). The gaming room is popular, the lounge area has big sofas, and is a quiet place to talk. There's also a pleasant beer garden, emptied at mealtimes by their good-value Italian restaurant, *Prego's*.

Nag's Head Hotel

Map 6, D4. 162 St Johns Rd, Glebe. Bus #470.

Mon–Sat 11am–midnight, Sun noon–midnight.

A good place for a quiet drink – no pool tables, no pokies – with British beers (pints available) and atmosphere; calls itself a "posh pub". The bistro dishes up excellent steaks and other grills.

The Rose Hotel

Map 6, G5. 54 Cleveland St, Chippendale. Bus #422, #423, #426, #427, #428.

Mon–Sat 11.30am–midnight, Sun 11.30am–10pm.

This pub is a real treasure, despite its location at the traffic-laden, arse-end of Cleveland St. The mock-Renaissance ceiling mural overlooks the pool table, while a bizarrely-decorated rocking horse is suspended over the beer garden out back. There's a modern Australian eatery with a huge blackboard menu, and a good wine list, with wines available by the glass.

BALMAIN

Exchange Hotel

Map 10, A6. Cnr Beattie and Mullens streets. Bus #441, #442.

Daily 10am–midnight.

Classic Balmain boozer, established in 1885. This backstreet corner pub has an enormous balcony, just perfect for the week-end morning Bloody Mary specials.

BALMAIN

London Hotel

Map 10, A6. 234 Darling St. Bus #433, #434, #442, #445.
11am–midnight, Sun noon–10pm.

Convivial British pub, with stools out on the verandah which overlooks the Saturday market. Attracts a mixed Balmain crowd.

Monkey Bar

Map 10, A5. 255 Darling St. Bus #433, #434, #442, #445.
Mon–Sat noon–midnight, Sun noon–10pm.

Stylish bar with an atrium restaurant overlooked by the bar. Twenty- and thirty-something professionals drink here, amongst loud music in a crowded space. There's a small stage for the free live music – blues, soul, jazz or acoustic rock – Wed, Fri, Sat nights and early Sunday evening. Bar menu $10–12.

Live music and clubs

There's an awful lot going on in Sydney, with bands hard at it in sweaty pubs and clubbers grooving in huge techno barns as well as tiny hidden rooms. It's easy enough to find out exactly what's on: you'll find comprehensive **listings** of music events in "Metro", a supplement in Friday's *Sydney Morning Herald*, "Time Out", a weekly entertainment lift-out in Sunday's *Sun-Herald*, or "Seven Days" in the *Daily Telegraph* every Thursday. For information on more alternative goings-on – clubbing, fashion, and the like – and band interviews and reviews, there is a plethora of free magazines which can be found in the cafés, record shops and boutiques of Darlinghurst, Glebe, Newtown and Kings Cross. *On the Street, Drum Media* and *Revolver* have weekly listings and reviews; *3D World* and *Beat* cover the clubbing scene. Best of all is *Revolver*, which offers informed and well-written critiques (as opposed to the more illiterate diary entries printed elsewhere). **Radio** station 2 MMM (FM 104.9MHz) details music gigs around town daily on the hour between 2–6pm. Also check the useful Web site *www.sydney.citysearch.com.au*

(a kind of listings mag on the net, with plenty about the music and club scene).

LIVE MUSIC

Australia in general, and Sydney in particular, has a well-deserved reputation for producing quality live bands: the thriving pub scene of the late 1970s and early 1980s produced a spectrum of great acts, from indie stars Nick Cave, The Church and the Triffids, to globe-straddling stadium-shakers like INXS.

Sadly, the passing of that era has seen the demise of many of Sydney's best live venues, with even famous places such as the *Strawberry Hills Hotel* being converted into dingy, poker-machine parlours. Otherwise, the live music scene in Sydney remains vibrant, nurturing its own top-class talent, and hosting a stream of interstate and overseas acts, peaking in summer with several huge open-air festivals (see p.213).

Besides the big concert halls, Sydney's live music action still centres around **pub venues** (see p.209). Pub bands are often free, especially if you arrive early (bands generally go on stage between 9.30–10.30pm, earlier on Sundays); otherwise, $5–10 is a standard entry fee, with $12–20 for smaller international acts or the latest interstate sensation. Sunday evenings are notably laid-back - an excellent time to catch some funk or mellow jazz somewhere around town.

CONCERT VENUES

Capitol Theatre

Map 5, B9. 13 Campbell St, Haymarket ℗9266 4800. Central CityRail.

Refurbished, older theatre with balcony seating and room for around 2000 people. The Capitol hosts musicals and even ballet, but crooners and mellow pop groups occasionally appear here.

Enmore Theatre

Map 6, B8. 130 Enmore Rd, Enmore ℂ9550 3666. Newtown CityRail.
A pleasingly intimate, old-world theatre venue for 1500 people
– dingier than the Capitol, a fact which sits comfortably with
its location, in inner-city Newtown. Elvis Costello and the
Cranberries are among notables to have played here.

Metro Theatre

Map 5, B8. 624 George St ℂ9264 2666. Town Hall CityRail.
Purpose-designed to handle everything from musicals to bands
and ambitious dance parties, the Metro is exceptionally well laid
out and has an excellent sound system – holds up to 1200 people.

State Theatre

Map 5, C7. 49 Market St ℂ9373 6655. Town Hall CityRail.
This 2000 seat theatre is decked out a bit too opulently in marble and statuary, but performers who insist on a bit of grandeur
(such as k.d.lang), play here.

Sydney Entertainment Centre

Map 5, A9. Haymarket, beside Darling Harbour ℂ9266 4800.
Pyrmont Light Rail.
Soulless, 12,000-seat arena with video screens and a good
sound system – Sydney's largest indoor venue, for big international acts.

....

**For advance credit-card bookings phone Ticketek
ℂ9266 4800, or Ticketmasters ℂ13 6100.**

....

PUB VENUES

The Basement

Map 5, C4. 29 Reiby Pl, Circular Quay ℂ9251 2797. Circular Quay
CityRail/ferry.

LIVE MUSIC: PUB VENUES

A great place to see jazz, acoustic and world music, as well as a roster of renowned blues performers. The best option here is to book a table and dine in front of the low stage; if you don't and it's a largish crowd, you'll probably find yourself in a cramped spot with an obstructed view, although the quality of the performance will probably seem like fair compensation.

BB's Wine Bar
Map 8, F1. 157 Curlewis St, Bondi Beach ©9365 3687. Bus #380. Mon–Fri from 5pm, Sat & Sun from 4pm.
A feral wine bar, *BB's* looks and feels as if squatters have taken over a duke's private den. Welcoming and open, it's pretty much the only place in Bondi Beach where you can see free live music every night. The bands are of variable quality, but unvarying enthusiasm. Good-value meals.

Beach Road Hotel
Map 3, H3. 71 Beach Rd, Bondi Beach ©9130 7247. Bus #380.
Huge, stylishly decorated pub with a bewildering range of bars and a beer garden. Massively popular with travellers, it has supplanted the rowdy *Bondi Hotel* as the place to imbibe after a day at the beach (even the goatee and black-frame glasses brigade are starting to give it a sniff). Entertainment, mostly free, ranges from DJs playing mellow grooves, to bands and a jazz supper club. There's also a cheap Italian bistro and an upmarket Thai eatery.

Bridge Hotel
Map 3, E3. 135 Victoria Rd, Rozelle ©9810 1260. Bus #501.
A legendary inner-west venue, specializing in blues and pub rock, with mostly local acts and occasional international artists. It doesn't look like your usual pub either, with its three-level courtyard a distinctive feature.

Cat and Fiddle Hotel

Map 10, A6. 456 Darling St, Balmain ℂ9810 7931. Bus #442.
Smallish venue with high standards, attracting informed indie
rock audiences who appreciate the quality interstate bands,
along with local gonnabes. Pool tables, pub-price beer and a
serious muso-crowd atmosphere. Music every night of the
week.

Excelsior Hotel (Glebe)

Map 6, E3. Pyrmont Bridge Rd, Glebe ℂ9660 7479. Bus #431,
#433, #434.
Not to be confused with the *Excelsior* in Surry Hills, the
Sunday afternoon sessions at the Glebe *Excelsior* inspired a
movement in quality songwriting and acoustic instruments.
Still one of the best places to experience Sunday afternoon
rock in Sydney – exponents to watch out for include
Leonardo's Bride and David Lane. The upstairs pool room
with interior balcony is a great feature and the food is good.
Usually free.

Excelsior Hotel (Surry Hills)

Map 7, B9. 64 Foveaux St, Surry Hills ℂ9211 4945. Central CityRail.
Muso's pub – songwriters nights and jam sessions are part of
the nightly live music line-up, usually folk/blues or plain old
pub rock; mostly free. Bar/Bistro until 3am, Fri and Sat.

The Globe

Map 6, C8. 379 King St, Newtown ℂ9519 0220. Newtown CityRail.
The epicentre of Newtown's – and perhaps Sydney's – musical
subculture. Top bands rub shoulders with DJs and the venue
isn't above putting on the occasional theme/retro night. The
two-level venue often has free entry downstairs, but otherwise
be prepared to pay $6–15 to mix with a varied inner-city
crowd. Big line-ups Thurs–Sun and more intimate gigs
Mon–Wed.

LIVE MUSIC: PUB VENUES

Harbourside Brasserie

Map 5, B1. Pier One, Hickson Rd, Millers Point ℂ9252 3000.
Circular Quay CityRail/ferry.

Great location on the harbour near The Rocks. Jazz, blues,
soul, fusion, world music or cabaret Mon–Sat from 10pm, and
Latin Dance Club, when frisky, foot-tapping girls get swept
around the floor by Latino boys who can actually dance, Sun
from 8pm. Cool, discriminating crowd; favoured by music-
industry types for album launches and get-togethers.

Hopetoun Hotel

Map 7, C9. 416 Bourke St (cnr Fitzroy St), Surry Hills ℂ9361 5257.
Central CityRail.

"The Hoey" is one of Sydney's best for the indie band scene,
with music Wednesday to Sunday in the small and always
crowded front bar. There's a popular pool room out back, a
drinking pit in the basement, and an ambitious little restaurant
upstairs. Cover charge Thurs–Sun $4–7, free Mon–Wed; closes
at midnight.

Iron Duke Hotel

Map 6, G9. 220 Botany Rd, Alexandria ℂ9990 9988. Bus #308.
Hard rock venue with big line-ups of amp-crashing local,
interstate and international bands Tues–Sun. A discerning
crowd of the inner-city music cognoscenti make this one a
genuine Sydney rock experience.

Round Midnight

Map 7, F5. 2 Roslyn St, Kings Cross ℂ9356 4045. Kings Cross
CityRail.

Intimate, late-night jazz and blues venue; Tues–Sun from 9pm.

Selina's

Map 8, A8. *Coogee Bay Hotel*, 212 Arden St, Coogee Bay ℂ9665
0000. Bus #314, #315, #372, #373.

Festivals

The big summer outdoor rock concerts are **Homebake** ($40; *www.homebake.com*), held early December in The Domain, with an all-Australian cast of some thirty bands, plus food- and market-stalls and rides; and the **Big Day Out**, (Australia Day weekend; $65) at the new showground at Homebush Bay – attracts international names like The Beastie Boys and Marilyn Manson, as well as local bands and DJs performing on various stages and dance floors, usually around sixty acts in all.

Woeful interior design has the audience peeping around pillars, and the acoustics are terrible. But a dearth of competition sees *Selina's* survive as Sydney's largest genuine pub venue. Room for 1100 punters.

CLUBS

Many of Sydney's best clubs are at **gay** or **lesbian** venues: although these are listed separately in "Gay Sydney" chapter, the divisions are not always clear – many places have particular gay, lesbian and straight nights scheduled each week. A long strip of thriving clubs stretches from Kings Cross to Oxford Street and down towards Hyde Park, with *DCM* (see p.235) perhaps the most popular place to go. The scene can be pretty snobby, with door gorillas frequently vetting your style. The year's big dance party is **Vibes on a Summer's Day**, a sweltering day of sultry beats, trip-hop, reggae flavours and excruciatingly beautiful bodies in and around the Bondi Pavilion (end of January; approximately $50).

Cauldron

Map 7, E6. 207 Darlinghurst Rd, Darlinghurst ©9331 1523. Kings Cross CityRail.

CLUBS

213

Wed–Sat 10pm–4am.

Stalwart club, that's as popular as ever with a new generation of well-heeled, eastern suburbs types.

Club 77

Map 7, D5. 277 William St, East Sydney ℂ9361 4981. Kings Cross CityRail.

Free midweek before 10pm, $4 before 11pm, $8 after. Weekends $10–15. Closes at 5am.

Just a quick flit down from the Cross: retro nights, techno beats and house sounds produce a hands-in-the-air rave atmosphere of the kind found on a rowdy harbour cruise; yet somehow, *Club 77* remains a favourite. They stop just short of letting in any old goose, so you may have to queue, but without too much anxiety. The crowd is mostly straight, the mood, that of an all-night party. The drinks are a little above pub prices, but not much.

Globe

Map 5, C7. Cnr Park and Elizabeth streets ℂ9282 8082. Town Hall CityRail.

Thurs–Sat 11pm–6am. $15.

After drinking boutique beers in the faux airport-lounge first-floor bar, head down to the club; a subterranean space with a low ceiling. Dress very cool or very hot – arriving with a supermodel on either arm will guarantee you entry. The music is energetic house, hip-hop and big beats; beers are pricey.

Home

Map 5, A7. Cockle Bay Wharf, Darling Harbour ℂ9266 0600. Town Hall CityRail.

Fri–Sun 10.30pm–5am. $10–20.

The first really BIG club venture in Sydney, *Home* is part of the new Cockle Bay Wharf development (see p.235), situated in Sydney's most heavily baited tourist trap, the Darling Harbour complex. Its acre or two of floor space can take 2000 punters at a time, which adds up to several suburbs' worth of youth grooving to house sounds and big beats. The decks are often manned by name DJs, but you get the feeling the crowd don't know or care too much. There's a mezzanine for those who prefer just to watch, as well as a chill-out room. Drinks are expensive, staff beautiful.

Palladium

Map 7, F5. Cnr Darlinghurst Rd and Roslyn St, Kings Cross ℗9331 0127. Kings Cross CityRail.

Sat–Sun 10.30pm–4am. $10.

On the top two floors of the old *Les Girls* theatre, the *Palladium* offers a succession of cool nights for a variety of crowds, from lounge cruisers to suburban breakdancers. Sunday night's "Tender Trap" has been a lounge club favourite for a few years, not least for the welcoming atmosphere, where non-clubbers rub nylon shirts with hardcore polyester smoothies, to produce just the right amount of static.

Powercuts Reggae Club

Map 5, C7. 150 Elizabeth St ℗9264 5380. Town Hall CityRail.

DJs play what they claim is "the smoothest reggae known to man" on Friday and Saturday nights 10pm–4.30am.

Q Bar Pool Club

Map 7, C7. 44 Oxford St, Darlinghurst ℗9360 1375. Town Hall, Museum or Kings Cross CityRail; bus #380.

Thurs–Sat 10pm–4am. $10.

Lots of pool tables and video games plus a dance floor make a popular combination. Swarms of young cuties and hopeful hair-cuts play pool by-the-hour; trendy but no reason to be scared.

Rhino Bar

Map 7, F5. 24 Bayswater Rd, Kings Cross. Kings Cross CityRail.

Thurs–Sat 9pm–3am. $10.

Cheap drinks and a fairly relaxed door policy mean that the

CLUBS

Rhino Bar is popular with a cheerful crowd that doesn't care too much about the "scene". Dancers and joggers mix on a smallish floor, jammed and jiving to a mix of dub and house grooves. The atmosphere throughout is lively, if a little beery in the front bar. A bit more glamorous on a Saturday night.

Sublime

Map 5, C7. 244 Pitt St ✆9264 8428. Wynyard CityRail.
Thurs–Sat 10pm–4am. $15.

Purpose-built basement club, popular with just about everyone for its selection of different theme nights. A hard, house feel is the bedrock for a serious club experience, and the vast dance area is crammed with hardcore clubbers, who take an occasional breather in the chill-out room before diving right back in.

Sugareef

Map 7, F5. 20 Bayswater Rd, Kings Cross ✆9357 7250. Kings Cross CityRail.
Thurs–Sat 9pm–3am. $10.

Ducking into *Sugareef* from next door's *Rhino Bar*, you find a contrastingly polished atmosphere, as if the sweat has been sucked from the air. With plenty of space to recline and reflect upon your hairstyle and shoes, conversation is also possible, as acid jazz maintains the pulse without inducing an aneurysm.

Underground Café

Map 7, F5. 22 Bayswater Rd. Kings Cross ✆9368 1067. Kings Cross CityRail.
Wed–Sun 9pm–4am. $5–10.

Beneath the low ceilings of this underground enclave, you'll find a mix of fashion-conscious travellers and young locals prowling the pool tables, lolling on high stools, or jammed into the snug corner stalls, while taking in some progressive house, big beats and a little garage. Often features national and international DJs. Thursdays for $2 entry and cheap drinks; gets going after midnight.

Performing arts and film

From Shakespeare to gay film festivals, Sydney's arts scene takes itself seriously while managing never to lose its sense of fun. Free summertime outdoor performances in The Domain, such as the Sydney Festival's **Opera in the Park** (see p.266), are among the year's highlights, as Sydneysiders turn out in their thousands to picnic and share in the atmosphere.

Check the *Sydney Morning Herald*'s Friday supplement "Metro", for **listings** of **what's on** at the venues below. The free *Sydney Arts and Cultural Guide*, published every six months and available from tourist offices, has information on upcoming theatrical productions and classical concerts. For theatre, concerts, opera and ballet, **cheap** tickets for that day's performance only are sold at the **Half-tix** kiosk in Martin Place (Mon–Sat noon–6pm).

> Credit-card bookings, for everything from concert events to circus performances, can be made through Ticketek ℡9266 4800 or Ticketmasters ℡13 6100.

CLASSICAL MUSIC, OPERA AND BALLET

The **Sydney Opera House** is the centre of high culture in Sydney, and while it's not necessary to don tie-and-tails or an evening dress when attending a performance, it's still about the only place you're likely to see locals in formal attire. The **Australian Ballet**, **Opera Australia**, **Sydney Theatre Company** and the **Sydney Dance Company** all have Opera House seasons.

The Australian Ballet (which features contemporary as well as classical dance; tickets $42–70), shifts between Sydney and Melbourne – it's based in the latter, but performs at the Opera House from mid-March to early May, and November through December. Opera Australia (tickets $42–145) also alternates between the two cities, with Opera House seasons from June to November and during February–March. The **Sydney Symphony Orchestra** performs variously at the Opera House, the Town Hall and St James Church, near Hyde Park.

Conservatorium of Music

Map 5, E4. Off Macquarie St, in the Botanic Gardens ℗9351 1263. Circular Quay CityRail/ferry.

Conservatorium students traditionally give free lunchtime recitals every Wednesday and Friday at 1.10pm during term time. Other concerts involving staff and students (some free, otherwise up to $25) are held at various venues around town; a programme is available from the music school.

Sydney Opera House

Map 5, E2. Bennelong Point ℗9250 7777. Circular Quay CityRail/ferry.

The Opera House is Sydney's prestige venue for opera, classical music, theatre and ballet. Forget quibbles about acoustics or ticket prices – it's worth going just to say you've been. The

Dance Companies

Aboriginal and Islander Dance Theatre ✆9252 0199. This company of young Aboriginal and Islander dancers stages about three productions per year at various venues; call for times and locations.

Bangarra Dance Theatre ✆9251 5333. Bangarra's innovative style fuses contemporary movement with traditional Aboriginal dances. Based at the Wharf Theatre, but performs at various Sydney venues.

Sydney Dance Company ✆9250 1777. Graeme Murphy, Australia's doyen of dance, has been at the helm since 1976, and continues to set the standard in ambitious sets and beautifully designed costumes. The company is based at the Wharf Theatre, with Opera House seasons April–May and Sept–Oct.

huge Concert Hall, seating 2690, is used for symphony orchestras, pop concerts and opera; the smaller Opera Theatre (1547 seats) has opera, ballet and dance. The Drama Theatre seats 544 people, the Playhouse 398.

Town Hall
Map 5, B7. Cnr Druitt and George streets ✆9265 9007. Town Hall CityRail.
Centrally located concert hall with a splendid high Victorian interior – hosts everything from chamber orchestras to bush dances.

THEATRE

MAJOR VENUES

Capitol Theatre
Map 5, B9. 13 Campbell St, Haymarket ✆9266 4800. Central CityRail.

Built in the 1920s, the Capitol was saved from demolition and then beautifully restored in the mid-1990s. The 2000-seater now hosts big-budget musicals and ballet, and is notable for its ceiling, painted midnight-blue and spangled with the stars of the Southern Cross. Tickets $48–62.

Footbridge Theatre

Map 6, D5. University of Sydney, Parramatta Rd ℗9692 9955. Bus #436–440.

Rich and varied repertoire, from *Cabaret* to Shakespeare; $16 for pantomime, other tickets $27–60.

Her Majesty's Theatre

Map 4, E6. 107 Quay St, Haymarket ℗9266 4820. Central CityRail.

The place to see big musical extravaganzas imported from the West End and Broadway.

Star City

Map 4, D3. 20–80 Pyrmont St, Pyrmont ℗9266 4800. Casino Light Rail.

Sydney's Vegas-style casino has two theatres catering to popular tastes. The technically advanced Lyric Theatre, seating 2000, stages hit musicals like *Showboat*, while the smaller theatre hosts an ongoing production of *The New Rocky Horror Show*.

Theatre Royal

Map 5, C6. MLC Centre, King St ℗9320 9191. Martin Place CityRail.

Imported musicals and blockbuster plays.

DRAMA & PERFORMANCE

Belvoir St Theatre

Map 7, B11. 25 Belvoir St, Surry Hills ℗9699 3444. Central CityRail.

Highly regarded venue for a wide range of contemporary Australian and international theatre. Tickets $22–34.

Ensemble Theatre

Map 10, C5. 78 McDougall St, Milsons Point ✆9929 0644. Milsons Point CityRail.

Australian contemporary and classical theatre. Tickets $29–39.

Marian Street Theatre

Map 2, E6. 2 Marian St, Killara ✆9498 3166. Killara CityRail.

Six to seven productions per year, often comedies – Australian dominated but also Broadway and West End. Tickets $32.

The Playhouse and Drama Theatre

Map 5, E2. Sydney Opera House, Bennelong Point ✆9250 7777. Circular Quay CityRail/ferry.

Modern plays and classics, many presented by the Sydney Theatre Company, and contemporary dance from the Sydney Dance Company.

Wharf Theatre

Map 5, B1. Pier 4, Hickson Rd, Millers Point, The Rocks ✆9250 1777. Circular Quay CityRail/ferry.

Home to the highly regarded Sydney Theatre Company, which produces works by Shakespeare as well as international and Australian playwrights. Superb waterfront location, with a restaurant, bar and café from which to check out the views. Also stages productions at the Opera House. Tickets around $48.

FRINGE & REPERTORY

New Theatre

Map 6, C9. 542 King St, Newtown ✆9250 1777. Newtown CityRail.

Amateurs and professionals work side-by-side (without pay) to present contemporary pieces with socially relevant themes.

NIDA Theatre

Map 3, G5. 215 Anzac Parade, Kensington ✆9697 7613. Bus #393–399.

THEATRE: FRINGE & REPERTORY

Australia's premier dramatic training ground – the National Institute of Dramatic Art – where the likes of Mel Gibson and Judy Davis started out. The three seasons of student productions (March–April, July–Aug & Sept–Oct) are open to the public. Tickets around $18.

The Performance Space
Map 7, A11. 199 Cleveland St, Redfern ℗9319 5091. Central CityRail.
Stages experimental performances. Tickets around $20.

Stables Theatre
Map 7, E6. 10 Nimrod St, Darlinghurst ℗9361 3817. Kings Cross CityRail.
Their mission is to develop and foster new Australian playwrights. Tickets around $18.

COMEDY

The inaugural **Sydney Comedy Festival** (*www.comedy. com.au*), held in October 1998, represents Sydney's first challenge to Melbourne's more famous March comedy extravaganza. It's set to become an annual event, based primarily at the Comedy Cellar (see below).

Bridge Hotel
Map 3, E3. 135 Victoria Rd, Rozelle ℗9810 1260. Bus #500–510.
Occasional comedy nights and pub theatre (see also p.210); major host for the Comedy Festival.

Comedy Cellar
Map 6, G4. *Off Broadway Hotel*, cnr Broadway and Bay St ℗9552 2999. Central CityRail.
Comedy nightly from 8.30pm in this cavernous modern venue (seats 350), offspring of the recently closed *Harold Park Hotel*. Not quite the intimate atmosphere of old, but the try-outs

each Monday remain and there's a varied programme of international, interstate and local comedians. Affordable pub restaurant upstairs where you can eat beforehand and DJs Mon–Sat after the shows. Tickets $15–20.

Comedy Store

Map 3, E3. 450 Parramatta Rd (cnr Crystal St), Petersham ℗9564 3900. Petersham CityRail.

International and Australian stand-up comics Wed–Sat nights in this comedy-devoted pub; bar open 5pm–midnight, show usually 8.30pm. You can have a meal inside the theatre with the show or out in the bar before. Fri & Sat nights there are two shows: dinner in the theatre for the early show, or in the pub for the later. Bookings recommended. Tickets from $10.

Theatresports

Map 7, B11. Belvoir Street Theatre, 25 Belvoir St, Surry Hills ℗9699 3444. Central CityRail.

Theatresports is the intellectual's answer to footy – pure performance improvisation on-the-run. The teams square off most Sunday evenings at Belvoir Street, and occasionally at other venues around town. Tickets $16.

CINEMAS

In 1998, Keanu Reeves could be seen roaming Sydney's streets during filming of *The Matrix*, and even appeared at the premiere screening in March 1999. Hollywood had come to town, in the shape of the new **Fox Studios** site (see box p.228) and US producers were already enthusing about the superb facilities and filming locations on offer in the heart of Sydney.

At the time of writing, a sixteen-screen cinema complex was under construction at Fox Studios; however, the commercial centre for Sydney filmgoers is still two blocks

Film Festivals

The **Sydney Film Festival**, held annually for two weeks in **early June**, is an exciting programme of features, shorts, documentaries and retrospective screenings from Australia and around the world: there are some seventy features and over a hundred shorts and documentaries in all. Founded in 1954 by a group of film enthusiasts at Sydney University, the festival struggled with prudish censors and parochial attitudes until freedom from censorship for festival films was introduced in 1971. From the early, relaxed atmosphere of picnics on the lawns, and hardy film-lovers crouching under blankets in freezing prefabricated sheds, over the years it gradually moved off-campus, to find a home from 1974 in the magnificent State Theatre (see p.209); other major screenings are at the Dendy Cinema in Martin Place and the Academy Twin on Oxford Street, Darlinghurst. Festival tickets are mainly sold by advance purchase, one- or two-week subscription, although there are some individual tickets available for special events, such as the day-long Dendy Award for Short Films ($20); a Flexipass covering three day-time films costs $21. As a subscriber, you have to choose whether you want to attend the festival for one week or two, for day or night sessions, and whether you want stalls or dress circle, and reserved or unreserved seating. It's more expensive to attend the night-time sessions, with a two week Gold Pass from $180 (stalls, unreserved) to $250 (dress circle, reserved); weekend daytime sessions are also included. You can watch films during the day for the entire festival on a Green Subscription ($145–$170) or come for just one week (night sessions plus weekend daytime) on a Red or a Blue Subscripton ($110–$145). For information and to subscribe, contact the Festival office at 405 Glebe Point Rd, Glebe (Mon–Fri 9am–5pm; ✆9660 3844 or 9660 9821, fax

9692 8793; postal address PO Box 950, Glebe NSW 2037; *www.sydfilm-fest.com.au*), or drop into the State Theatre box office.

There are now also two Short Film festivals in Sydney, both of which echo the young and irreverent attitude that once fuelled the Sydney Film Festival. Stars above and the sound of waves accompany the week-long **Flickerfest International Short Film Festival** (☏9211 7133; *flicker fest@bigpond.com*), held early January in the amphitheatre of the Bondi Pavilion; foreign and Australian productions are screened, including documentaries. **Tropfest**, held in late February, showcases short films which must be specifically made for the festival; (films are also required to include a particular motif, which in 1999 was "chopsticks"). Launched in 1993 at the *Tropicana Café*, the festival began almost by chance, when young actor John Poulsen persuaded his local coffee spot to show the short film he had made. He pushed other filmakers to follow suit, and the following year a total of 15,000 punters attended café screenings of around twenty films (notables such as Nicole Kidman have also turned up to watch the proceedings). Tropfest is now so popular that it occupies most of the trendy Victoria St café strip in Darlinghurst, and the outdoor screenings in the Domain attract around 20,000 people. (For details, contact Tropfest, Suite 24, 2A Bayswater Rd, Kings Cross, NSW 2011 ☏9368 0434, fax 9356 4531, *www.tropfest.au*).

Other, less high-profile festivals include the **Women on Women Film Festival** (☏9332 2408; single ticket $11.50, day ticket $29, weekend pass $49), held over three days in late September at the Chauvel Cinema (see p.227). The festival showcases short films and videos by women directors, highlighting female characters and themes. The **Gay & Lesbian Film Festival** is part of the Mardi Gras festivities in late February (see "Gay Sydney" chapter.

south of Town Hall on George Street. There you'll find **Hoyt's** (✆9267 9877), **Village** (✆9264 6701), and **Greater Union** (✆9267 8666) complexes. Others nearby are **Pitt Centre**, at 232 Pitt St (✆9264 1694); a new **Hoyt's** multiplex at the Broadway Shopping Centre, on Broadway near Glebe (✆9211 1911); and **Reading Cinemas**, in Market City Shopping Centre, Haymarket (✆9280 1202). There is a giant **Imax** theatre at Darling Harbour, and an outdoor cinema in Centennial Park.

....

Tuesday is cheap movies day ($7–8) at mainstream cinemas; Monday and/or Tuesday at art-house cinemas.

....

MAINSTREAM

Epson Moonlight Cinema
Map 7, I12. Centennial Park Amphitheatre, Oxford St (Woollahra entrance) ✆1900/933 899; 40¢ per minute. Bus #378, #380, #382. From Nov to mid-Feb, an open-air cinema glows in the hot dark, showing classic, art-house and cult films. Films run at 8.45pm, Tues–Sun; tickets on sale from 7.30pm (advance bookings through Ticketmaster ✆13 6100).

Hayden Orpheum Picture Palace
Map 10, E3. 380 Military Rd, Cremorne ✆9908 4344. Bus #228–230. Charming Heritage-listed cinema with Art Deco interior. The main cinema has Wurlitzer organ recitals preceding the Saturday and Sunday night films (also sometimes Tues & Fri nights). Mainstream and new releases.

Walker Cinema
Map 10 C4, 121 Walker St, North Sydney ☎9959 4222; North Sydney train station.

Although a small screen, this oasis amongst the 'burbs is a North Sydney institution showing both mainstream and art-house.

Panasonic Imax Theatre

Map 5, A7. Southern Promenade, Darling Harbour ℭ9281 3300. Town Hall CityRail.

Giant surround-screen, and films designed to thrill your senses. Tickets $13.95.

ART HOUSE

Academy

Map 7, D8. 3a Oxford St, Paddington ℭ9361 4453. Bus #378, #380, #382.

Twin cinema, running mostly independent, art-house and foreign-language films. Located in the heart of gay Sydney, it's home to the Mardi Gras' Gay & Lesbian Film Festival (see box pp.224–225).

Chauvel Twin Cinema

Map 7 E9 Paddington Town Hall, corner of Oatley Rd and Oxford St, Paddington ☎9361 5398. Bus #378, #380, #382.

This recently renovated Town Hall is a beautiful setting to taste the varied programme of Australian and foreign films plus classics. A notorious cineaste haunt. Discounts on Monday and Tuesday.

The Dendy

Map 5, C5. MLC Centre, Martin Place ℭ9233 8166. Martin Place CityRail.

Cinema, café, bar and pool-room complex (daily noon–midnight), showing prestige new-release films.

CINEMA: ART HOUSE

227

Map 6, D7. **Dendy Newtown**, 261 King St, Newtown ©9550 5699.
Newtown CityRail.

With attached café, bar and bookshop.

Govinda's Movie Room

Map 7, E7. 112 Darlinghurst Rd, Darlinghurst ©9380 5162. Kings
Cross CityRail.

Attached to a funky, Hare Krishna-run vegetarian restaurant.
There's an assortment of lounge-chairs and scatter-cushions on
which to recline and watch classic, art-house, and quality independent films. The $13.90 movie-and-dinner deal is very pop-
ular and you may need to book.

Verona

Map 7, D8. 17 Oxford St, Paddington ©9360 6099. Bus #378, #380,
#382.

Has a groovy first-floor bar/café, and shows mainly art-house
and foreign-language films.

Fox Studios

Since Fox Studios opened at Moore Park (see p.91) in May,
1998, Universal Pictures and Warner Bros have made use of
their superb production facilities to make, respectively, *Babe:
Pig in the City*, and *The Matrix*. Parts of the *Star Wars* saga are
scheduled to be filmed there in 2000, by which time visitors
may be able to take a peek at the film set from an elevated
walkway. (For latest information call Fox Studios ©9383 4000).
An Entertainment and Retail Precinct is to include a sixteen-
screen cinema complex, inside an Art Deco building designed
to emulate the classic 1930s Hollywood picture palaces.

Gay Sydney

I t's not hard to work out why Sydney is one of the most popular destinations in the world for gay and lesbian tourists: the people are gay-friendly and so is the weather, which gets steamiest in February – just in time for the **Gay & Lesbian Mardi Gras**.

Oxford Street is Sydney's official "pink strip", and here you'll find countless pairs of tight-T-shirted guys strolling hand-in-hand, or checking out the passing talent from a hip, streetside café. **King Street**, Newtown, is another burgeoning centre of gay culture, while lesbian communities have carved out territory of their own in **Erskineville** and **Leichhardt** (known affectionately as "Dykehart"). The free weeklies *Sydney Star Observer* and *Capital Q* (available from shops and newsagents), are handy for **listings** including details of dance parties, as is *Lesbians on The Loose*. Two monthly gay and lesbian magazines – *Outrage* and *Campaign* – are available at newsagents. For general browsing, **The Bookshop** stocks various gay and lesbian titles as well as magazines and flyers with information on upcoming events.

MARDI GRAS

The first Sydney Gay & Lesbian Mardis Gras was held in 1978 as a **gay-rights** protest. Today, it's the biggest celebration of gay and lesbian culture in the world. The festival goes for three weeks, starting the first week of **February**, and culminating in the parade and party on the last weekend of the month.

The parade begins at 7.30pm (finishing around 10.30pm), but people line the barricades along Oxford Street from mid-morning. Around a million people will have taken up vantage points along the route before the Dykes on Bikes, traditional leaders of the parade, roar into view. There are new floats every year, and recent entries have included a group of Monica Lewinsky lookalikes, and fifty marching Shirley Basseys. If you can't get to Oxford Street until late afternoon, your best chance of finding a spot is along Flinders Street near Moore Park Road, where the parade ends. Otherwise, AIDS charity The Bobby Goldsmith Foundation (©9283 8666) has 7000 **grandstand seats** on Moore Park Road, at $75 each.

THE MARDI GRAS PARTY

This is the post-parade, wild-and-sexy dance party, and it's one of the hottest tickets in Sydney. Twenty-thousand people sashay and strut through five dance spaces at Fox Studios, Moore Park. The two biggest are the Hordern Pavilion and the Royal Hall of Industries, where past performers have included Kylie Minogue, Boy George and Grace Jones.

Don't plan to buy a ticket upon arrival – they sell out in January, and you need to be a member of the Sydney Gay & Lesbian Mardi Gras to get them. Visitors from overseas can apply for international membership, which costs $40, and allows you to buy one ticket ($95). Application forms for membership are available from the Gay & Lesbian Mardi Gras via Web site (*www.mardigras.com.au*); post (P.O. Box 557, Newtown, NSW 2042); ©61-2-9557 4332, or fax 61-2-9516 4446. They can also send you a copy of the

The Sleaze Ball

This was set up as a fundraiser for the first Mardi Gras Party twenty years ago, and has since become an annual fixture. There's not quite the same frenzied build-up as Mardi Gras, but it's just as wild and can be every bit as much fun. It's held the first Saturday night in October, and is attended by up to 15,000 people. Tickets cost $75 and again, you have to be a member of Mardi Gras to get one.

official *Festival Guide* (published in December), for an additional $20.

CAFÉS AND RESTAURANTS

Café 191
Map 7, D8. 191 Oxford St. Bus #373, #378, #380.
Daily 8am–midnight (Fri, Sat & Sun until 2am). Licensed.
Perfectly positioned for watching the Oxford Street crowd, *191* is a popular meeting place for gays and lesbians heading out for the evening. Pasta or a burger costs around $11.

The Californian
Map 7, C7. 177 Oxford St ℘9331 5587. Bus #380.
Wed–Thur 8am–1am, Fri–Sun 24-hour, closed Mon–Tues.
Marilyn gazes down at you from the front counter in provocative pose, while Fifties rock jitterbugs from the jukebox. The all-day Californian breakfast ($7.90) is fuel for the boys streaming in from the clubs at 5am.

Nova Restaurant and Bar
Map 7, D8. Level 1, 191–195 Oxford St ℘9380 4400. Bus #373, #378, #380.

Lunch Wed–Fri noon–3pm, dinner Wed–Mon 6–10pm.
Licensed.
Fine dining, in a bright, Art Deco space. The huge windows
look down over Taylor Square, and there's a quiet, loungey
cocktail bar, open Tues–Sun 6pm–3am. Tasty entrees such as
sautéed red-claw yabbie spaghettini or wild mushroom risotto
for around $12.

Thai Panic

Map 7, C7. 80 Oxford St ✆9361 5577. Bus #380.
Daily noon–11pm.
This corner eatery is very popular day and night, with young
gays and lesbians. It's noisy, and the big wall-mirrors give the
illusion of space which really isn't there. Main dishes $9.50;
lunch special $6.50 (noon–4pm).

PUBS AND BARS

Apart from a few pubs in the inner west, these are all concentrated around Oxford Street. Start at the *Albury* and
keep on going, for days if you like!

Albury Hotel

Map 7, D8. 6 Oxford St, Paddington. Bus #380.
Mon-Fri 2pm–2am, Sat 2pm–1am, Sun 2pm–midnight. Free entry.
Energetic performances on the huge, horseshoe bar of this stylish, Art Deco hotel. Regulars get here in time for the show,
then move on to the other pubs and clubs. The *Albury* attracts
a lively and very mixed crowd – gay or straight, you'll feel pretty welcome. Shows nightly from 10.30pm (Sunday 6.30pm).

Bank Hotel

Map 6, C8. 324 King St, Newtown. Newtown CityRail; bus #422.
Daily 11am–1.30am.
This stylish bar has become a dyke favourite, although it has a

mixed inner-city crowd. Wednesday night women's pool competition draws large crowds.

The Barracks

Map 7, D8. Patterson Lane (off Bourke St), Surry Hills. Bus #380.
Daily 8pm–3am. Usually free.
This is a very popular, four-level gay venue. Drinking by dimly-lit pool tables on the two lower levels, DJs and dancing on the third, and a relaxed bar on the fourth. It draws big crowds on Friday, Saturday and Sunday nights after 11pm. Traditionally a haunt for leather men, its appeal has broadened recently.

Beauchamp Hotel

Map 7, D8. 267 Oxford St, Darlinghurst. Bus #378, #380.
Daily noon–midnight.
Traditional Aussie pub decor with a male, rough-trade crowd. This is essentially a drinking and meeting venue, especially popular on Sunday afternoons, when it gets very crowded. In summer, the guys come here straight from the beach.

Imperial Hotel

Map 6, D8. 35 Erskineville Rd, Erskineville. Newtown CityRail; bus #422.
Thurs–Sun noon–8am, Tues–Wed, noon–2am, closed Mon.
This is where the film *Priscilla, Queen of the Desert* both started and ended. It was the *Imperial*'s finest hour, and the theme is revived with *Priscilla* drag shows on Thursday (after midnight & 1.30am), Friday and Saturday nights (10.30pm & 11.30pm, 1.15am & 2.15am, all shows free). It's a notorious late-night venue, and the dance floor is popular, hot and sweaty with gay men.

Leichhardt Hotel

Map 3, E3. Cnr Short and Balmain roads, Leichhardt. Bus #436–438, #440.
Sun–Tues noon–10pm, Wed–Sat 10am–midnight.

PUBS AND BARS

The focus of the large Leichhardt lesbian social scene. The pool tables are very popular and there are decent pub meals.

Midnight Shift Hotel

Map 7, C7. 85 Oxford St, Darlinghurst. Bus #378, #380.
Mon–Fri noon–6am, Sat 2pm–midday, Sun 2pm–10am.
A large drinking and cruising space for men of varied ages. The front bar is busy on Friday and Saturday nights, and revellers cram onto the tiny dance floor in the early hours of Sunday morning.

Newtown Hotel

Map 6, D7. 174 King St, Newtown. Newtown CityRail; bus #422.
Mon–Sat 11am-midnight, Sun 11am–10pm.
The *Newtown* is decked out in kitsch decor, and attracts mostly suburban, down-to-earth gays and lesbians. Tuesday to Sunday you can enjoy a good, cheap, modern Australian meal in the restaurant (6-9pm), then stick around for the 9.30pm drag show. Friday and Saturday nights the crowd comes to dance.

Oxford Hotel

Map 7, D7. 134 Oxford St, Darlinghurst. Bus #378, #380.
Sun & Mon 3pm–1am, Tues–Thurs 3pm–2am, Fri & Sat 3pm–3am.
One of Sydney's oldest established gay men's bars, which attracts businesspeople during the afternoon and a mixed leather/denim crowd in the evening. It's dark and dingy, with a pool table and a friendly atmosphere. More of a dyke crowd on a Sunday night, lured in by popular lesbian DJs.

Stonewall Hotel

Map 7, C7. 175 Oxford St, Darlinghurst. Bus #378, #380.
Daily noon–8am. Free entry.
The newest pub on the strip, the *Stonewall* is a big hit with young gay men and their female straight or lesbian friends. There's TV screens flashing video clips, and theme nights with gay bingo, "Mr

Gay Sydney" heats or go-go dancing. The cocktail bar upstairs is particularly popular with dykes on Thursday nights (Riot Girls, Thursdays, 8pm–5am; a funky, soul, talent-quest night).

Like anywhere else in the world, it is important to take precautions against HIV. The Australian Government responded early to AIDS, and the Sydney community has embraced the safe-sex message. Support networks are well established: for information, contact the AIDS Council of NSW (ACON), 9 Commonwealth St, Surry Hills ✆9206 2000. There is a handy medical centre at Holdsworth House, 320A Oxford St, Darlinghurst ✆9331 7228. (Mon–Fri 8am–7pm, Sat 9am–2pm). They'll help whether you have the flu, an HIV-related inquiry, or if you just need a repeat on your Viagra or Propecia.

CLUBS

DCM
Map 7, C7. 31–33 Oxford St, Darlinghurst ✆9267 7380. Bus #378, #380, #382.
Thurs–Sun 11pm–6/8am. $15.
Popular with the gay crowd, *DCM* draws lots of straights too, with its "if you've got it, flaunt it" ethos. Energetic techno, lots of lycra-covered hardbodies (both boys and girls); nobody comes overdressed.

Home
Map 5, A7. Cockle Bay Wharf, Darling Harbour ✆9266 0600. Town Hall CityRail.
Sun, 6pm–8am. $10–20.
This is the biggest, newest, trendiest nightclub in Sydney, and it

gets taken over by a gay/lesbian crowd on Sunday night.
Cocktails at 6pm on the terrace (with local drag identities),
then the club doors open at 10pm for some of Sydney's hottest
DJs playing garage and disco. (Gay and lesbian night also on
one Friday each month – check gay press for details).

Midnight Shift

Map 7, C7. 85 Oxford St, Darlinghurst ©9360 4319. Bus #380.
Thurs–Sun 11pm–7am. $10 (Sat only).

Commonly known as "The Shift", this is the "mainstream"club
for gay men. In the early hours of Sunday morning you can
hardly move on a dance floor full of gym-pumped men, sweat-
ing it out with their shirts off; drag show Thursday nights.

Spicy Friday

Map 6, G5. *Lansdowne Hotel*, cnr City Rd and Broadway ©9211
2325. Central CityRail; bus #422, #423, #426, #428.
Fri 5pm–3am. $5.

The crowd is about 80 per cent lesbian for this funky soul and
cabaret theme night, which doesn't really liven up until after
10pm. There are pool tables and an upstairs chill-out lounge.

Stonewall Hotel

Map 7, C7. 175 Oxford St, Darlinghurst ©9360 1963. Bus #380.
Fri–Sat, 11pm–5am. Free.

The third floor of this popular pub becomes a nightclub on
Friday and Saturday nights, with high energy dance music. The
crowd is young and groovy – 70 percent gay boys, 20 percent
lesbian, 10 percent straight.

Taxi Club

Map 7, D8. 40 Flinders St, Surry Hills ©9331 4256. Bus #373, #377,
#392–394.
24-hour. $10 (disco only).

It's a Sydney legend, but don't bother before 2 or 3am – and

Travel Agents

The following Darlinghurst travel agents specialize in travel and accommodation arrangements for gay travellers:

FOD Travel Level 2, 77 Oxford St ℰ9360 3616, fax 9332 3326. (Mon–Fri 9am–5pm, Sat 9am–noon).

Jornada Level 1, 263 Liverpool St ℰ9360 9611, fax 9326 0199; *www.jornada.com.au* (Mon–Fri 8.30am–5.30pm).

Silke's Travel 263 Oxford St ℰ9380 6244, fax 9361 3729; *www.silkes.com.au* (Mon–Sat 9am–5pm).

you need to be suitably intoxicated to appreciate it fully. There's a weird mix of drag queens, taxi drivers, lesbians, boys (straight and gay), and the cheapest drinks in gay Sydney. The first-floor restaurant has meals under $10, as well as poker machines and a bar; the second level is a disco/bar.

GYMS

Bayswater Fitness
Map 7, E5. 33 Bayswater Rd, Kings Cross ℰ9356 2555.
Mon–Thurs 6am–midnight, Fri 6am–11pm, Sat 7am–10pm, Sun 7am–9pm. $15.
Clientele of mostly gay men, although lesbians are also welcome. Weights, circuit-fitness, aerobics classes and a sauna.

City Gym
Map 7, C6. 107–113 Crown St, East Sydney ℰ9360 6247.
24-hour. $10.
Unbelievably popular (at all hours) among gay men, lesbians

and straights. There's plenty of free weights, aerobics classes and a sauna – which can be cruisey.

Fitness Network

Map 7, C8. 256 Riley St, Surry Hills ℂ9211 2799.
Mon–Fri 7am–9pm, Sat & Sun 8am–8pm. $10.

A predominantly gay male clientele plus gay-friendly staff. The sauna is accessed from both the men's and women's locker rooms. Relatively cruisey.

Newtown Gym

Map 6, C8. Level 1, 294 King St, Newtown ℂ9519 6969.
Mon–Fri 6am–l0pm, Sat & Sun 8am–8pm. $8.

Large lesbian membership. Step, stretch, and yoga classes, weight training, solarium and sauna. Childcare facilities available.

Beaches

During Sydney's hot summer, a popular choice among the gay set is **Tamarama**, (known locally as Glama-rama), a 15-minute walk from the southern end of Bondi Beach. But if showing off is not your thing, Bondi or nearby Bronte may suit you better. The calm, harbour waters of Red Leaf at Double Bay (see map 10, E7) also lure a big gay crowd, and if you want to get your gear off, try Lady Jane Beach at Watsons Bay (map 10, G–H5). Coogee Women's Baths (map 8, B9) is Sydney's women-only pool.

Kids' Sydney

With its sunny climate, fabulous beaches and wide-open spaces, Sydney is a great place to holiday with kids. There are lots of parks, playgrounds, sheltered bays and public pools for safe swimming, and a range of indoor options for rainy days. Museums (which can often be dire places for kids) are mostly child-friendly, in particular the **Powerhouse Museum** and the **Australian Museum**, both of which have exhibits and activities designed to entertain as well as educate. The **Historic Houses Trust**, consisting of Elizabeth Bay House, Vaucluse House, Government House, Susannah Place, the Justice and Police Museum, Hyde Park Barracks, the Sydney Museum and Elizabeth Farm, offer a huge range of school holiday programmes for ages 6–12; $6 per child (details ©9518 6866).

Darling Harbour is never short of kids' amusements, with rides and games, free basketball and outdoor entertainment, and **Sega World**, an indoor theme park with a huge range of the latest video games (see p.247). **Manly Wharf**, too, offers a variety of distractions including a ferris wheel, dodgem cars and an amusement arcade (see p.123). *Sydney's Child* is an excellent free monthly magazine providing a detailed **listing** of what's on, and advertises a range of services including babysitting. You can pick up a copy at libraries and major museums, or check *www.family.com/Local/sydc*

School holidays

Summer, six weeks, beginning roughly ten days before Christmas, to last week in Jan; **Autumn**, two weeks coinciding with Easter (normally early to mid-April); **Winter**, two weeks, beginning the second week of July; **Spring**, two weeks, beginning the last week of Sept.

MUSEUMS AND GALLERIES

The Art Gallery of NSW

Map 5, F6. The Domain ©9225 1740. Martin Place or St James CityRail.

Daily 10am–5pm. Free, except for special exhibitions.

Holds free Sunday performances (2.30pm) for families, exploring art appreciation through drama, storytelling, dance and mime. During school holidays, practical art workshops ($10) are held for children 6–12 years, and there are free storytelling or performance sessions – often mime or Aboriginal dance.

The Australian Museum

Map 5, D8. College St (cnr William St). Museum or Town Hall CityRail.

Daily 9.30am–5pm. $5, child $2, student $3, family $12.

The people here clearly know a thing or two about the special relationship kids have with dinosaurs – their dino exhibition is aimed squarely at the 5–12-year-olds. The museum's biodiversity section has a Search and Discover room, complete with microscopes, specimens (and books to help with identifying them), and a child-size kitchen where kids can learn about being environmentally friendly. Kids Island, overlooked by a colourful model of a hot-air balloon with its own slippery slide, is for under-fives; the island has a shipwreck boat and all sorts of crawling pits and cubby houses to explore, plus a baby change area. The museum's shop is full of model dinosaurs and other creatures.

The Powerhouse Museum

Harris St, Ultimo. Haymarket Monorail.
Daily 9.30am–5pm. $8, child $2; free first Sat of the month.

Has a huge range of hands-on interactive exhibits, many aimed at small children. Most weekends, coinciding with events such as Design Week, there are supervised activities (free with entry), from crafts to storytelling sessions, plus a similar but expanded programme during school holidays.

PARKS AND WILDLIFE

Sydney and the surrounding area provides plenty of opportunities to see – and in some cases touch – native wildlife. **Taronga Zoo** (p.111) occupies an enviable position right over the harbour; children's concerts are featured during school holidays. You can visit the original filming locations for the famous television series *Skippy* at **Waratah Park** (p.294), cuddle koalas at the **Featherdale Wildlife Park** (p.136), meet a giant crocodile and watch snakes and spiders being milked at the **Australian Reptile Park** near Gosford (p.304).

Centennial Park

Map 7, I12.

Offers typical park pleasures like feeding ducks and climbing trees, but also has bike paths (and a learners' cycleway) and bridleways. You can rent kids' bikes and rollerblades nearby (see p.91) and an Equestrian Centre offers horse and pony rides (p.283). There are guided walks in the school holidays ($5; information ✆9339 6699), and the restaurant even

PARKS AND WILDLIFE

serves up "babyccinos" (hot frothy milk – cappuccino for kids).

Cumberland State Forest

Map 2, E6. 95 Castle Hill Rd, West Pennant Hills ℃9871 3377. Pennant Hills CityRail, then bus #631–635.

Free ranger-guided tours on weekends at 11am & 2pm. There's an activities programme during school holidays which includes introductions to bushtucker, camel and pony rides, and wildlife surveys. Walks are free; crafts and other activities around $5.

National Parks and Wildlife Service

Map 5, C3. Sydney Harbour National Park ℃9247 5033.

Offers ranger-led walks in the school holidays; they also lead ghost tours of the Quarantine Station near Manly ($10; 2hr; see p.125) and trips to Sydney Harbour's Goat Island (last Fri each month 6pm; adult $16, child $13, family $45; see box p.104).

Royal Botanic Gardens

Map 5, F5.

Runs Kids' Branch on the last Saturday of each month (℃9231 8134; noon–1.30pm & 2.30–4pm; 5–10 years, $10). There's always an imaginative botanical theme, which might involve picking herbs and making a magical potion (such as a foot rub for tired parents feet!). During Easter and the September school holidays there's participatory musical theatre ($10 child or adult); winter and summer holiday programmes feature Aboriginal storytelling sessions and twilight walks for possum- and bat-spotting.

....

Three other great kids' attractions are the Sydney Aquarium (see p.80), Oceanworld (see p.124) and the Maritime Museum (see p.81).

....

PARKS AND WILDLIFE

SHOPS

ABC Shop
Map 5, B7. Level 1, Albert Walk, QVB ℗9333 1635. Town Hall CityRail.
Mon–Fri 9am–5.30pm (Thurs to 8pm), Sat 10am–4.30pm.
ABC television's merchandizing outlet – books, audio, video,
toys, clothing and accessories – sells all the Australian
favourites, from Bananas in Pajamas to The Wiggles.

Gleebooks Children's Books
Map 6, E3. 191 Glebe Point Rd, Glebe ℗9552 2526. Bus #431,
#433, #434.
Daily 10am–9pm.
Children's bookshop, attached to the well-respected Gleebooks
secondhand store (see p.250).

Hobbyco
Map 5, C6. Gallery Level, Mid-City Centre, Pitt St Mall ℗9221 0666.
Town Hall CityRail.
Mon–Sat 9am–6pm (Thurs to 9pm), Sun 11am–5pm.
Hobby shop with everything from dolls houses to kites,
Meccano sets, trains and slot cars. The working model railway
is a major attraction.

The Kids' Room
Map 7, E8. 83 Paddington St, Paddington ℗9328 6864. Bus #378,
#380, #382.
Mon–Fri 10.30am–5.30pm, Sat 10am–4.30pm.
Quality clothes and shoes, for babies through to early teens. All
Australian brands like Fred Bare, Scooter, Gumboots.

Play House Toyshop
Map 5, B6. 152 Clarence St ℗9299 5498. Town Hall CityRail.
Mon–Fri 9am–5.30pm (Thurs to 7pm), Sat 9am–4pm.

Catering for younger children, from babies up to about nine years. Playhouses, lots of handmade wooden toys, and attentive service and advice.

SWIMMING AND WATER SPORTS

Beware Sydney's **strong surf** – young children are safer swimming at sheltered harbour beaches or ocean pools. Public swimming pools (typically outdoor and unheated), generally have a toddlers' **paddling pool**. For year-round swimming there's a heated pool at North Sydney (p.282), right beside Luna Park, or at the indoor Sydney International Aquatic Centre (p.283) which has a rapid water ride and slides. NSW Sport & Recreation conduct inexpensive **Swimsafe courses** for kids from 18 months (information and bookings ℅13 1302). Manly Surf School (℅9970 6300) offers group lessons in **board-riding** and **surf safety** for kids from age seven (2hr; $30), as well as family lessons. Balmoral Windsurf, Sail and Kayak School at Balmoral Beach (℅9960 5344), has a **learn to sail** camp (ages 5–16) during summer and Easter holidays (one, three or five days, $90/200/275).

Sun protection

A broad-spectrum, water-resistant sunscreen (with a minimum SPF of 20) is a must, and colourful zinc cream on nose and cheeks is a good extra protectant when swimming. Most local kids wear UV-resistant lycra swim tops or wetsuit-style all-in-ones ($20–35) to the beach, and schoolchildren wear hats in the playground – the legionnaire-style ones ($5) are especially popular, as they shade the face and the back of the neck. All these items can be purchased at surfwear shops, department stores, or at the NSW Cancer Council Shop in Glasshouse shopping centre, Pitt St Mall.

BEACHES

Balmoral
Map 10, F3.
On the north side of the harbour, around the corner from Taronga Zoo, this is the pick of the family beaches for its wide sandy bays, sheltered from the wind and waves. See p.113.

Bronte
Map 8, D4.
The most popular of the eastern beaches for families, fronted by an extensive and shady park with picnic shelters and BBQs, a mini-train ride ($1.50; 4 rides for $5) and an imaginative children's playground – a sandpit wrapped in the arms of a mosaic octopus, colourful cubby houses, a roundabout using pedal-power. A natural rock enclosure provides a calm area for swimming. See p.119.

Coogee Bay
Map 8, B9.
Coogee's beach is fronted by a big grassy park, complete with picnic shelters, barbecues and an adventure playground. Just past the southern end of the beach is Coogee Women's Pool, for women and children only (boys up to age 12); the pool is run by kindly volunteers, who'll look after your baby while you swim. See p.121.

Manly
Map 9.
On the north side of the harbour, tucked in beside Manly Wharf, Manly Cove has a small harbour beach with a netted-off swimming area. The ferry ride over is lots of fun, and there are plenty of attractions for kids in the area, including an aquarium and a funfair. Another attractive option here is to fol-

BEACHES

low the footpath from the southern end of Manly's surf beach around the headland to sheltered and picturesque Shelley Beach. See p.122.

Healthland Fitness (p.284) have gyms in Mosman and Bondi Junction offering childcare (max 2hr; infants accepted) with the price of a $15 casual visit.

THEATRE

Marian Street Theatre
Map 2, E6. 2 Marian St, Killara ℂ9498 3166. Killara CityRail
Popular 1pm Saturday kids' matinee *Merlin's Magic Kingdom*; also school holiday weekdays at 10.30am & 1pm (suitable for 3–10-year-olds; adult $8.50, child $6.50).

Rocks Puppet Cottage
Map 5, C3. Kendall Lane (off Argyle St), The Rocks ℂ9255 1788. Circular Quay CityRail/ferry.
Free weekend and school holiday puppet shows (11am, 12.30pm & 2pm); also theatre performances (such as *Toad of Toad Hall*; 10am & 2pm; child $4, family $13).

Storytelling

Local libraries hold storytelling sessions throughout the year, which often involve crafts or films. South Sydney Libraries are particularly good, and there are sessions for pre-schoolers at their Kings Cross library (in Fitzroy Gardens, off Macleay St ℂ9358 4962), Wed at 11am (1hr). For details of other libraries, contact the State Library ℂ9273 1414.

THEATRE

THEME PARKS

Australia's Wonderland
Map 5, C3. Wallgrove Rd, Rooty Hill. Rooty Hill CityRail, then Busways service.
Daily 10am–5pm. Wildlife park only, $13, child $9; entry including all rides, $37, child $26.

Huge family entertainment complex with shows, waterslides, roller coasters, and the Australian Wildlife Park, where you can "meet the animals" – koalas, kangaroos, echidnas, wombats, emus, goannas, saltwater crocodiles, and forest birds in simulated natural habitats.

Sega World
Map 5, A8. Darling Walk, Darling Harbour. Haymarket Monorail.
Mon–Fri 11am–10pm, Sat & Sun 10am–10pm; unlimited rides $25, child $20.

Darling Harbour's high-tech, indoor theme park. Time zones – past, present and future – are the theme, with rides including a roller coaster, a haunted house where you're let loose with a ghost-hunter zapper, dodgem cars, plus two virtual reality experiences, one in a galactic battle zone, the other under the ocean on another planet. The nine huge screens of the Visionarium provide 360° views, and you have to strap yourself into your moving seat for the Magic Motion Theatre. In addition, there are over 200 video games, from old favourites to the very latest.

Sydney's biggest annual funfair is at the Royal Easter Show (see p.268).

THEME PARKS

247

Shopping

The rectangle bounded by Elizabeth, King, York and Park streets is Sydney's prime shopping area, with a number of beautifully restored **Victorian arcades** and the main **department stores**. The city also has plenty of sparkling shopping complexes where you can hunt for fashion and accessories without raising a sweat. Still in the centre, The Rocks is packed with Australiana and **souvenir shops**, where you can satisfy the urge to buy boomerangs, didgeridoos and stuffed toy koalas.

Paddington is best for stylish one-stop shopping, with its enticing array of designer shops, funky fashion, some of the city's most appealing bookshops – and the best weekend market in town. The more avant-garde **Darlinghurst** and **Surry Hills** (notably the stretch of Crown Street between Devonshire and Oxford streets) have become a focus for retro-influenced interior design and clothes shops. Still heading east, down-at-heel **Bondi Junction** is good for chainstore shopping, with branches of the main stores clustered into a hideous suburban mall-frenzy. Down at the beach, **Bondi Pavilion** has an excellent souvenir shop, and the Campbell Parade strip offers lots of beachwear and surf shops – handy for when you've forgotten your togs, or if you simply must have some Speedos with "Bondi" emblazoned on them.

Opening Hours

Most stores are open Monday to Saturday from 9am or 10am until 5.30pm or 6pm, with late-night shopping on Thursdays and Fridays until around 9pm.

Many of the larger shops and department stores are also open on Sunday from 10am or noon until 4pm or 5pm, as are most malls and shopping centres at tourist hotspots such as Darling Harbour and The Rocks.

In the inner west, **Balmain** has chic shops and gourmet delis to supplement its Saturday market, while cheerfully grungy **Newtown** is filled with secondhand and speciality shops; the King Street drag becomes more subdued on the St Peters (south) side of the train station, but is well worth a stroll to look at the more unusual shops, where you might encounter inflatable dinosaurs, train memorabilia and cowboy high-style.

The main **sales** happen immediately post-Christmas and in August, although there are also stock clearances throughout the year, often around public holidays.

BOOKS

The ubiquitous book **superstore** has arrived in Sydney, and some offer extras like Internet terminals, discounted best sellers, author appearances and book signings, even coffee outlets. For extended opening hours and knowledgeable staff, however, you'll still do better with the smaller independents. In addition to the places listed below, there is a concentration of **secondhand bookshops** on King Street in Newtown, and New South Head Road in Double Bay.

Berkelouws

Map 7, E8. 19 Oxford St, Paddington ☏9360 3200. Bus #378, #380, #382.

Daily 10am–midnight.

Catering to collectors as well as casual browsers, Berkelouws has been dealing in antiquarian books since 1812. New books are downstairs, and their upstairs coffee shop, with huge windows overlooking the busy Oxford Street strip, is a popular pre- and post-movie meeting place.

Dymocks

Map 5, B6. 428 George St ☏9235 0155. Town Hall CityRail.

Mon–Fri 9am–6pm (Thurs until 9pm), Sat 9am–5pm, Sun 10am–5pm.

Sprawled across several floors, Dymocks has a particularly impressive Australian selection, and an upstairs café where you can slurp generous smoothies. There's another branch at level 2, Harbourside, Darling Harbour (near Harbourside Monorail station), with longer hours (Mon–Sat 10am–9pm, Sun 10am–7pm) and an espresso bar (daily 10am–6pm).

Gleebooks

Map 6, F4. 49 Glebe Point Rd, Glebe ☏9660 2333. Bus #431–433.

Daily 8am–9pm.

Specializes in academic and alternative books, contemporary Australian and international literature, plus author appearances and book-signings. Just along the street is Gleebooks Secondhand and Children's Books, at 191 Glebe Point Rd ☏9552 2526.

Gould's Book Arcade

Map 6, E7. 32–38 King St, Newtown ☏9519 8947. Newtown CityRail.

Daily 7am–midnight.

Chaotic piles of books and magazines greet you in this near

legendary secondhand bookshop. The incredible range of non-fiction includes a whole host of Leftie political tomes, but it's tough to find anything specific here unless you're incredibly lucky – the best in Sydney for browsing.

The Travel Bookshop

Map 5, D9. Shop 3, 175 Liverpool St ℰ9261 8200. Museum CityRail.

Mon–Fri 9am–6pm, Sat 10am–5pm, Sun noon–5pm.

The place for maps, guides, phrasebooks and travelogues, plus a good selection of Australiana and specialist walking and cycling books, as well as travel accessories.

Also see The Bookshop (p.229), a specialist gay and lesbian bookshop in Darlinghurst.

CLOTHES AND ACCESSORIES

For interesting **fashion** to suit a range of budgets, Oxford Street in Paddington is the place, along with the glitzy Sydney Central Mall in the city (see p.58). With more time to explore, take a stroll down Crown Street, near the junction with Oxford Street, where there are great stores stuffed with Hawaiian shirts, frocks from the Fifties and cool clubbing gear. Or check out the **secondhand** stores on Newtown's King Street – though you'll probably find that prices are higher than for similar stuff in the UK or US. And if you like **designer labels**, but not the price tags, there are several factory outlets for samples and seconds on Regent Street in Redfern and, more conveniently, in the city centre at Market City (see p.259).

Country Road

Map 5, C6. 142–144 Pitt St ℰ9232 6299. Town Hall CityRail.

Mon–Fri 9am–5.30pm (Thurs until 9pm), Sat 9am–5pm, Sun 11am–5pm.

Classic but stylish (if a little preppy) Australian-designed clothes for men and women, plus a high-quality range of shoes and accessories.

Mambo

Map 7, D8. 17 Oxford St, Paddington ℘9331 8034. Bus #378, #380, #382.

Mon–Fri 9am–6pm (Thurs until 9pm), Sat 9am–5pm, Sun 11am–5pm.

Influenced by comic-strip and graffiti art, Reg Mombassa's designs are now emblazoned on T-shirts, surf gear, beach towels, watches and wallets around the world, promoting his tongue-in-cheek philosophy of "salvation through shopping".

Marcs

Map 5, C6. Pitt St Mall ℘9221 4583. Town Hall CityRail.

Mon–Fri 9.30am–6pm (Thurs until 9pm), Sat 9am–5pm, Sun noon–4pm.

The place to buy great shirts for men and women. Also stocks a selection of hip European and US lines such as Diesel.

R. M. Williams

Map 5, B6. 389 George St ℘9262 2228. Central CityRail.

Mon–Fri 9am–5.30pm (Thurs until 9pm), Sat 9am–4.30pm, Sun 11am–4pm.

This quality bush outfitters is great for moleskin pants and shirts, Drizabone coats and superb leather riding and dress boots.

Strand Hatters

Map 5, B6. Strand Arcade, 412 George St ℘9231 6884. Town Hall CityRail.

Mon–Sat 9am–5pm.

For the widest range of Akubra hats and other Australian classics, this old-fashioned store is the place.

Zomp

Map 5, C6. Mid-City Centre, Pitt St Mall ℂ9221 4027. Town Hall City Rail.

Mon–Fri 9am–5.30pm (Thurs until 9pm), Sat 9am–5pm, Sun 11.30am–4pm.

A shoe-fetishist's heaven, with styles (and prices) that run the gamut from sensible to extravagant.

SECONDHAND

The Look

Map 6, D7. 230 King St, Newtown ℂ9550 2455. Newtown CityRail.

Mon–Thurs 10am–6pm, Fri–Sat 10am–10pm.

A stylish variant on the charity shop, run by the Wesley Mission and worth a look for bargain buys. Also branches in various suburbs; call ℂ9773 5188 for nearest location.

Pretty Dog New and Recycled Clothing

Map 6, D7. 1A Brown St, Newtown ℂ9519 7839. Newtown CityRail.

Mon noon–6pm, Tues & Wed 11am–6pm, Thurs 11am–8pm, Fri 11am–5pm, Sat 10am–6pm, Sun noon–5pm.

Wild and wonderful clubbing gear, plus a good selection of retro and secondhand clothes – and fancy cosmetics "for fussy bitches".

Route 66

Map 7, C7. 255–257 Crown St, Darlinghurst ℂ9331 6686. Bus #378, #380, #382.

Mon–Fri 10.30am–6pm, Sat 10am–6pm, Sun 11.30am–4.30pm.

Taking its inspiration from America's legendary highway (Route 66) to the Wild West, this is where you'll find US vintage gear, and cowgirl-chic leather boots just made for line-dancing.

SECONDHAND

Zoo Emporium

Map 7, C8. 332 Crown St, Surry Hills ℡9380 5990. Bus #378, #380, #382.

Mon–Sat 11am–6pm (Thurs until 8pm), Sun noon–5pm.

The very best in Seventies disco gear, from a world where day-glo never died.

ACCESSORIES

In addition to the following, it's worth checking out the **markets** (see p.261), **museum shops** (especially the MCA, see p.57, the Powerhouse Museum, see p.82 and the Art Gallery of New South Wales, see p.71) for unusual treasures, trinkets and trivia, as well as the smaller, **private galleries** (see p.256) for art and crafts.

Dinosaur Designs

Map 5, B6. Strand Arcade ℡9223 2953. Town Hall CityRail.

Mon–Fri 9.30am–5.30pm (Thurs until 8.30pm), Sat 10am–4pm.

Dinosaur's trademark chunky resin and silver jewellery, and beautifully tactile tableware in muted shades of amber and earth, are terribly hard to resist.

Done Art and Design

Map 5, C3. 123 George St, The Rocks. ℡9251 6099. Circular Quay CityRail/ferry.

Mon–Fri 9.30am–9pm, Sat 9.30am–6.30pm, Sun 10am–6pm.

Love the stuff or loathe it, there's no doubt that Ken Done's loud and colourful knitwear, T-shirts and other design oddments are as identifiably Sydney as the Harbour Bridge. Appropriately, the bridge, Opera House and harbour scenery feature prominently in his artwork, which graces items from duvet covers to swimwear.

Love and Hatred

Map 5, B6. Strand Arcade ℡9233 3441. Town Hall CityRail.

Mon–Fri 10am–5.30pm (Thurs until 9pm), Sat 10am–4.30pm.
Funky Australian jewellery incorporating gothic and medieval
imagery – they also do commissioned pieces.

FOOD AND DRINK

The handiest **supermarkets** for the **city centre** are
Woolworths Metro, opposite the Town Hall, and Coles
Express, in the Wynyard station complex. The Asian supermarkets on Sussex and Burlington streets in Chinatown offer more
exotic alternatives, and for deli items and impromptu **picnic
supplies**, head for the splendid food hall at David Jones (see
p.260), or one of the gourmet stores listed below. In the **suburbs**, the big supermarkets such as Coles stay open until about
10pm or midnight, and there are plenty of 24-hour, 7-Eleven
convenience stores in the inner-city and suburbs.

Australian Wine Centre
Map 5, C4. Cnr George and Alfred streets, Circular Quay ℗9247
2755. Circular Quay CityRail/ferry.
Mon–Sat 9.30am–6pm, Sun 11am–5pm.
Stocks more than a thousand wines from over 300 wineries
around Australia, and holds regular tastings.

Infinity Sourdough
Map 7, E6. 225 Victoria St, Darlinghurst ℗9380 4320. Kings Cross
CityRail.
Daily 6am–7pm or later.
A great place for breakfast on the fly, and for the sheer luxury
of bread baked on the premises. Sourdough, wholemeal,
Guinness rye bread and oatmeal polenta loaves are specialities.

Jackson's on George City Bottle Shop
Map 5, C4. 176 George St ℗9247 2727. Circular Quay CityRail/ferry.
Daily 10am–midnight.

FOOD AND DRINK

Conveniently located bottle shop, perfect for city-centre BYO restaurants and picnics in the Botanic Gardens.

jones the grocer

Map 7, I11. 68 Moncur St, Woollahra ℂ9362 1222. Bus #389.
Mon–Sat 9am–5pm.

Stylishly packaged, outlandishly priced and utterly delicious groceries and gourmet treats to eat in or take away. Sip a soothing latte at the long central table while you recover from the moment of reckoning at the cash register.

Russell's Natural Food Markets

Map 6, F4. 53–55 Glebe Point Rd, Glebe ℂ9552 4055. Bus #431–433.
Mon–Fri 9.30am–7pm (Thurs until 8pm), Sat 9am–6pm, Sun 10am–5pm.

Vast range of wholefoods, organic fruit and vegetables, speciality honeys and tahini.

Simon Johnson

Map 6, G1. 181 Harris St, Pyrmont ℂ9552 2522. Pyrmont Light Rail; bus #21, #443.
Mon–Sat 9am–5pm.

When only the best will do, try Simon Johnson's superb cheeses (in a dedicated conditioning room), teas and coffees, top-of-the-range pastas, oils and vinegars, as supplied to discriminating restaurateurs.

GALLERIES

Sydney's diverse arts scene is reflected in a myriad of **small art galleries,** which are concentrated in Paddington and Surry Hills, with a few smaller ones in King Street, Newtown. The useful *Guide and Map to Art Galleries in Paddington and Environs* is published by the Josef Lebovic Galleries (see opposite). If you're interested in buying **Aboriginal art** and crafts, try some of the galleries that direct profits back to Aboriginal communities, rather than settling for the standard tourist tat. Shops attached to Sydney's major galleries and museums are detailed in the various guide reviews.

Australian Galleries: Painting & Sculpture

Map 7, H8. 15 Roylston St, Paddington ℗9360 5177. Edgecliff CityRail; bus #330, #365, #387.

Tues–Sat 10am–6pm.

Serene gallery, exhibiting and selling contemporary Australian art, including works by Margaret Olley, Jeffrey Smart and John Coburn.

Australian Galleries: Works on Paper

Map 7, E8. 24 Glenmore Rd, Paddington ℗9380 8744. Bus #378, #380.

Tues–Sun 10am–6pm.

Works for sale here include drawings by Brett Whiteley and Arthur Boyd, as well as prints and sketches by young Australian artists.

Caspian Gallery

Map 7, H10. 469 Oxford St, Paddington ℗9332 1840. Bus #378, #380, #382.

Mon–Sun 11am–6pm.

Great place to pick up ethnic and exotic artefacts to grace the coffee table or that bare corner in the hallway.

Josef Lebovic

Map 7, H10. 34 Paddington St, Paddington ℗9332 1840. Bus #378, #380, #382.

Tues–Fri 1–6pm, Sat 11am–5pm.

Renowned gallery specializing in graphics, prints from the nineteenth and twentieth centuries and vintage photography.

GALLERIES

Ray Hughes Gallery

Map 7, C11. 270 Devonshire St, Surry Hills ℂ9698 3200. Central CityRail.

Tues–Sat 10am–6pm.

Stable of high-profile contemporary Australian and New Zealand artists. Openings monthly, with two artists per show.

ABORIGINAL ART

Duncan MacLennon's Boomerang School

Map 7, E5. 200 William St, Kings Cross ℂ9358 2370. Kings Cross CityRail.

Mon–Sat 9am–6.30pm, Sun 2–6pm.

Boomerangs sold here are mostly made by Aboriginal people from around Australia. You can try them out during the free boomerang-throwing lessons, which have been held every Sunday (10am–noon) since 1958 in Yarranabbe Park, near Rushcutters Bay.

Gavala Aboriginal Art and Cultural Education Centre

Map 4, D4. Level 2, South Harbourside, Darling Harbour ℂ9212 7232. Harbourside Monorail.

Daily 10am–6pm.

Highly credible Aboriginal arts and crafts store – all profits go to the artists and their communities, while the centre aims to raise awareness of indigenous cultures through education programmes, dance and theatre.

Hogarth Galleries Aboriginal Art Centre

Map 7, F8. 7 Walker Lane (off Brown St), Paddington ℂ9360 6839. Bus #378, #380, #382.

Tues–Sat 11am–5pm.

This long-established gallery has a sound reputation for its support of contemporary Aboriginal artists, and its broader commitment to reconciliation.

Quadrivium

Map 5, B7. Gallery Level, QVB, George St ℂ9264 8222. Town Hall CityRail.
Mon–Sat 10am–6pm (Thurs until 9pm), Sun 11am–5pm.
Upmarket gallery specializing in Aboriginal painting, sculpture and drawings; guest artists sometimes demonstrate their work on site. Also showcases Asian art and silver jewellery.

MALLS AND DEPARTMENT STORES

Australia has followed the American trend in shopping and you're bound to find yourself in mall-land at some stage. Although lacking in neighbourhood character, big city and suburban malls and department stores are handy for familiarizing yourself with prices and variety, especially if time is short. Mall air-conditioning, too, can be a big plus on hot, sticky days.

MALLS

Broadway Shopping Centre

Map 6, G4. Cnr Broadway and Bay streets, Broadway. Bus #431–440.
On Broadway, between Central Station and Glebe, this spanking new mall benefits from its proximity to Sydney Uni and the arty enclave of Glebe, with a less run-of-the-mill mix of street fashion and chain stores. A Hoyts multiplex cinema shows art-house and mainstream movies, there's a Collins book superstore, and an extensive Asian section in the Coles supermarket.

Market City

Map 5, A9. 9–13 Hay St, Haymarket. Haymarket Light Rail.
This cavernous mall above Paddy's Markets houses two food courts, a multiplex cinema (the Reading) and a bar. The shop-

ping centre has a distinctly Asian feel, with Chinese lanterns
hanging from the ceiling and resident shiatsu masseurs. There
are Asian supermarkets, factory outlets for big-name stores like
Esprit and Osh Kosh and smaller boutiques selling street and
club wear.

QVB (Queen Victoria Building)

Map 5, B7. 455 George St. Town Hall CityRail.
Mon–Sat 9am–6pm (Thurs until 9pm), Sun 11am–5pm.
This splendid Victorian arcade is an attraction in its own right,
receiving more visitors than either the Harbour Bridge or the
Opera House. The interior is magnificent, with polished
woodwork, elevated walkways and antique lifts. Brave the
weekend hordes for a look at the designer stores upstairs (the
third level has several boutiques featuring the work of young
Australian designers. Or come just for a coffee in *Bar Cupola* or
Jet, both at street level. From Town Hall Station you can walk
right through the basement level (mainly bustling food stalls)
and continue via the Sydney Central Plaza to Grace Bros,
emerging on the Pitt St Mall.

Strand Arcade

Map 5, B6. 412 George St (through to Pitt St). Town Hall CityRail.
Built in 1892, this elegant arcade with its wrought-iron
balustrades houses tiny boutiques, jewellers, watchmakers,
Sydney's best hat shop (see p.252), plus gourmet coffee shops
and tea rooms.

DEPARTMENT STORES

David Jones

Map 5, C7. Cnr Elizabeth and Castlereagh streets ©9266 5544. St
James or Museum CityRail.
Mon–Sat 9am–6pm (Thurs until 9pm), Sun 11am–5pm.
Straddling Market St, David Jones' twin buildings are linked

by a walkway above street level. An utterly civilized shopping experience, the ground floor of this flagship store is graced with seasonal floral displays and a coiffed pianist playing tasteful tunes. A less salubrious version is located at Bondi Junction.

Gowings

Map 5, B7. Cnr Market and George streets ✆9264 6321. Town Hall CityRail.

Mon, Wed & Fri 8.30am–6pm, Thurs 9am–9pm, Sat 9am–6pm, Sun 11am–5pm.

For Australian workwear, the place to go is this delightfully old-fashioned department store, which has become a beloved Sydney institution. It has everything a bloke (or indeed a sheila) could want, from Bonds T-shirts to Speedo swimwear, blundstone boots and a range of Akubra hats at the best prices in town – plus cheap haircuts. With a floor devoted to outdoor pursuits, it's also a useful pitstop for basic camping equipment. Other branches are located at 319 George St, Wynyard and 82 Oxford St, Darlinghurst.

Grace Brothers

Map 5, B7. 436 George St ✆9238 9111. Town Hall CityRail.

Mon–Sat 9am–6pm (Thurs until 9pm), Sun 11am–5pm.

Traditionally seen as the more workaday of Sydney's two main department stores, the reborn Grace Bros store, at the heart of Sydney Central, has sharpened up its act, with several floors of designer fashion and a tranquil Well-ness Spa flanked by elegant minimalist homewares.

MARKETS

Weekend markets have become a feature of the leisurely lives of Sydneysiders, so be prepared for **crowds**. The best for general **browsing** are Paddington Bazaar, the more **arty**

Balmain market and the **downbeat** weekend market on Glebe Point Road. Apart from the markets listed below, there is a Sunday art and craft market in Kings Cross (see p.92), a monthly flea market in Surry Hills, and Aboriginal crafts sold outdoors at La Perouse on Sundays.

Balmain Markets

Map 10, A6. St Andrews Church, cnr Darling St and Curtis Rd, Balmain. Bus #433, #442.

Sat 7.30am–4pm.

An assortment of books, CDs, handmade jewellery, clothing and ceramics, plus herbs and organic produce. The highlight is an eclectic array of food stalls in the church hall where you can snack your way from the Himalayas to the Middle East.

Glebe Market

Map 6, F4. Glebe Primary School, Glebe Point Rd. Bus #431–433.

Sat 9am–4.30pm.

The market is shady, relaxed and quietly sociable, like Glebe itself. A mixture of funky new and secondhand clothes and accessories, including beach dresses, handbags, jewellery – plus plants, records and CDs, and the inevitable New Age knick-knacks and secondhand books. Chinese masseurs ply their therapeutic trade, while a small range of food stalls serves cheap ethnic eats.

Paddington Bazaar

Map 7, G10. 395 Oxford St, Paddington. Bus #378, #380, #382.

Sat 10am–4pm.

As well as being a great location for people-watching, these markets offer leather goods, jewellery and original fashion – old and new. Even if you're just here to browse, the atmosphere, music and buskers come free, and it's all conveniently located in the middle of an excellent shopping and grazing strip.

The Rocks Market

Map 5, C2–C3. George St, The Rocks. Circular Quay
CityRail/ferry.
Sat & Sun 10am–5pm.
Completely taking over The Rocks end of George Street this
collection of more than a hundred stalls offers jewellery,
antiques and art and crafts, mostly with an Australiana/
souvenir slant. Sheltered from the sun and rain by huge canvas
sails.

Sydney Fish Markets

Map 6, F2. Pyrmont Bay, Pyrmont. Fish Markets Light Rail.
Daily 7am–4pm.
Sydney's seafood comes off the fishing boats right here. Also
excellent fruit and veg, flowers, a reliable deli, a bottle shop,
plus takeaway sushi and fish and chips for the picnic tables by
the water's edge (watch out for marauding seagulls and
pelicans).

MUSIC

Tyranny of distance has traditionally kept many big-name
bands from including Sydney on their world tours. As a
result, perhaps, there is fierce loyalty here to home-grown
music. In addition to specialist **Australian music** shops,
you'll find a smattering of places catering for **jazz** and **folk**
aficionados, as well as the usual megastores.

Fish Records

Map 7, E9. 33 Oxford St, Darlinghurst ©9267 5142. Bus #378, #380,
#382.
Mon–Sat 9am–11.30pm, Sun 10am–9.30pm.
Excellent music store catering to eclectic tastes – indie, drum
and bass, acid jazz, top 40, soundtracks and some classical. Also
at Bondi Junction, Broadway Shopping Centre and Newtown.

MUSIC

HMV

Map 5, C6. Mid-City Centre, Pitt St Mall ℂ9221 2311. Martin Place or Town Hall CityRail.

Mon–Fri 9am–6pm (Thurs until 8pm), Sat 9am–5.30pm, Sun 11am–5pm.

The most conspicuous of the city-centre music shops, this megastore stocks just about everything, including extensive classical and world music sections.

Sounds Australian

Map 5, C3. Shop 33, 16–23 Playfair St (off Argyle St), The Rocks ℂ9247 7290. Circular Quay CityRail/ferry.

Daily 10am–5.30pm.

Specialist Australian music store, that covers genres from classical through jazz and folk to traditional Aboriginal music and experimental sounds. With its relaxed, listen-before-you-buy policy and knowledgeable staff, this is a great place to get a taste for antipodean music.

Waterfront Records

Map 5, B6. 89 York St ℂ9262 4120. Town Hall CityRail.

Mon–Sat 10am–6pm (Thurs until 9pm), Sun 10am–4pm.

The place to track down your favourite grunge bands on hard-to-find independent labels. This is also where you can plug into the live music scene, with heaps of flyers as well as in-store ticket sales for the best gigs.

Festivals and events

![T]he Sydney year is interspersed with festivals, both sporting and cultural, with summer the peak time for big events. The **Sydney to Hobart Yacht Race** starts on Boxing Day (December 26); then there's the **New Years Eve fireworks**, eclipsed by the big extravaganza of the **Australia Day** celebrations (January 26). Running throughout January is the **Sydney Festival** whose highlight is the free outdoor **Opera in the Park** concert. The summer winds up in a whirl of feathers and sequins at the **Gay & Lesbian Mardi Gras**, held in late February/early March. An entirely different side of Sydney life is on view at the impressive summer **surf carnivals**, staged regularly by surf life saving clubs; check the newspapers for details.

City Infoline (℡9265 9007; *www.sydneycity.nsw.gov.au*) has details of events including the rundown of the Sydney Festival, and *The Official Sydney Events Guide,* published quarterly, is an excellent source for **listings** and festival information (available at newsagents; $2.95).

JANUARY

New Year
The New Year begins with a spectacular fireworks display on Sydney Harbour. People crowd out vantage points including North Head, South Head, The Rocks, Cremorne Point, Blues Point and Neutral Bay (✆9265 9333 for more details).

Sydney Festival
After the New Year celebrations, there's a brief hiatus before the start of the Sydney Festival on January 2, an exhaustive (and exhausting) arts event that lasts until the Australia Day celebrations (Jan 26). Highlights include Opera In The Park and Symphony in the Park (both free), in The Domain; the outdoor cinema at Mrs Macquarie's Chair; and a fantastic roster of international performers and exhibitions. Many events are free, and happen in public spaces such as Circular Quay, The Domain and Darling Harbour. International shows tend to be quite expensive. A weekly listing of events appears in the *Sydney Morning Herald* during the festival, and the full, 80-plus page programme is available from early January. Darling Harbour also hosts its own festival (Dec 26–Jan 31); most attractions are aimed at children, but there's also a free promenade jazz festival (✆1900/121 999 for Darling Harbour events).

Sydney Fringe Festival
Held at the Bondi Pavilion for two weeks from late January, the Fringe Festival includes a riotous Nude Surfing competition at Bondi Beach – both sexes welcome (festival events and bookings ✆9130 3325 or 9368 1253; see p.118).

Flickerfest International Short Film Festival
Week-long outdoor film festival, held outdoors in the

amphitheatre of the Bondi Pavilion in early January (©9211 7133; see p.225).

Big Day Out

Sydney's biggest outdoor rock concert, held at the Showgrounds at Homebush Bay the weekend before or after Australia Day (Jan 26) Features around sixty of the best local and international acts (tickets $65 through Ticketek ©9266 4800; see p.213).

Australia Day

January 26 is the anniversary of the arrival of the First Fleet in Sydney Harbour in 1788 (see p.339), and Australia Day activities are focused on the harbour. (Australia Day Events Infoline ©1900/920 455; *www.adc.nsw.gov.au*). Sydney's passenger ferries race from Fort Denison to the Harbour Bridge; there is a Tall Ships Race, from Bradley's Head to the Harbour Bridge; a 21-gun salute fired from the Man O'War steps at the Opera House; and a military air show over the harbour. The Australia Day Regatta (©9955 7171) takes place in the afternoon, with hundreds of yachts racing at various harbour locations. There are also events and activities in The Rocks, Hyde Park and at Darling Harbour, where there's a 9pm fireworks display to rival the New Year's Eve extravaganza (©9258 0044). The Survival concert (at Waverley Oval, Bondi ©9331 3777) features many of Australia's best Aboriginal bands and performers, as they celebrate Aboriginal culture (in pointed opposition to the mainstream Australia Day festivities). Coogee Beach hosts an outdoor jazz festival (©9399 0999), and many Sydney museums have free entry all day.

Vibes on a Summers Day

At the very end of January, the Bondi Pavilion hosts an outdoor daytime dance party with international DJs (©9130 3325 or 9368 1253; tickets aound $50).

FEBRUARY

Chinese New Year

Towards the end of January or in the first weeks of February, Chinese New Year is celebrated in Chinatown – firecrackers, dragon and lion dances, food stalls and music.

Tropfest

End of February; hugely popular competition festival for short films (☎9368 0434; see box p.225).

Sydney Gay and Lesbian Mardi Gras

The festival runs through February, and features films, theatre and exhibitions that range from cheeky to outrageous. It all culminates in one of the world's biggest street parades, when up to a million people line the streets on the last Saturday in February or the first Saturday in March (☎9557 4332; see p.229).

MARCH/APRIL

Royal Easter Show

The Royal Easter Show, an agricultural and garden show, moved in 1998 to the Sydney Showground at the new Olympic site at Homebush Bay (Show Infoline ☎9704 111). For twelve consecutive days in late March/early April (the Easter weekend is neatly sandwiched in between), there is a frantic array of amusement-park rides, parades of prized animals and various farm/agriculture related displays. There are usually horse-related events in the main arena during the day; at night, there's a fireworks display, rodeos and even a giant robotic dinosaur on show ($17, child $9.50, rides extra).

Norton St Festival

Sunday street festival in mid-March (10am–7pm), celebrating Sydney's most stridently Italian community. It's held along the Norton St (see box p.100) strip of cafés and restaurants. Lots of food stalls and entertainment, culminating in a fireworks display over Leichhardt Town Hall (✆9692 0051).

MAY

Sydney Writers Festival

Week-long high profile mid-May event with readings, work-shops and discussions, mostly free; Australian and international writers. Takes place in a very scenic location at the Wharf Theatre, Hickson Rd, Millers Point.

JUNE

Sydney Film Festival

Takes over several of the city's screens for two weeks from early June (✆9660 3844; see box p.224).

AUGUST

City-to-Surf Race

A 14km fun-run from Park Street in the city to Bondi, held on the second Sunday of August. Around 30,000 participants; entry $20 (✆9224 2742).

SEPTEMBER–OCTOBER

Festival of the Winds

In September, as the skies get bluer, Australia's largest kite festival takes over Bondi Beach (✆9130 3325 or 9368 1253).

Carnivale

Carnivale is a multicultural festival, celebrating the diverse talents of the ethnic peoples of Sydney through theatre, music and dance. Held each spring, September to early October (free call ©1800/064 534).

Biennale of Sydney

Every alternate (even-numbered) year, this international contemporary art festival takes place over six weeks from mid-September until early November. Provocative contemporary exhibitions at various venues and public spaces around town, including the Art Gallery of New South Wales and the Museum of Contemporary Art, featuring artists from thirty countries.

Women on Women Film Festival

Held over three days in late in September at the Chauvel Cinema, Paddington (©9332 2408; see p.225).

Manly International Jazz Festival

The Labour Day weekend in early October; mostly free outdoor, waterfront events with some indoor concerts charging entry for some of the bigger Australian and international acts. As Sydney gets into the swim of summer, and the beaches officially open for the year, this jazz-fest by the sea is a wonderful way to enjoy the warming weather (©9977 1088).

Blessing of the Fleet

Labour Day weekend. Most of Sydney's fishing industry workers come from the Italian community, hence this very Italian festival at Darling Harbour. Brightly decorated fishing boats are blessed for their life at sea, and revellers dress in traditional fancy dress (©9286 0100).

Taste of a Nation

In mid-October, Fitzroy Gardens, Kings Cross, is host to a food fair, with Kings Cross restaurateurs showing their stuff (℡9264 1399).

City of Sydney Food and Wine Fair

In late October, Hyde Park is overtaken for a day by around eighty stalls representing restaurants, wineries, cheese-makers and the like (℡9265 9007).

Newtown Festival

Organized by the Newtown Neighbourhood Centre (℡9516 4755; *www.newtownfestival.org.au*), this is one of Sydney's biggest community festivals. Around Oct 8–Nov 8, various local venues host events, and shop windows lend themselves to the work of some young, irreverent, in-your-face artists. The highlight is the Fair Day (second Sun in Nov) when Camperdown Park is overtaken by a bazaar with market stalls and live music.

NOVEMBER

Glebe Street Fair

Second-last Sunday in November. Thousands flock to one of Sydney's great eat-streets, Glebe Point Road, for a vibrant street festival – notably fabulous food for sale, representing the local restaurants and cafés, plus lots of arts and crafts (℡9692 0051).

DECEMBER

Homebake

Australian music is celebrated in The Domain (℡9266 4800; $40; see box p.213) with a line-up of bands from around the country.

Sydney to Hobart Yacht Race

It seems almost half of Sydney turns out on December 26 to cheer the start of this classic regatta, and watch the colourful spectacle of two hundred or so yachts setting sail on their 630-nautical-mile slog. The toughest bit is the crossing of Bass Strait, which is swept by the "Roaring Forties". (Conditions were so rough in 1999 that many crews abandoned the race, and six sailors tragically died.) Good vantage points include South Head and Nielson Park or Georges Head and Bradleys Head on the North Shore.

Christmas Day on Bondi Beach

Backpackers and Christmas on Bondi Beach have long been synonymous. The behaviour and litter had been getting out of control over several years, and after riots in 1995, the local council took control of what had for many years been an ad hoc beach party. Their objective now is to keep a spirit of goodwill towards the travellers, while tempting local families back to the beach on what is traditionally regarded as a family day. Alcohol has been banned from the beach, with the exception of a fenced-off section that has a bar, bands and other entertainment for boisterous revellers; a $15 fee gets you in, and you're issued a plastic beer-glass attached to a string tied around your neck. In 1998, only 3000 crammed into it at the height of the festivities, compared to the 12,000 of 1996. The great drunken backpacker clan has dispersed to other beaches, notably Coogee further south. Waverley Council (©9369 8000) is not sure whether to dispense with organized proceedings in future, though the alcohol ban will certainly remain in place: it looks to be the end of an era.

Sporting Sydney

Sydneysiders are sports mad, especially for the ostensibly passive spectator sports of rugby league, Aussie Rules football, cricket, tennis and horse racing. No matter what it is, from surf lifesaving competitions to yacht races, it'll draw a crowd. They're keen participants too, whether it's a game of squash or the latest infatuation with yoga, but getting into (or onto) the water is their greatest joy. The *Sydney Morning Herald*'s Friday **listings** supplement, "Metro", has a Sport and Leisure section, with details of the best events around town. Most seats can be booked through Ticketek ✆9266 4800.

Sydney stadiums

The $640 million **Stadium Australia**, the Olympic Stadium in Homebush Bay (**map 3, C3**), is the nation's newest and largest sporting venue. It opened in March 1999, with the kick-off of the Rugby League season, to a packed house of 105,000 fans – a world record rugby league crowd. Previously, the **Sydney Cricket Ground** (**map 7, F12**) and the **Sydney Football Stadium** (both located in Moore Park; **map 7, F11**) were Sydney's key sporting venues; however, judging by the popularity of Stadium Australia, it may soon be taking away some of their biggest events, including rugby league, rugby union, AFL, soccer, and possibly even one-day cricket matches.

RUGBY LEAGUE

Rugby League is *the* football code in Sydney, and was for many years a bastion of working-class culture. Formerly run by the Australian Rugby League (ARL), the game was split down the middle in 1996, when Rupert Murdoch launched Super League in an attempt to gain ratings for his Foxtel TV station. It quickly became obvious, however, that the game could not support two separate competitions, and in 1997 they united to form the **National Rugby League** (NRL; ©9339 8500). The season starts in early March, and the **Grand Final** is played at the end of September – when huge crowds pack out the Football Stadium or Stadium Australia. There are seventeen clubs (scheduled to be cut to fourteen) – Brisbane is the glamour club, while Sydney's best teams are Sydney City, Cronulla and Parramatta. The **State of Origin** series, where Queensland and NSW battle it out over three matches (at least one of which is held in Sydney), is incredibly hard-fought, and coverage of these matches consistently produces the highest ratings on Australian television.

AUSTRALIAN RULES

Victoria has traditionally been the home of **Australian Rules** ("Aussie Rules") football, and Victorian sides are still expected to win the AFL Flag – decided at the Grand Final in Melbourne in September – as a matter of course. However, the enormously popular **Sydney Swans**, NSW's contribution to the AFL, have ensured Aussie Rules a place in Sydney, helped along by legendary goalkicker Tony "Plugger" Lockett. (During the 1999 season, Plugger finally broke the game's all-time goal scoring record, which had stood for 62 years). The game itself is a no-holds-barred, eighteen-a-side brawl, closely related to Gaelic football.

The objective is to kick the ball through the uprights for a goal, which is worth six points, or the short posts either side for a "behind" – one point. There are four 25-minute quarters, plus lots of time added on for injury. Despite the violence on the pitch, crowds tend to be very well-behaved; you'll be surrounded by boisterous fans, but perfectly safe, if you go to watch the Swans at their home base at the Sydney Cricket Ground (see *www.afl.com.au*).

RUGBY UNION

Rugby union, in spite of the huge success of the national team (the Wallabies), still lags behind rugby league in popularity. However, the introduction of the **Super 12** competition, which runs from the end of February to the end of May, and involves regional teams from Australia, New Zealand and South Africa, has generated broader interest in what has traditionally been an elitist game. The state's contribution to the Super 12 is the **NSW Waratahs**, who play at the Sydney Football Stadium about six times per season. (For more details contact the Australian Rugby Union ©9955 3466; otherwise you can find all the latest rugby info at *www.rugby.com.au*).

SOCCER

Soccer is still a minority sport in Australia. Around half the **Australian National League** (ANL) soccer clubs evolved from communities of postwar immigrants – mainly Italians, Greeks and Yugoslavs. (In the mid-1990s, a ban on clubs with these nation's flags in their team logos won considerable support, but also came in for accusations of "ethnic cleansing".) The four Sydney teams who compete in the ANL competition (October–May) for the Ericsson Cup are: Sydney United, Marconi-Fairfield, Sydney Olympic and Northern Spirit. Details of matches and grounds through **Soccer Australia** (©9241 6199). Australia's national team, the **Socceroos,** play in the Oceania group, against teams such as Fiji and Western Samoa. Their home matches at the Sydney Football Stadium still generate only limited interest, although recent, high-profile games against a FIFA eleven and Manchester United created huge interest, particularly as Australia's best players returned from Europe to play with the Socceroos.

CRICKET

Sydney's cricket season runs Oct–March, and offers some of the year's best sporting days out (locals go for the atmosphere, the sunshine and the beer as much as the game). The **Sydney Cricket Ground** (SCG) is the venue for four-day, interstate Sheffield Shield matches (not much interest from spectators, but a breeding ground for Australia's Test cricketers); five-day international **Test matches**; and the colourful, crowd-pleasing **one-day internationals**. Ideally, you would observe proceedings from the Members Stand while sipping an icy gin and tonic – but unless you're invited by a member, you'll end up elsewhere, drinking beer from a plastic cup. Cricket spectators aren't a sedate lot in Sydney, and the noisiest barrackers come from "the Hill" – or the Doug Walters stand, as it's officially known. Still the cheapest spot to sit, the now concreted area was once a grassy hill, where rowdy supporters threw beer cans at players and each other. The Bill O'Reilly Stand gives comfortable viewing (until the afternoon, when you'll be blinded by the sun), whereas the Brewongle Stand provides a consistently good vantage. Best of all is the Bradman Stand, with a view from directly behind the bowler's arm. For information, scores, prices and times, call Match Information ©0055/63132. You can buy tickets in advance, or at the gates on the day (subject to availability). Cricket fans can take a **tour** of the SCG on non-match days (Mon–Sat 10am, 1pm & 3pm; 1hr 30min; $18, children $12, family $48; ℂ9380 0383).

TENNIS

Sydney's major tennis event is the **Adidas International**, held during the second week of January as a lead-up to the Australian Open in Melbourne; it's played at the **NSW Tennis Centre**, at the Olympic site in Homebush Bay. Tickets are available from September; contact the NSW Tennis Association for more details (ℂ9331 4144). You can also visit the tournament's former long-time home, at White City, and even have a game on a lawn or synthetic court as part of a tour which includes the tennis museum, a coaching session and a match with your guide (Mon & Thurs 10.30am; 1hr 30min; $25; bookings ℂ9360 4113; Edgecliff CityRail; **map 7, H7**). Another place to play nearby is **Rushcutters Bay Tennis Centre**, Rushcutters Bay Park, New South Head Road ℂ9357 1675. The clay courts (daily 8am–9/10pm; **map 7, G5**) are in a picturesque park by the marina ($14 per hour, $16 after 4pm and on Sat & Sun; racquet hire $3).

A central place to play squash is Hiscoe's Fitness Centre, 525 Crown St, Surry Hills ℂ9699 3233 (Mon–Fri 6am–10pm, Sat 8am–8pm, Sun 9am–noon & 4–8pm; $16–20 per 45min; racquet $2.50; map 7, C10).

RACETRACKS

Australians lose $1000 a head each year succumbing to the temptation of a flutter. This eagerness to bet, coupled with relaxed gambling laws, has tax-collectors rubbing their hands as the revenue rolls in. Sydney offers plenty of opportunities for any punter heading for the fast lane to millionares row – or the slippery slope to the poorhouse.

There are **Horseracing** meetings on Wednesday, Saturday and most public holidays. This is due mainly to the accessibility of courses, high quality of racing, the presence of bookmakers and cheap admission prices. The venues are well maintained, peopled with colourful racing characters, and often massive crowds. Best times to hit the track are during the Spring and Autumn Carnivals (respectively Aug–Sept and March–April), when prize money rockets, and the quality of racing rivals the best in the world. The principal racecourses are: **Royal Randwick** (Alison Rd, Randwick ✆9663 8400; $6; carnivals $10); **Rosehill Gardens** (James Ruse Drive, Rosehill ✆9930 4070; $6; carnivals $10–$20); and **Canterbury Park** (King St, Canterbury ✆9930 4000; $6), which has midweek racing, plus floodlit night racing from September to March. There are also plenty of picturesque country venues to choose from (contact the Australian Jockey Club for more details on ✆9663 8400).

Every Friday the *Sydney Morning Herald* publishes its racing guide, "The Form". Bets are placed at TAB shops; these are scattered throughout the city, and most pubs also have TAB access.

If the chariot scenes of *Ben Hur* are more to your taste, a trip to the trots might be the ticket. **Harness racing** occurs at **Harold Park Paceway**, Ross St, Glebe (**map 6, C4**; ✆9660 3688; $6), on Tuesday afternoons and Friday evenings, though Tuesdays are best avoided unless you need to escape human contact for a few hours. There is more of a buzz on Friday nights, the excitement reaching its peak on the last Friday of November when the Miracle Mile is run. For some, watching horses lope around the fibresand course is too sedate, but just around the corner money is thrown away at greater speed as the **greyhounds** hurtle around **Wentworth Park** (**map 6, F3**; ℂ9960 3688; $5) every Monday, Wednesday and Saturday.

SURFING AND SURF CARNIVALS

One peculiarly Australian institution is the **surf carnival**, where teams of lifesavers demonstrate their skills (see box p.117). Call Surf Life Saving NSW ℂ9663 4298 for details of

Beach and sun safety

Sydney's beaches do have perils as well as pleasures: most are protected by shark nets, but these don't keep out stingers such as bluebottles. Loudspeaker announcements will alert you in the event of a (very rare) shark sighting, or a more common insurge of bluebottles. Pacific **currents** can be very strong – inexperienced swimmers would do better sticking to the sheltered **harbour beaches**, or **sea pools** at the surf beaches. Ocean beaches are patrolled by lifeguards during October–April (all year at Bondi), generally 6am–7pm. The red-and-yellow flags indicate the safe areas to swim; if you do get into difficulty, stay calm, raise one arm above your head, and a lifeguard will assist you.

It's easy to underestimate the strength of the southern **sun**: follow the local slogan and Slip (on a shirt), Slop (on the sun block), Slap (on a hat). The final hazard, despite the apparent cleanliness of Sydney beaches, is **pollution**. Storms, currents and onshore breezes occasionally wash sewage and rubbish onto beaches, making them unsuitable for swimming. Harbour swimming spots tend to be the worst, particularly South Sydney beaches; the northern ocean beaches are generally Sydney's cleanest. To check pollution levels, call the Beachwatch Information Line ℂ9901 7996.

the current season's carnivals. **Surfing** competitions are good opportunities to catch some hot wave-riding action. The NSW Surfriding Association ©9970 7066 can tell you where to find them.

Surf schools can teach you the basic skills, and enlighten you on surfing etiquette and lingo: Let's Go Surfing at Bondi (©9365 1800) and Manly Surf School (©9977 3777) are two of the best, charging around $40 for a two-hour group lesson, including boards and wet suit. You can **hire boards** from surfshops for $20–30 per day (wet suit may cost extra): try Aloha Surf, 44 Pittwater Rd, Manly ©9977 3777 or Bondi Surf Company, 72 Campbell Parade, Bondi Beach ©9365 0870. Listen to radio station 2MMM (FM 104.9 MHz) for a **surf report** at 7am, 9am and 3.40pm weekdays and 7am, 9am & noon on weekends.

CANOEING, KAYAKING, SAILBOARDING AND SAILING

Balmoral Windsurf, Sail and Kayak School
Map 10, F3. Balmoral boatshed, southern end of the Esplanade, Balmoral ©9960 5344.
Rents sailboards, kayaks and catamarans as well as giving lessons. Sailboard hire from $20 per hour; kayaks $10; catamarans $30.

Northside Sailing School
Map 10, F1. Spit Bridge, Mosman ©9969 3972;
www.northsidesailing.com.au
Specializes in weekend sailing courses on Middle Harbour (Sept–April); tuition is in groups of up to four and the two-day courses cost $280, leading to Australian Yachting Federation Certificate. Boats for rent (daily during the season) are $25 for the first hour and $15 for subsequent hours.

Rose Bay Aquatic Hire

Map 10, F7. 1 Vickery Ave, Rose Bay © 9371 7036.

Rents out catamarans ($25 first hour, $15 thereafter), windsurfers ($15 per hour), and motorboats (weekends $40 for the first two hours, $10 for each subsequent hour, plus charge for petrol; midweek $40 half-day, $60 full-day; no boat licence required).

The big event on the yachting calendar is the Sydney to Hobart Yacht Race, each Boxing Day, December 26. One of the best ways to watch the start is from on board a boat – Sydney Ferries (©13 1500) put on special services which book out early.

DIVING AND SNORKELLING

Visibility in the waters around Sydney is good – and divers can expect to see to a distance of 10–15m. One of the best places to dive is at Gordon's Bay in Clovelly, where there is easy access to Sydney's only **underwater nature trail** – a sort of beneath-the-sea bushwalking track, marked by a series of chains connected to conrete drums. The trail includes typical Sydney shoreline life: sponges, sea jellies, anemones, shrimps and crabs, molluscs, cuttlefish, octupus, sea stars and sea squirts. The 700m trail takes around 35–40 minutes to cover, and has a maximum depth of 14m. It is one of Sydney's most dived locations.

Manly Dive Centre

Map 9, B4. 10 Belgrave St, Manly © 9977 4355. Manly ferry.

Offers shore dives at Shelley Beach, Fairlight, Little Manly and Harbord, plus boat dives off North and South Head (boat dive with full gear $70, shore dive with gear $50).

Pacific Coast Divers Clovelly

Map 8, B6. 355 Clovelly Rd, cnr Beach St, Clovelly © 9665 7427.

Closest dive shop to Gordons Bay, so naturally they run lots of trips there. Double boat dive $70; two shore dives $55 (equipment $40). Snorkelling sets $15 per day.

Prodive Coogee
Map 8, A8. 27 Alfreda St, Coogee ℘9665 6333. Bus #323, #324.
Boat and shore dives anywhere between Camp Cove and La Perouse (double boat dive $135, shore $105; gear included).

SWIMMING POOLS

Most pool complexes are outdoors and have a fifty-metre pool, a smaller children's pool and a wading pool, all usually unheated. The swimming season is generally the warmer months, from the long weekend in October, until Easter. There are over seventy public pools, plus 74 enclosed sea pools at beaches and on the harbour; several of the latter are detailed in the text, including the Women's Pool (p.122) and Wylie's Baths (p.122), both in Coogee.

Andrew "Boy" Charlton
Map 5, G4. The Domain. ℘9358 6686. Martin Place CityRail.
Daily Sept–April 6.30am–8pm (Fri until 7pm). $3.50.
An open-air, 50m saltwater swimming pool in a great waterside setting, with views across to the Garden Island Naval Depot. Solar-heated to take the chill off slightly.

North Sydney Olympic Pool
Map 10, C5. Alfred St South, Milsons Point ℘9955 2309. Milsons Point CityRail.
Mon–Fri 5.30am–9pm, Sat & Sun 7am–7pm. $3, child $1.40.
The heated, 50m outdoor pool is open all year (covered in winter). Situated by the water, in the shadow of the harbour bridge, it's one of Sydney's best pools.

Sydney International Aquatic Centre

Map 3, C2. Olympic Boulevarde, Homebush Bay ℰ9752 3666.
Strathfield CityRail then bus #401–404, or Olympic Park CityRail.
Mon–Fri 6am–9.15pm, Sat & Sun 6am–6.45pm. Swim and spa
$4.50, child $3.50 ($9 includes steam rooms and sauna).
As well as being a great place to swim laps, there are amusements such as the rapid river-ride, as well as waterslides. Also
spas, steam rooms and saunas.

Victoria Park Pool

Map 6, F5. Cnr City Rd and Broadway. ℰ9660 4181. Central City Rail.
Mon–Fri 6am–7.15pm, Sat & Sun 7am–5.45pm. $2.50.
Heated outdoor pool next to Sydney University and close to
Glebe Point Rd, in a landscaped park. Great café.

....

**For thrill sports, from rap jumping to skydiving and
aerobatic flights, contact the Adrenalin Sports Club
ℰ9959 3834.**

....

CYCLING, ROLLERBLADING AND HORSE RIDING

The narrow maze of streets in Sydney's CBD, combined with
traffic congestion, means that **cycling** has never been too
popular. Bicycles can be carried free on trains (outside of peak
hours), and on ferries at all times. The best source of information is Bicycle NSW, Level 2, 209 Castlereagh St (Mon–Fri
9am–5.30pm; ℰ9283 5200). For leisure cycling, head for
Centennial Park (p.91) or the cycleway at Manly (p.122). Hire
bikes from Centennial Park Cycles, 50 Clovelly Rd,
Randwick ℰ9398 5027 (mountain bikes $8 per hour, standard
and kids' bikes $6); Clarence Street Cyclery, 104 Clarence St,
City ℰ9299 4962 (mountain bikes $65 per day, $110 weekend) and Inner City Cycles, 31 Glebe Point Rd, Glebe ℰ9660
6605 (mountain bikes $30 for 24 hours, $50 weekend).

Rollerblading is banned in the CBD. The two most popular areas for bladers are along the bike track at Manly, and in Centennial Park. Teenagers also use the skateboarding ramp at Bondi Beach. Hire places charge $10 for the first hour, then $5 per hour, inclusive of protective gear: Total Skate, corner Oxford and Queen streets, Woollahra (✆9380 6356) is handy for Centennial Park; Bondi Boards and Blades, 230 Oxford St, Bondi Junction (✆9365 6555; also skateboards); and Inline Action, 93 North Steyne, Manly (✆9976 3831).

Several stables at Centennial Park offer **horse riding**, including Centennial Stables, corner Cook and Lang roads (✆9360 5650; one-hour escorted rides $35).

GYMS AND YOGA

Most gyms charge $15 for a casual visit, which applies all day, and includes access to aerobics and even yoga classes. Healthland Fitness is recommended, with several centres including one at Bondi Junction (110 Spring St; Mon–Thurs 6am–10pm, Fri 6am–9pm, Sat 7am–7.30pm, Sun 9am–7.30pm; free childcare available; ✆9389 3999). Also see gyms reviewed in the "Gay Sydney" chapter, including Bayswater Fitness (p.237), which offers daily **yoga classes**.

Yoga is very popular in Sydney, and specific **yoga schools** offering casual visits include Glebe Yoga School, 2/23 Glebe Point Rd, Glebe ✆9552 6597 ($13, 2hr experienced; $10, 1hr 30min beginner); Yoga Synergy, at 115 Bronte Rd, Bondi Junction and 196 Australia St, Newtown – bookings for both ✆9389 7399 (classes 1hr 30min, beginners to advanced; $14 at Bondi Junction, $10 at Newtown).

After you've got all sweaty, try a traditional ginseng bath and skin-scrub treatment at the wonderful **Korean Bathhouse**, *Hotel Capital*, 1st floor, 111 Darlinghurst Rd, Kings Cross ✆9358 2755.

City Directory

Airlines (domestic) Ansett Australia and Kendell, 19 Pitt St, and 32 Martin Place ✆13 1300; Qantas, 70 Hunter St, and 468 Oxford St, Bondi Junction ✆13 1313; Sydney Harbour Seaplanes, Lyne Park, Rose Bay, free call ✆1800/803 558.

Airlines (international) Air Canada ✆9232 5222; Air New Zealand ✆13 2476; Alitalia ✆9922 1555; All Nippon ✆9367 6700; British Airways ✆9258 3200; Canadian Airlines ✆1300/655 757; Cathay Pacific ✆13 1747; Continental ✆9244 2242; Delta ✆9251 3211; Emirates ✆9279 0711; Finnair ✆9244 2299; Garuda ✆1300/365 330; Gulf Air ✆9244 2199; Japan Airlines ✆9272 1111; KLM ✆9231 6333; Lauda Air ✆9251 6155; Malaysia Airlines ✆13 2627; Olympic ✆9251 1048; Qantas ✆13 1211; Royal Brunei ✆9223 1566; Sabena ✆9344 2135; Scandinavian Airlines ✆9299 9800; Singapore Airlines ✆13 1011; Swissair ✆9232 1744; Thai Airways ✆9251 1922; United ✆13 1777.

Car rental Most car-rental firms have a branch in William St, Kings Cross; the big four, which rent late-model cars, are also at the airport. Average daily charge is $55–70 for a small manual: Avis, 214 William St ✆9357 2000; Budget, 93 William St ✆13 2727; Hertz, cnr William and Riley streets ✆13 3039; and Thrifty, 75 William St ✆9331 1385.

There are cheaper deals with Bayswater, 120 Darlinghurst Rd, Kings Cross ☎9360 3622; Kings Cross Rent-A-Car, 169 William St ☎9331 1366; and Network, 51 William St ☎9361 0022.

Consulates British, Level 16, 1 Macquarie Pl ☎9247 7521; Canadian, Level 5, 111 Harrington St ☎9364 3000; New Zealand, 1 Alfred Pl, Circular Quay ☎9247 1344; US, Level 59, MLC Centre, Martin Place ☎9373 9200.

Disabled travellers ACROD (Australian Council for the Rehabilitation of the Disabled), 24 Cabarita Rd, Cabarita, NSW 2137 ☎9743 2699, fax 9743 2899, provides a list of organizations, accommodation, travel agencies and tour operators. Barrier Free Travel, 36 Wheatley St, North Bellingen, NSW 2452 ☎ & fax 6655 1733, is a travel consultant service that plans trips and gives advice; their guide to Sydney is also available from the NSW Tourism Commission ☎13 2077. For taxis, try Wheelchair Accessible Taxis ☎9332 0200 or ABC ☎13 2522.

Electricity Australia's electrical current is 240/250v, 50Hz AC. British appliances will work with an adaptor; American and Canadian 110v appliances need a transformer.

Email The *Well Connected Café* on Glebe Point Road (see p.169) is the best place for a cybercafé experience, while Darlinghurst Rd in Kings Cross is crammed with places you can access your email. You can use the Internet for free at the State Library (p.68), or as part of your admission to the Australian Museum (p.66).

Emergency ☎000 for fire, police or ambulance.

Health See "Medical Centres" in the Yellow Pages. Broadway Medical Centre, 185–211 Broadway ☎9212 2733, open Mon–Sat, no appointment necessary. Sydney

Sexual Health Centre, Sydney Hospital, Macquarie St ℘9382 7440. Women's Health Clinic, 139 Macquarie St ℘9247 1555. Travellers Medical and Vaccination Centre, 7th floor, 428 George St ℘9221 7133.

Hospitals Sydney Hospital, Macquarie St ℘9382 7111; St Vincents Hospital, Victoria St, Darlinghurst ℘9339 1111.

Laundries Most accommodation will have a coin-operated laundry; a load of washing costs about $3 at any laundromat.

Left luggage Cloakrooms at Town Hall and Central stations (both Mon–Sat 9am–4.40pm; $1.50 per 24hr); lockers at the airport and Sydney Coach Terminal (both $4 per 24hr).

Motorbike hire Sydney Motorcycle Hire, 23 Euston Rd, Alexandria ℘9565 5788, from $38 per day.

Newspapers The two daily (Mon–Sat) Sydney papers are the reliable broadsheet *Sydney Morning Herald* and the tackier tabloid *Daily Telegraph* (the latter publishes a morning and an afternoon edition); Melbourne's *Age* is readily available, as is *The Australian*, the only national newspaper – both are strong on international news, and maintain generally high standards of journalism. Saturday editions of the *Herald* and the *Australian* feature travel and arts sections as well as entertainment listings. Sunday papers (*Sun Herald*, *Sunday Telegraph*) are fairly low-brow and packed with advertising. The City of Sydney Public Library, behind the Town Hall (Mon–Thurs 9am–7pm, Fri 9am–6pm, Sat 9am–noon), keeps a large selection of overseas newspapers.

Pharmacy (late-night) Blake's Pharmacy, 28 Darlinghurst Rd, Kings Cross (daily 8am–midnight ℘9358 6712). Late-night pharmacy information ℘9235 0333.

Police Headquarters at 14 College St ℗9339 0277.

Post office The GPO building in Martin Place is being redeveloped into a luxury hotel, and the post office is to take up the ground floor. Meanwhile, it is located nearby at 130 Pitt St (Mon–Fri 8.15am–5.30pm, Sat 9am–1pm). Poste restante is available at the post office inside Hunter Connection shopping arcade, opposite Wynyard Station (Mon–Fri 8.15am–6pm). Poste Restante, c/- Sydney GPO, NSW 2000.

Public toilets Free public toilets are found at beaches, in parks, shopping arcades, train stations and department stores.

Radio ABC stations: Radio National (576 AM), offers a popular mix of arty intellectual topics; 2BL (702 AM), intelligent talk-back radio; ABC Classic FM (92.9 FM) for classical; 2JJJ ("Triple J"; 105.7 FM), supports local bands and alternative rock – aimed squarely at the nation's youth. 2JJJ competes with commercial mainstream rock station 2MMM ("Triple M"; 104.9 FM).

Television There are five terrestrial TV stations: three commercial (Channels Ten, Nine and Seven) and two non-commercial (ABC and SBS) – plus two pay TV stations (Optus and Foxtel). The ABC, on Channel Two, is a national, non-commercial station, and has the best of British sit-coms and mini-series as well as excellent news coverage. SBS, a government-sponsored, multicultural station, is best for world news and quality current affairs, and screens foreign-language films nightly.

Telephones Local calls (untimed) from public phones cost 40¢; 25¢ from private phones. Call boxes do not accept incoming calls. Most public phones take both Telstra phonecards (sold through newsagents for $5, $10, $20 or

$50) and coins. Crediphones accept most major credit cards, and can be found at international and domestic airports and many hotels. The Telstra Pay Phone Centre, 231 Elizabeth St (Mon–Fri 7am–11pm, Sat & Sun 7am–5pm) has private booths.

Many businesses and services have free-call numbers, prefixed ℂ1800; six-digit numbers beginning ℂ13 are charged at the local-call rate. Numbers starting ℂ0055 are private information services, costing between 35¢ and 70¢ a minute. Directory assistance calls (ℂ013 for local area, ℂ1225 for international) are free, as are calls to the operator. Calls within Australia are generally cheapest between 7pm & 7am Monday to Saturday, and all day Sunday. One.Tel cards, for discounted international calls, are widely available at newsagents. Global Gossip, (770 George St, and 111 Darlinghurst Rd, Kings Cross; both open daily 8am–midnight), offers discount-rate international calls from private phone booths.

To phone out of Australia, dial 0011, followed by the country code (UK 44, US and Canada 1, Ireland 353, New Zealand 64), then the area code, minus its zero. Reverse charge calls can be made through the international operator (ℂ0107 from a payphone, ℂ0101 from a private phone), but this is easier with Country Direct, which allows you to speak directly with an operator in your home country; the call is charged to the receiving number, or to your credit card. Country direct numbers: Canada ℂ1800/881 150; USA ℂ1800/881 011; UK ℂ1800/881 440; Ireland ℂ1800/881 353; and New Zealand ℂ1800/881 640.

Trains Central Station; info and bookings ℂ13 2232.

Travel agents STA Travel, does international and domestic flights, tours and accommodation; branches include 855 George St ℂ9212 1255 and Springfield Ave, Kings Cross ℂ9368 1111. YHA Travel, 422 Kent St, City ℂ9261 1111,

TELEPHONES

offers domestic and international travel services: transport, tours and accommodation (branch at *Sydney Central YHA*, 11 Rawson Pl ✆9281 9444). Backpackers Travel Centre, Imperial Arcade, off Pitt St Mall ✆9231 3699.

BEYOND THE CITY

Around the Hawkesbury River

North of Sydney the picturesque sandstone-lined **Hawkesbury River** widens and slows as it approaches the South Pacific, joining **Berowra Creek**, Cowan Creek, **Pittwater** and Brisbane Water in the system of flooded valleys that form **Broken Bay**. The bay and its surrounding inlets are a haven for anglers, sailors and windsurfers, while the surrounding bushland is virtually untouched. Several national parks surround the Hawkesbury River: the three most major are **Ku-Ring-Gai Chase** to the south, facing **Brisbane Waters National Park** across Broken Bay, and **Dharug** inland to the west.

The area covered in this chapter is on colour map 2

KU-RING-GAI CHASE NATIONAL PARK

Ku-Ring-Gai Chase is much the best known of Sydney's national parks and, with the Pacific Highway running all the way up its west side, is also the easiest to get to with a car. The bushland scenery is crisscrossed by walking tracks, which you can explore to seek out Aboriginal rock paintings, or wander through to spot its wildlife. Only 24km from the city centre, the huge park's unspoilt beauty is enhanced by the presence of water on three sides: the Hawkesbury, its inlet Cowan Creek, and the expanse of **Pittwater**, an inlet of Broken Bay. There are four road entrances to the park and $7.50 car entrance fee; public transport options are detailed below.

Bobbin Head

From Palm Beach (p.127) you can take a boat cruise to the park's most popular picnic spot, **Bobbin Head**, with its colourful boat marina on Cowan Creek (Palm Beach Ferries ©9918 2747; hourly 9am–5pm, Sun 9am–6pm; $7 one-way). At the **Kalkari Visitor Centre** (daily 9am–5pm), on the Ku-Ring-Gai Chase Road, there's information about bush trails, guided walks led by volunteers, and screenings of videos about the area's Aboriginal heritage and wildlife. From here the signposted Birrawanna Walking Track leads to the NPWS **Bobbin Head Information Centre** (daily 9am–4pm; ©9457 1049; also approached by car further along Ku-Ring-Gai Chase Road), inside the Art Deco *Bobbin Inn* which has a very pleasant restaurant, popular for weekend breakfasts and Sunday afternoon jazz. Without your own transport, apart from the ferry, the best way to get here is by train to Turramurra Station then the Hornsby Bus #577 (©9457 8888) to the Bobbin Head Road entrance; some buses continue down to Bobbin Head itself.

WARATAH PARK

Daily 10am–5pm; $12.90, family $34; koala cuddling hourly 11am–4pm & 4.30pm; ©9968 1111. Chatswood CityRail then bus #284.

One of Sydney's oldest wildlife reserves, **Waratah Park** sits in the middle of stunning national park scenery on Namba Road, off Mona Vale Road. Waratah is most famous as the home of **Skippy**, the bush kangaroo, television's first marsupial star. The TV series was filmed here in the 1960s and the specially constructed sets that made up the ranger station now form the wildlife reserve office, which was set up after filming finished in the late 1960s. You can still meet Skippy (or at least his descendants) amongst the free-ranging kangaroos, and visit the office where most of the emergency calls were taken by ranger Matt Hammond before Skippy hopped off to the rescue. A video showing scenes from the show should get the nostalgic tears flowing. Apart from the showbiz associations, the main pull of the reserve is getting up close to the wildlife – you can pat the kangaroos and the koalas.

PITTWATER

The beauty of Pittwater is best appreciated with a spot of bush camping or a spell at the quite wonderful, isolated youth hostel, or else as a day ferry trip from Palm Beach, or Church Point via Scotland Island. The Palm Beach Ferry Service from Barrenjoey Road, Palm Beach Wharf (hourly 9–11am & 1–5pm, Sat & Sun until 6pm; $7 return; ✆9918 2747) heads to *The Basin* campsite (see overleaf). Nearby, the **Garigal Aboriginal Heritage Walk** (3.5km circuit) to the park's most accessible Aboriginal art site with rock engravings and hand art, heads from West Head Road, at the northeastern corner of Ku-Ring-Gai Chase, where there are superb views back across Pittwater to the Barrenjoey Lighthouse at Palm Beach. From Church Point, another ferry service goes to Halls Wharf from where it's a ten-minute walk uphill to the youth hostel (last departure Mon–Fri 7.15pm, Sat & Sun 6.30pm; ✆9999 3492 for times; $6 return). For no extra charge the same friendly ferry service will also drop you off and pick you up from **Scotland Island** at the southern end of Pittwater, which it stops at on the 40-minute round trip from Church Point. The bush-clad island is residential only with no sealed roads or shops, just a school, a kindergarten and a bush fire brigade, and makes for an interesting wander. Otherwise, there's a 24-hour service to Halls Wharf with Pink Water Taxi (mobile ℂ018/238 190). There are two **direct buses** to Church Point: #E86 from Central Station or #156 from Manly Wharf. Alternatively, bus #190 from Wynyard runs up the coast to Newport, where you can have a drink at the *Newport Hotel* and then catch a water taxi.

Pittwater Accommodation

The Basin Campground (bookings ℂ9451 8124).
Minimal facilities so bring all food supplies with you; book in advance.

YHA Hostel, ten minutes' walk uphill from Halls Wharf ℂ9999 2196, fax 9997 4296.
This rambling old house is surrounded by bush, with a verandah where you can feed rainbow lorikeets and look down onto the water. Bring supplies with you – the last food (and bottle) shop is at Church Point. Bookings are essential. Rooms ①, dorms ①.

THE HAWKESBURY RIVER

One of New South Wales' prettiest rivers, with bush covering its sandstone banks for much of its course and some interesting old settlements alongside, including **Richmond** and **Windsor**, the **Hawkesbury River** has its source in the Great Dividing Range and flows out to sea at Broken Bay.

One of the rivers inlets, **Berowra Creek**, and its settlement of **Berowra Waters** is particularly delightful, and easily reached from Sydney's northern suburbs. For information about the many national parks along the river, contact the the NPWS in Sydney (*©*9247 8861) or at 370 Windsor Rd in Richmond (*©*4588 5247). Short of chartering your own boat, the best way to explore the river system is to take a cruise (see box p.299). You are advised not to swim in the river during or three days after heavy rain due to potential agricultural run-off and sewerage overflows, or if you see rubbish or the greenish tinge associated with a toxic algae.

Downstream: Berowra Waters

Sydneysiders have long escaped for a day-trip of culinary and scenic pleasure to the seclusion of **Berowra Waters**, a small boat-filled settlement on narrow **Berowra Creek** off the lower Hawkesbury. It can be reached by a 24-hour car ferry from Berowra Waters Road, which runs west off the Pacific Highway, 6km away (the turn-off is 12km north of Hornsby). Berowra train station is by the turn-off from the highway, and it's possible to walk along bush tracks to get to the ferry, though after lunch (see below) you'd face another 6km trek back. If you really want to lash out, you could charter a sea-plane to take you here from Rose Bay (see p.105).

....

For a good lunchtime nibble with a view try *Berowra Waters Boatshed Restaurant* **Berowra Waters Road** *©*9456 **1025. Lunch Wed–Sat, dinner Fri & Sat.**

....

Upstream: Wisemans Ferry

The first ferry across the Hawkesbury River was started by Solomon Wiseman in 1827, some way inland at the spot now known as **Wisemans Ferry**. The crossing forged an inland connection between Sydney and the Hunter Valley via the convict-built Great North Road. Unfortunately, travellers on this isolated route were easy prey for marauding bushrangers and it was largely abandoned for the longer but safer coastal route. Today it's a popular recreational spot for day-trippers – just a little over an hour from Sydney by car, and with access to the **Dharug National Park** over the river by a free 24-hour car ferry. Dharug's rugged sandstone cliffs and gullies shelter Aboriginal rock engravings which can be visited only on ranger-led trips during school holidays; there's a camping area at Mill Creek (call Gosford NPWS on ℗4324 4911 for details of both walks and camping bookings, which are essential for weekends and holidays). Open to walkers, cyclists and horse-riders but not vehicles, the **Old Great North Road** was literally carved out of the rock by hundreds of convicts from 1829.

Driving north of Wisemans Ferry along **Settlers Road**, another convict-built route, you'll come to **St Albans**, where the hewn sandstone *Settlers Arms Inn* was built in 1836, The pub is set on two-and-a-half acres and much of the fruit and veg for the delicious home-cooked food is organically grown on site.

The Upper Hawkesbury: Windsor and Richmond

About 50km inland from Sydney and just a few kilometres apart, Windsor and Richmond are two of five towns founded by Governor Macquarie in the early nineteenth century to capitalize on the fertile soil of the Upper Hawkesbury River area. You can take a **train** to Windsor and Richmond from Central Station.

Windsor is probably the best preserved of all the historic towns on the river, with a lively centre of narrow streets,

River Cruising

Cruises

Brooklyn, just above the western mass of Ku-Ring-Gai Chase National Park, and easily reached by train from Central Station, is the base for Hawkesbury River Ferries (bookings ©9985 7566) whose **River Boat Mail Run** still takes letters, as well as tourists, up and down the river. Departures are from Brooklyn Wharf on Dangan Road (Mon–Fri 9.30am; $25). They also offer coffee cruises towards the mouth of the river (Mon, Tues & Thurs 1.30pm, Sat 11am & 1.30pm, Sun 11am; 2hr; $12), plus a ferry service to Patonga at the edge of Brisbane Waters National Park (Mon–Thurs 1.30pm, Sat 11am & 1.30pm, Sun Brooklyn 11am; $5 one-way, $10 return; bikes $2).

Gosford's Public Wharf is the starting point for the *MV Lady Kendall* – also taking on passengers at **Woy Woy** – which cruises both Brisbane Water and Broken Bay (bookings ©4323 1655; Mon–Wed, Sat & Sun, daily during school holidays, Gosford 10.15am & 1pm, Woy Woy 10.35am and 12.10pm; 2hr 30min).

Windsor is the base for Windsor River Cruises (©9831 6630), with cruises Sun & Wed only: the coffee cruise (2hr 15min; $15), the Bridge to Bridge cruise from Windsor to Kangaroo Point in Brooklyn ($55 includes lunch at Wisemans Ferry; 8.30am–5.30pm), and the Tizzana Winery cruise including wine tasting and a smorgasboard lunch ($50; 6hr).

Boat and Houseboat rentals

The **Hawkesbury Boating Centre**, on Dangar Road, opposite the railway station in Brooklyn (©9985 7252) hires out small boats which seat up to eight people. For houseboats, the **New South Wales Travel Centre** in Sydney (©9667 6050) has details of operators with prices ranging from around $600–850 for a weekend.

spacious old pubs and numerous colonial buildings. The **Hawkesbury River Museum and Tourist Information Centre** on Thompson Square (daily 10am–4pm; ©4577 2310; museum $2.50) is a good place to start exploring, and the *Macquarie Arms Hotel*, claiming to be the oldest in Australia, is the best place to end up for a beer. From Windsor, Putty Road (Route 69) heads north through beautiful forest country, along the eastern edge of the Wollemi National Park (p.324), to the Hunter Valley (p.309).

Richmond's attractions include its unspoilt riverside setting, an old graveyard and settlers' dwellings. Cinema buffs could take in a bargain-priced film at the beautifully preserved Regent Twin Cinema (©4578 1800; Mon–Sat $7, Sun $5). Moving on, the **Bells Line of Road** (Route 40), from Richmond to Lithgow via Kurrajong, is a great scenic drive; all along the way are orchard fruit stalls stacked with produce from the valley. There's a wonderful view of the Upper Hawkesbury Valley from the lookout point at Kurrajong Heights, on the edge of the Blue Mountains, and you can take it all in from the *Balcony View Café*. Another scenic drive from Richmond to the Blue Mountains, emerging near Springwood (p.318), is south along the Hawkesbury Road, with the Hawkesbury Heights Lookout halfway along providing panoramic views.

Hawkesbury Accommodation

Del Rio Riverside Resort, Webbs Creek across the Webbs Creek ferry, 3km south of Wisemans Ferry ©4566 4330, fax 4566 4358.

Campsite also with en-suite cabins, a Chinese restaurant, swimming pool, tennis court and golf course. Cabins ③–④.

Hawkesbury Heights YHA Hostel, Hawkesbury Rd, Hawkesbury Heights ©9261 1111.

Not far from the Hawkesbury Heights Lookout is the brand-new solar-powered youth hostel with good views from its secluded bush setting, and no crowds. ①.

Rosevale Farm Resort 3km along Wisemans Ferry Rd en route to Gosford ©4566 4207.

Inexpensive camping in extensive bushland close to Dharug National Park; vans ②.

Settlers Arms Inn Settlers Road, St Albans ©4568 2111.

Colonial inn; rooms come with brass beds and other old-fashioned touches but with modern en-suite bathrooms. ⑤–⑥.

Wisemans Ferry Inn, Old Great North Rd, Wisemans Ferry ©4566 4301.

An old inn dating from 1817, with characterful rooms upstairs sharing bathrooms and en-suite motel-style rooms outside at the back. Bistro meals are served daily. ②–③.

The Central Coast

The shoreline between Broken Bay and Newcastle, known as the **Central Coast**, is characterized by large **coastal lakes** – saltwater lagoons almost entirely enclosed, but connected to the ocean by small waterways. To travel anywhere on the Central Coast, you need to go through **Gosford**, perched on the north shore of Brisbane Water and just about within commuting distance of Sydney. Its proximity to the city has resulted in uncontrolled residential sprawl which has put a great strain on the once-unspoilt lakes. Around Gosford are two excellent **national parks**, one giving an insight into Sydney's past in the form of **Old Sydney Town**, and the other, the nearby **Australian Reptile Park**, offering lots of native creepy crawlies and scaly things. Beyond the national parks, **Pearl Beach** and nearby **Patonga** are idyllic bay beach retreats while on the ocean, **Terrigal**, **Avoca** and **The Entrance** are all enjoyable holiday resorts. For tourist information on the whole region, and accommodation bookings, call **Central Coast Tourism** (free call ✆1800/806 258) or drop into their offices near Gosford CityRail at 200 Mann St (Mon–Fri 9am–5pm, Sat 9.30am–3pm, Sun 10am–2pm; ✆4385 4074), or at Terrigal and The Entrance.

Transport on the coast

If you're **driving**, and want to enjoy the coastal scenery and lakes, follow the Pacific Highway rather than the speedier Sydney–Newcastle Freeway. The **train** to Gosford or Woy Woy also follows a very picturesque route. Central Coast Airbus (✆4332 8655) gets you to the area direct from Sydney airport on several **bus** services daily (also picking up in the city): stops include Gosford, Terrigal and The Entrance. The fit and intrepid can go by **bike**: from Manly head up the northern beaches, hop on the Palm Beach Ferry from Barrenjoey Road, Palm Beach Wharf (✆9918 2747) to Patonga, then continue up through Woy Woy and Gosford to the coast.

Within the Central Coast area a well-developed **bus service** is run by a collection of operators: Busways Peninsula (✆4362 1030), Busways Central Coast (✆4392 6666), Gosford Bus Service (✆4325 1781), Peninsula Bus Lines (✆4324 1255 or 4362 1188) and The Entrance Red Bus Services (✆4332 8655).

You can also take a **ferry** from Palm Beach to Patonga and walk from there to Pearl Beach. For **taxis**, call ✆13 1008.

OLD SYDNEY TOWN

Map 2, E5. Wed–Sun 10am–4pm, daily school & public holidays; $17. Peninsula Bus Lines #38 from Gosford CityRail.

Old Sydney Town, southwest of Gosford just off the Pacific Highway, is a reconstruction of Sydney as it looked in the early years of the penal settlement. "Everyday" scenes, such as a convict's escape or a flogging, are acted out, and a token gesture towards Aboriginal culture has been made in the form of a Koorie Trading Post, which sells souvenirs. Many bus companies include it in their itineraries (see box above).

OLD SYDNEY TOWN |

AUSTRALIAN REPTILE PARK

Map 2, E5. Daily 9am–5pm; $11.95. ©4340 1022 for feeding times and wildlife shows.

Next door to Old Sydney Town, is the **Australian Reptile Park**. Over the years the park has provided a very useful public service producing serum from snake and spider venom. You can watch snakes and funnel web spiders being milked of their venom, but less fearsome hands-on interaction is also available: you can pat Eric, the giant crocodile, touch a python, or hand-feed kangaroos – the landscaped bush setting is also home to a bunch of furrier native creatures.

BRISBANE WATER AND BOUDDI NATIONAL PARKS

Brisbane Water National Park, immediately south of Gosford, is the site of the **Bulgandry Aboriginal engravings**, which are of a style unique to the Sydney region featuring figurative outlines scratched boldly into sandstone. The site, no longer frequented by the Guringgai people – whose territory ranged south as far as Sydney Harbour and north to Lake Macquarie – is 7km southwest of Gosford off the Woy Woy Road. Tiny **Bouddi National Park** is 20km southeast along the coast, at the northern mouth of Broken Bay, and is a great spot for bushwalking with camping facilities at Putty Beach, Little Beach and Tallow Beach: book through the NPWS office at 207 Albury St, Gosford (©4324 4911), which has information on both parks.

PEARL BEACH AND PATONGA

Surrounded by Brisbane Water National Park, undeveloped **Pearl Beach** is a small community which expands with holiday-makers on weekends. The place is decidedly friendly and very peaceful – not even a bottle shop – so don't expect wild beach parties. But the very pretty, sheltered beach, popular with families, has a relaxing open access saltwater pool at one end (perfect for a discreet night-time skinny-dip). You can walk from the end of Crystal Avenue to the neighbouring beach settlement of **Patonga** visiting a lookout and the open access **Crommelin Native Arboretum** en route. The best day to undertake the 45-minute walk is the last Sunday of the month when the **Patonga Beach market** is held (8am–4pm) with arts and crafts, food stalls and buskers.

To get to Pearl Beach or Patonga, you can take the Busways Peninsula **bus** (℗4362 1030) from Woy Woy train station; you can also get to Patonga by ferry from Palm Beach (p.127). If you want to stay, contact Pearl Beach Real Estate next to the general store (℗4341 7555, fax 4341 9665), a friendly establishment dealing in **holiday lets** ($400–700 per week). The **general store** (daily 8am–6pm) also sells petrol and gas, and there are a couple of phones and a post box outside.

Eating

Pearls on the Beach ℗4342 4400 bookings advised. Closed Mon–Wed, no dinner Sun.
Prime beachfront location offering well-priced Australian fare with plenty of seafood on the menu. Licensed & BYO.

Sit 'n' Chats Beach Cafe ℗4341 3686. Daily 8am–5pm, dinner Fri–Sun and daily school holidays.
Opposite the restaurant, you can get gourmet burgers, oysters and calamari, or just coffee and cake. There's a special Sunday brekkie for $15 and Sunday afternoon jazz. BYO.

EATING

Central Coast outdoor activities

The Central Coast offers endless aquatic antics. Central Coast Adventures (©4381 0326) organizes abseiling and canyoning; Central Coast Kayak Tours (©4381 0342) offers kayaking trips from $75; Central Coast Surf School (©4382 1541) gives surfing lessons (1hr 30min; $15, including gear) on weekends at local beaches. Erina Sail & Ski Hire (©4365 2355) offer beginners' sailboarding lessons on Terrigal Lake on summer weekends (1hr 30min; $15). There's also good diving around The Entrance (p.308) with Pro Dive Central Coast, 96 The Entrance Rd (©4334 1559), arranging scuba-diving lessons and daily boat dives.

TERRIGAL

Twelve kilometres southeast of Gosford, **Terrigal** is one of the most enjoyable spots on the Central Coast, a family-oriented, laid-back, beach resort having a well-developed café culture with foodie inclinations. **Central Coast Tourism** at Rotary Park, Terrigal Drive (summer daily 9am–5pm, winter closed Sun; ©4385 4074; free accommodation bookings), is a good source of information on the whole region. To **get** to Terrigal, take Peninsula Bus Lines #80, #81 or #82 from Gosford CityRail; #81 also links Terrigal and Avoca Beach.

Accommodation

Holiday Inn Resort Cnr The Esplanade and Pine Tree Lane ©4384 9111, fax 4384 5798.
Huge swanky beachfront hotel with three restaurants and a nightclub; facilities include a pool, gym and tennis courts. Rates rise on weekends, with a two-night minimum stay. ⑦, Fri & Sat ⑧.

Hunters Real Estate 104 Terrigal Esplanade ℂ4384 1444.
Holiday unit lets; around $350–950 weekly, depending on season
and number of rooms.

Terrigal Beach Backpackers Lodge 12 Campbell Crescent ℂ &
fax 4385 3330.
De luxe friendly YHA-affiliated hostel footsteps from the beach, also
offering a pleasant dining room and garden with BBQ. There are
facilities for the disabled. Bikes provided free. Rooms ①, dorms ①.

Eating

The Boatshed 84 The Esplanade. ℂ4384 1049. Daily
8am–5.30pm.
Specializing in good-value all-day breakfasts and gourmet
sandwiches and burgers.

Galley Beach House East end of Terrigal Beach ℂ4385 3222.
Fabulous views over the water compete with fabulous contemporary
cuisine given a Mediterranean/Middle Eastern twist. BYO.

Patcino's Church St near the YHA hostel ℂ4385 1960. Daily
8am–5.30pm, Fri & Sat until 9pm.
Terrigal's best café, tucked away in a side street, offers good cakes,
excellent coffee and open sandwiches. On Fri and Sat nights an
Indonesian chef takes over. BYO.

AVOCA BEACH

Six kilometres to the south of Terrigal, and altogether quieter, **Avoca Beach** is especially popular with surfers. A
large, crescent-shaped and sandy beach between two headlands, it has its own surf lifesaving club – and a safe children's rock pool. A pleasant smalltown atmosphere is
enhanced by the cute **Avoca Beach Theatre** on Avoca

AVOCA BEACH

Drive (©4382 2156), a well-preserved early-1950s cinema. Peninsula Bus Lines serves Avoca Beach: take **bus** #79 from Gosford CityRail.

Accommodation and eating

There's no accommodation right on the beach at Avoca, unless you go through an agent such as George Brand Real Estate ©4382 1311, where weekly holiday house rental rates start at $350.

The Palms 160 The Round Drive, Avoca ©4382 1227.
Upmarket cabin park (no camping) 1.5km from the beach but with a pool. Poolside cabins and bush-set villas are all two-bedroom en-suites. Weekends are dearer. Villas ③, cabins ④.

Beachfront Café and Restaurant Avoca Beach ©4382 1622.
Daily 9am–late. A good place to hang out on the beachfront and chow down suitably fishy dishes. The café also lays on weekend entertainment, ranging from bands to poetry readings.

THE ENTRANCE

Further north of Avoca, Tuggerah and Munmorah lakes meet the sea at **The Entrance**, a beautiful spot with water extending as far as the eye can see. Naturally it's a favourite fishing spot and a posse of **pelicans** turn up for the daily fish-feeds at 3.30pm at Memorial Park, on Marine Parade. The **Entrance Visitors Centre**, Marine Parade (daily 9am–5pm; ©4385 4074), can help with accommodation.

The beaches and lakes along the coast from here to Newcastle are crowded with caravan parks and motels, and with places offering the opportunity to fish, windsurf, sail or waterski: although less attractive than places further north, they make a great day-trip or weekend escape from Sydney.

The Hunter Valley

I n Australia, and, increasingly, worldwide, the **Hunter Valley** is synonymous with fine **wine**: the first vines were planted 150 years ago, and are mainly the two classic white-wine varieties of Semillon and Chardonnay, with Pinot Noir and Shiraz dominating the reds. The reason to come here is to indulge in some **wine tasting** at some of the more than sixty wineries that fill the lower and the upper valley. Alongside them, there's some very salubrious accommodation and a fine-dining scene – all well enjoyed by weekending Sydneysiders out to pamper themselves.

In what seems a bizarre juxtaposition, the Hunter is also a very important coal-mining region, in the upper part of the valley especially. By far the best-known area, however, is in the **Lower Hunter Valley** around the old country town of **Cessnock,** which lies more or less due west of Newcastle, in an area of small creeks and tributaries of the Hunter River. But even in the main valley of the Hunter, followed by the New England Highway as it heads up towards the mountains of the Great Dividing Range and the New England Plateau, the impression is overwhelmingly rural, with green meadows and pastures interspersed with corn-fields, vegetable patches, forested ridges, red-soiled dirt tracks, and, of course, vineyards. Old mansions and sleepy hamlets, dating back to colonial times, complete the seemingly idyllic pastoral scene. Yet nearby coal is extracted from several enormous open-cast mines to feed Newcastle's power stations. The area is dotted with interesting old country towns: even **Maitland** and **Singleton**, two of the main centres of the coal industry in the Upper Hunter Valley, boast buildings that help retain a beguilingly colonial flavour.

....

The area covered in this chapter is on colour map 2

....

WOLLOMBI, CESSNOCK AND POKOLBIN

Wollombi, a homesteading settlement 30km south of Cessnock, is the gateway to the Hunter Valley on the scenic inland route from Sydney, which involves leaving the freeway at Calga and heading north via Mangrove and Bucketty. The *Wollombi Tavern*, home of Dr Jurd's Jungle Juice (have a free taste and find out), makes a fine refreshment stop, sitting out on the wooden verandah looking over the creek to trees, fields and hills beyond. Wollombi was once a ceremonial meeting place, and there are **Aboriginal rock carvings** and cave paintings throughout the area, some of which can be visited on horseback with the Wollombi Horse Riding Centre (℡4998 3221; 2hr including 30min lesson; $30), 4km past the tavern on the Singleton Road. They also offer fully equipped cabin accommodation (④) and riverside camping.

The Lower Hunter's main town, **Cessnock**, is uninteresting in itself, and surprisingly unsophisticated given the wine culture surrounding it; its big old country pubs are probably its best feature and staying in one provides a taste of Australian rural life. Most of the vineyards and accommodation is around **Pokolbin**, at the centre of the vineyards, 12–15km northwest of Cessnock, and with your own transport you'd be better off basing yourself out here. Pick up the excellent free maps and brochures on the Hunter Valley from the NSW Travel Centre in Sydney or the **Cessnock Visitors Centre**, at Turner Park, Abedare Road (Mon–Fri 9am–5pm, Sat 9.30am–5pm, Sun 9.30am–3.30pm; ©4990 4477; *www.winecountry.com.au*); the latter can also book accommodation.

To get to Cessnock, catch a **train** from Central Station to Newcastle and then a bus to Cessnock with Rover Motors (©4990 1699). By **bus**, Keans Travel Express (©9281 9366) goes direct from Sydney to the Hunter Valley once daily, taking just over two hours with stops including Kurri Kurri, Neath, Cessnock and Pokolbin. Otherwise there is no public transport in the valley. Instead of **hiring a car** in Sydney, you could pick one up in Newcastle: Ara (©4962 2488), or Thrifty (©4942 2266) do reasonable deals.

WINERIES

More than sixty wineries cluster around the Hunter Valley, and almost all of them offer tastings and are interesting to visit. There are also a few gems in the upper valley, around Wybong and Denman, west of Muswellbrook. Try to tour the wineries during the week; at weekends both the number of visitors and the prices go up. In February, when the place is flooded with wine-lovers enjoying the Dionysian delights of the **Hunter Valley Vintage Festival** accommodation becomes difficult to find. Another lively time is October, when Wyndham Estate hosts **Opera in the Vineyards** (free call ©1800/675 875), followed by the **Jazz in the Vines Festival** held on the last Saturday in October (©4938 1345) based at Tyrrell's.

Vineyard Tours

If you don't have wheels – or would prefer not to meander off-road after excessive wine-tasting – **vineyard tours** are a

Hunter Valley wineries

Lower Hunter

Allandale Winery Lovedale Rd, Pokolbin ©4990 4526. Mon–Sat 9am–5pm, Sun 10am–5pm. Picturesque small winery with great views overlooking the vineyard, the Lower Hunter and the Brokenback Range. They're happy for you to visit during vintage time, when you can see the small operation in action; try their prize-winning Chardonnay.

Drayton's Family Wines Oakey Creek Rd, Pokolbin ©4998 7513. Mon–Fri 8am–5pm, Sat & Sun 10am–5pm. Friendly, down-to-earth family winery, established for over 140 years. In that time they've become well known for their ports: the lucky might get a taste of Old Decanter, aged 21 years.

Hermitage Road Cellars and Winery Hunter Resort, Hermitage Rd, Pokolbin ©4998 7777. Daily 10am–5pm; tour 11am & 2pm. The largest commercial winery, lacking in atmosphere but offering informative wine tours: booking essential.

Kevin Sobels Wines Cnr Broke and Halls roads, Pokolbin ©4998 7766. Daily 9am–5pm. Set up in 1992, the welcome at this small, simple winery is wonderfully down to earth, and includes a greeting by Bacchus, the resident St Bernard.

Lindemans Wines McDonalds Rd, Pokolbin ©4998 7684. Mon–Fri 9am–4.30pm, Sat & Sun 10am–4.30pm. One of the best-known names in the valley; Dr Lindeman first planted vines in the valley in 1842. Its museum has a collection of winemaking paraphernalia.

Scarborough Wine Co Gilliards Rd, Pokolbin ©4998 7563. Daily 9am–5pm. Small, friendly winery specializing in

Chardonnay. Relaxed tastings are held in a small cottage with prime valley views.

Tamburlaine Wines McDonalds Rd, Pokolbin ℂ4998 7570. Daily 9.30am–5pm. The jasmine-scented garden outside gives a hint of the flowery elegant wines within. The range is too small even for the domestic market, so you can only buy it here.

Tyrrell's Family Vineyard Broke Rd, Pokolbin ℂ4998 7509. Mon–Sat 8am–5pm, with tour Mon–Fri 1.30pm. Oldest independent family vineyards, producing consistently good wines. The tiny slab hut, where Edward Tyrrell lived when he began the winery in 1858, is still on the grounds.

Verona Vineyard & The Small Winemakers Centre McDonalds Rd, Pokolbin ℂ4998 7668. Daily 10am–5pm. Sells wines produced by four other small vineyards; $2 tasting charge on some wines is refunded on purchases. Excellent café.

Upper Hunter

Cruikshank Callatoota Estate Wybong Rd, Wybong, 18km north of Denman ℂ6547 8149. Daily 9am–5pm. Winemaker John Cruikshank is a real character who unapologetically only makes his favourite, red wine.

Reynolds Yarraman Yarraman Road, Wybong ℂ6547 8127. Mon–Sat 10am–4pm, Sun 11am–4pm. Tucked away in the upper valley, but worth seeking out for the beautiful location and the excellent, prize-winning wines.

Rosemount Estate Rosemount Rd, Denman ℂ6547 2467. Mon–Sat 10am–4pm, Sun 10.30am–4pm. Producer of some of Australia's best-known, award-winning wines, and with an excellent vineyard brasserie (closed Mon).

good option. Hunter Vineyard Tours (©4991 1659) runs small group bus tours visiting five well-chosen wineries over six hours, all offering tastings ($29, including pick-up from Cessnock; with Newcastle pick-ups $34; $16 extra with lunch). The more expensive Hunter Valley Day Tours (©4938 5031) will tailor-make tours to also include surrounding scenic areas such as Barrington Tops. Pedal power is also popular: either **rent bikes** from Grapemobile, corner of McDonalds and Gilliards roads, Pokolbin (© & fax 4991 2339; $25 per day, $15 half-day), or go on their **bicycle tour**, and take in six wineries ($89). You can also choose horsepower: Brokenback Trail Horse and Carriage Tour (©6574 7207) offers leisurely trips for up to eight people visiting 3–4 wineries; the $55 day-trip includes lunch with vineyard views. Wonderbus (©9555 9800; *www.wonderbus. com.au*) offer a $99 day-tour from Sydney to the Hunter Valley which also includes a dolphin cruise around Port Stephens.

ACCOMMODATION

Since the Hunter Valley is a popular weekend trip for Sydneysiders, accommodation **prices** rise on Friday and Saturday nights when many places only offer two-night deals; advance **booking** is essential.

Belford Country Cabins 659 Hermitage Rd, Pokolbin © & fax 6574 7100.
Family-run, fully equipped wooden bungalows for up to eight people. Great bushland location, with lots of wildlife spotted, small pool and playground. ③, Fri & Sat ⑤.

Bellbird Hotel 388 Wollombi Rd, Cessnock ©4990 1094.
Great classic country pub, circa 1900, with wide iron-lace verandah, 5km southwest from the centre of Cessnock. The public bar is full of country characters. Eat inexpensive no-frills bistro food in the

vine-covered and flower-filled beer garden. Rates include a generous cooked breakfast. ②, Fri ③, Sat ④.

The Convent Halls Rd, Pokolbin ©4998 7764, fax 4998 7323.
The swankiest place to stay in the Hunter Valley, but at a price (from $290 per night). The guesthouse has heaps of cosy cachet, fireplaces and low beams and is part of the Pepper Tree winery. Attached is the fine restaurant, ***Robert's at Pepper Tree***. B&B ⑧.

Elfin Hill Motel Marrowbone Rd, Pokolbin ©4998 7543, fax 4998 7817.
Friendly, family-run hilltop motel with extensive views. Comfortable units in timber cabins, all air-con. Facilities include a saltwater pool and barbecue area. Breakfast available. ④, Fri & Sat ⑥.

Neath Hotel Cessnock Rd, Neath ©4930 4270, fax 4930 4195.
B&B in a nicely furnished listed pub, 6km east of Cessnock. Only packages are offered on weekends (one or two nights), including full cooked breakfasts and dinner in the antique-filled restaurant. ②, Fri & Sat ④–⑥.

Pokolbin Cabins Palmers Lane, Pokolbin ©4998 7611, fax 4998 7873.
Extensive complex has two- and three-bedroom log cabins and five-bedroom homesteads, fully equipped with everything from linen to firewood. Swimming pool and tennis court in the shady grounds. ③, Fri & Sat min two nights ⑥.

Sussex Ridge Off Deaseys Rd, Pokolbin ©4998 7753, fax 4998 7359.
Guesthouse in a classic two-storey, tin-roofed homestead among extensive bushland, with great views from the balcony. All rooms are en-suite and facilities include open fires, a BBQ area and a pool. Cooked breakfast included. ⑥, Fri & Sat ⑦.

EATING

Most of the Hunter's many excellent restaurants are attached to the various wineries or are among the vineyards, while in the towns large old pubs dish out less fancy but more affordable grub. Over a mid-May weekend several wineries around Lovedale Road team up with local restaurants to host the gourmet **Lovedale Long Lunch** (©4930 7611), served amongst the vines. You can taste free samples of the Hunter Valley Cheese Company's handmade wares at their outlet at McGuigan Bros Winery, Broke Road, Pokolbin.

Amicos 138 Wollombi Rd, Cessnock ©4991 1995.

A popular cheap eat, this BYO restaurant serves Italian and Mexican food in a casual atmosphere; $5 pasta night Mon. Daily from 6pm.

Blaxlands Restaurant Broke Rd, Pokolbin ©4998 7550.

More than a hundred wines from the Hunter Valley are available at this well-regarded restaurant in an 1829 sandstone cottage. You can eat outside on the verandah. Licensed. Expensive. Booking advised.

Chez Pok *Pepper's Guesthouse*, Ekerts Rd, Pokolbin ©4998 7596.

Popular restaurant stylishly using local produce. The views overlooking vineyards are very pretty as is the antique-filled cottage interior. Daily breakfast to dinner. Licensed. Expensive.

Hermitage Restaurant Hunter Estate, Hermitage Rd, Pokolbin ©4998 7777.

Pleasant, rustic-style dining room with an imaginatively cooked menu focusing on NSW produce. Expensive. BYO & licensed.

The Hoot Café 115 Vincent St, Cessnock ©4991 2856.

Sydney style and prices in this bright and airy café with soul music playing. Gourmet sandwiches, tasty cakes and delicious stuffed potatoes. Mon–Fri 8am–4pm, Sat 8am–1pm.

Il Cacciatore Hermitage Lodge, cnr of McDonalds and Gillards roads, Pokolbin ©4998 7639.

EATING

Excellent upmarket Italian restaurant with a wide choice, including
fish dishes. Licensed & BYO.

Roberts at Pepper Tree The Convent, Halls Rd, Pokolbin ©4998
7330.
The place to head for a treat in a beautiful old farmhouse filled with
flowers. French rustic-style food emerges from wood-fired ovens.
Expensive; licensed.

Rothbury Café Rothbury Estate, Broke Rd, Pokolbin ©4998 7363.
A good, unpretentious lunch spot overlooking the vineyards of this
winery. Well-priced pizza and pasta of the day plus interesting
modern Australian dishes. Lunch daily.

The Blue Mountains

The section of the Great Dividing Range nearest Sydney gets its name from the blue mist that rises from millions of eucalyptus trees and hangs in the mountain air. In the early days of the colony, the **Blue Mountains** were believed to be an insurmountable barrier to the west and it was only in 1813, when the explorers Wentworth; Blaxland and Lawson finally conquered the mountains that the western plains were opened up for settlement. The range is surmounted by a plateau at an altitude of more than 1000m where, over millions of years, rivers have carved deep valleys into the sandstone creating a spectacular scenery of sheer precipices and walled canyons. Tourism snowballed after the arrival of the railway in 1868 and by 1900, the first three mountain stations of Wentworth Falls, Katoomba and Mount Victoria had been established as fashionable resorts.

All the villages and towns of the **Blue Mountains** – Glenbrook, Springwood, Wentworth Falls, Katoomba and Blackheath – lie on a ridge, connected by the Great Western Highway. Around them is the **Blue Mountains National Park**, to many, the best national park in New South Wales. The region makes a great weekend break from the city, with stunning views and clean air complemented by a wide range of accommodation, cafés and

Blue Mountains tours

From Katoomba

Fantastic Aussie Tours 283 Main St, Katoomba, by the train station ☏4782 1866. Their hop-on, hop-off Blue Mountains Explorer Bus links Katoomba, Leura, the Three Sisters, the Skyway and other lookouts via 18 stops (departs Katoomba hourly; day-ticket $18). Blue Mountains Highlights is a half-day coach tour ($34). There's a day-tour to the Jenolan Caves (daily $64–73) and a combined bushwalk and cave visit ($85).

Katoomba YHA (☏4782 1416; p.326) and **WonderBus** (below) both do less touristy Jenolan Caves tours from Katoomba (both around $50).

From Sydney

Blue Mountains Canyon Tours ☏ & fax 9371 5859. Exploring the Blue Mountains' deep canyons requires a mixture of abseiling down waterfalls, swimming through caves, and bushwalking. Wet canyoning is offered Oct–April, dry canyoning is available all year. Trips range from $79–219.

Wildframe ☏9314 0658. Two tours, the first for fit walkers, the second for lazier types. The Grand Canyon Eco-tour is a small group bushwalk through the Grand Canyon. You'll see kangaroos in the National Park and learn how to throw a boomerang; day-tour (8am–6pm; $55). The Blue Mountains Bush Tour ($76) more relaxed trip, with lunch at *Jemby-Rinjah Lodge* (see p.328).

Wonderbus ☏9555 9800 or 9261 1111. Good-value day-tours, including wildlife-watching and a satisfying bushwalk ($60). Overnight packages include abseiling ($180), the Jenolan Caves ($170), or horse-riding ($230).

restaurants. **Katoomba** is particularly good for those on a budget since it has four **hostels** to choose from, but with more cash you can indulge in some of the more unusual and characterful guesthouses in **Blackheath** and **Mount Victoria**.

Transport and information

CityRail trains leave from Central Station to Mount Victoria and follow the highway, stopping at all the major towns en route (frequent departures until about midnight; 2hr; $9.40 one-way to Katoomba, $11.20 return). If you're dependent on public transport, Katoomba makes the best base: facilities and services are concentrated here, and there are **buses** to local attractions and to other centres: the Katoomba–Woodford Bus Co (✆4782 4213) and Mountainlink (✆4782 3333). Buses leave town from Katoomba Street outside the *Carrington Hotel*.

Glenbrook has the **Blue Mountains Information Centre**, on the Great Western Highway (daily 9am–5pm; ✆4739 6266; *www.bluemts.com.au*), the place to pick up a huge amount of information about the area, including the very useful *Blue Mountains Wonderland Visitors Guide*, which has several detailed maps and the free listings guide *This Month in the Blue Mountains*. The other official tourist information centre is at **Echo Point**, near Katoomba (p.323); neither office books accommodation but they do issue vacancy listings. The **NPWS** has ranger stations at Wentworth Falls (see below) and Blackheath (p.327) where you can get comprehensive walking information.

WENTWORTH FALLS

The small village of **Wentworth Falls**, named after the explorer William Wentworth (see p.351), is home to the restored nineteenth-century **Yester Grange** (Mon–Fri 10am–4pm, Sat & Sun 10am–5pm; $5), filled with Victorian-era antiques and a fine watercolour collection, its neat gardens set off by their rugged bush backdrop (and there's a good tearoom).

Nearby, a signposted road leads from the Great Western Highway to the **Wentworth Falls Reserve**, with superb views of the waterfall tumbling down into the Jamison Valley. You can reach this picnic area from Wentworth train station by following **Darwin's Walk** – the route followed by the famous naturalist in 1836.

Most of the other bushwalks in the area start from the **Valley of the Waters Conservation Hut**, about 3km from the station at the end of Fletcher Street. Bus services are infrequent; a taxi from the station costs $6. The NPWS Hut, with a great café (daily 9am–5pm; ℰ4757 3827), is in a fantastic location overlooking the Jamison Valley. A wide selection of bushwalks, detailed on boards outside, ranges from the two-hour **Valley of the Waters track**, which descends into the valley, to a two-day walk to **Mount Solitary**. One of the most rewarding is the quite strenuous, six-kilometre **National Pass**, a walk which will conveniently get you back to the train station and takes in Wentworth Falls en route.

After the bushwalk stop off for a calories-horrific German-style pastry at *Patisserie Schwarz* **Renae Arcade, 30 Station St, Wentworth Falls. Closed Tues.**

LEURA

Just 2km east of Katoomba, the more upmarket **Leura**, packed with great cafés, art galleries and small boutiques, retains its own distinct identity and a real villagey atmosphere. The main street – The Mall – is secluded from the highway and its green median strip qualifies as a small park. Even the flower-filled station manages to look pretty, and indeed Leura is renowned for its beautiful **gardens**, some of which are open to the public during the **Leura Gardens Festival** (early to mid-Oct; $10 for visits to 8 gardens; details ⓒ4739 6266). Open all year round, though, is the **Everglades Gardens** (daily 9am–sunset; $5), situated in the grounds of an elegant mansion at 37 Everglades Ave. There are enjoyable views from its formal terraces, with a colourful display of azaleas and rhododendrons, an aboretum, and peacocks strutting among it all.

Not far from the village, the flowers give way to the bush: **Leura Cascades** can be viewed from the picnic area on Cliff Drive or take the two- to three-hour return walk to the base. A popular walking track from Leura Cascades is the **Federal Pass**, skirting the cliffs between here and **Katoomba Falls** (6km one-way; 2hr 30min). Other waterfalls in the area include the much-photographed **Bridal Veil Falls**, accessible from the Cascades picnic area, and **Gordon Falls**, which you can walk to from Lone Pine Avenue. To the east of Gordon Falls, Sublime Point Road leads to the aptly named **Sublime Point** lookout, with panoramic views of the Jamison Valley.

Eating

The Bakery Café 179 The Mall. Daily 7.30am–7.30pm.
A tiny but thriving place consisting of a counter with a few stools – and heavenly bakery products to consume with excellent coffee.

Brad's Mountain Deli 134 The Mall. Mon–Fri & Sun 9am–6pm, Sat 8am–6pm.
A big range of food at reasonable prices makes this a popular one

with the locals. Good-value sandwiches, yummy home-baked cakes, and friendly staff.

Landseers 178 The Mall. Daily 7.30am–5pm.
Small café with a very striking, cosy interior, and a sunny courtyard, offering big sandwiches and lasagne, plus choice cakes and puds.

KATOOMBA

Katoomba, the biggest town in the Blue Mountains and the area's commercial heart, is also the best located, though for all its surrounding charms, café culture and secondhand clothes and bookshops, it can still seem a little raw and characterless. When the town was discovered by fashionable city dwellers in the late nineteenth century, the grandiose **Carrington Hotel**, prominently located near the train station on the main strip, **Katoomba Street**, was the height of elegance, with its leadlighting and wood panelling. It has been beautifully renovated and now has accommodation, a restaurant and two cocktail bars. Also worth checking out on the main street, is the **Paragon Café** further downhill at 65 Katoomba St (Tues–Sun 10am–4pm), with its listed Art Deco interior and fabulous window and counter display of handmade chocs.

Edge Maxvision Cinema

The **Edge Maxvision Cinema**, at 225–237 Great Western Highway (℡4782 8928), has a huge six-storey cinema screen. The cinema was created as a venue to show *The Edge – The Movie*, a visually stunning introduction to the ecology of the Blue Mountains – and the joys of canyoning (daily 10am, 11.40am, 12.30pm, 2.50pm & 5.15pm; $12.50 new-releases cheap tickets Tues $6). The film's highlight is the segment about the "dinosaur trees", a stand of thirty-metre-high **Wollemi Pine**, previously known only from fossil material over sixty million years old. The trees – miraculously still existing – remain deep within a sheltered rainforest gully in the **Wollemi National Park**, north of Katoomba, and made headlines when they were first discovered in 1994.

Echo Point

A 25-minute walk south from the Katoomba train station (or by the Mountainlink bus departing daily 8am–2pm from outside the Savoy Theatre) will bring you to **Echo Point**, the location of the **information centre** (daily 9am–5pm; ✆4782 0756). From here you have breathtaking vistas that take in the Blue Mountains' most famous landmark, the **Three Sisters** (910m). These three gnarled rocky points take their name from an Aboriginal Dreamtime story which relates how the Katoomba people were losing a battle against the rival Nepean people: the Katoomba leader, fearing that his three beautiful daughters would be carried off by the enemy, turned them to stone, but was tragically killed before he could reverse his spell. They have stood here ever since, subjected to the indignities of persistent abseilers and kept awake at night by spectacular floodlighting. The Three Sisters are at the top of the **Giant Stairway**, the beginning of the very steep stairs into the three-hundred-metre-deep **Jamison Valley** below, where there are several walking tracks to places with such intriguing names as **Orphan Rock** and **Ruined Castle**. There's a popular walking route, taking about two hours and graded medium, down the stairway and partway along the **Federal Pass** to the **Landslide** and then taking the Scenic Railway (below) back up to the ridge.

The **Scenic Railway** at the end of Violet Street (daily 9am–5pm; last train up leaves at 4.50pm; $3, $4.50 return) can spare you entirely from the trek down into the Jamison Valley. Originally built to carry coal, this funicular railway glides down an impossibly steep gorge to the valley floor. Even more vertiginous is the **Skyway** (daily 9am–5pm; $4.50), a rickety-looking cable-car contraption that starts next to the railway and travels 350m across to the other side of the gorge and back again – you can't actually get off – giving those who can bear to look a bird's-eye view of Orphan Rock, Katoomba Falls and the Jamison Valley. The Scenic Railway complex features some divinely tacky structures from the 1970s, including a greasy-spoon **revolving restaurant** with great views.

Accommodation

The Cecil Guesthouse 108 Katoomba St ⓒ4782 1411, fax 4728 5364.

Very central choice, but back from the main drag. Has an old-fashioned 1940s atmosphere, with log fires, games room and tennis courts. No en-suite rooms. A hearty breakfast is included. B&B ④, weekends ⑤.

The Clarendon Cnr of Lurline and Waratah streets ⓒ4782 1322, fax 4782 2564.

Classic 1920s guesthouse with its own cocktail bar and restaurant, and cabaret shows on weekends. The guesthouse rooms are best – avoid the Seventies-style motel rooms. Budget rooms without bathroom are available. ③–⑤, weekend packages only ⑥–⑦.

Hydro-Majestic Hotel Great Western Highway, opposite Medlow Bath CityRail, 7km west of Katoomba ⓒ4788 1002, fax 4788 1063.

Luxurious, restored Art Deco hotel with magnificent views of the Megalong Valley, especially from the café balcony. Breakfast included; café (daily until 6pm) and restaurant (nightly). All rooms are en suite with hot drinks and telephone. ⑦, weekends ⑧.

ACCOMMODATION

Katoomba Mountain Lodge Church Lane, off Katoomba St ℭ & fax 4782 3933.

Central budget accommodation with great views over the town. Four-bed dorms and attractive doubles (sharing bathrooms) with window seats. Breakfast and dinner available. Rooms ②, ③ weekends, dorms ①.

Katoomba YHA Hostel 66 Waratah St ℭ4782 1416, fax 4782 6203.

Large, pleasant hostel in a charming old guesthouse with wood-combustion fires and a games room. Rooms are en suite and linen is supplied. Convenient for both town centre and Echo Point walks. Bike rental for guests and trips arranged. Reception open all day. Rooms ①, weekends ②, dorms ①.

Eating

Arjuna 16 Valley Rd, off the Great Western Highway ℭ4782 4662.
Excellent, authentic Indian restaurant. A bit out of the way, but positioned for spectacular sunset views, so get there early. BYO; non-smoking. Evenings from 6pm; closed Tues & Wed.

Avalon Restaurant First floor, 98 Main St, opposite Katoomba CityRail ℭ4782 5532. Dinner daily, plus lunch Thurs, Fri & Sun.
Stylish restaurant with the ambience of a quirky café. Moderately priced menu, but big servings and desserts to die for. BYO.

Blues Café 57 Katoomba St, Katoomba. Daily 9am–9pm.
Bakery and cosy vegetarian café – this place has been going for years and is as popular as ever.

Siam Cuisine 172 Katoomba St, Katoomba ℭ4782 5671.
Tues–Sun 11.30am–2.30pm & 5.30–10pm.
Crowded, inexpensive BYO Thai restaurant with $6 lunch specials.

Zuppa 36 Katoomba St, Katoomba ℭ4782 9247. Daily 8am–5pm and Fri & Sat night to 11pm.

Katoomba's trendiest café – amiable staff, Art Deco interior,
generous servings. Nothing over $7 during the day; different
menu on Fri and Sat night (bookings advised) but never more
than $15. Live music Fri night.

Drinking

The best place for a civilized **drink** is the *Carrington Bar* on
Katoomba Street, which features a piano player on Friday
nights and jazz on Saturday; or you could try your luck at
The Clarendon's salubrious little bar, mostly reserved for
guests, where there are also cabaret acts. On the other side
of the railway line, the huge late-opening *Gearins Hotel* is a
hive of activity, with several bars where you can play pool
and see bands.

BLACKHEATH

North of Katoomba, there are more lookout points at
Blackheath – just as impressive as Echo Point and much
less busy. One of the best is **Govetts Leap**, near the
NPWS **Blackheath Heritage Centre** (daily
9am–4.30pm; ✆4787 8877). The centre has good interpre-
tive material on history, flora and fauna, as well as practical
information (with plenty on the adjacent Wollemi and
Kanangra Boyd parks too). The two-kilometre **Fairfax
Heritage Track** from the NPWS Centre takes in the
Govett's Leap Lookout with its marvellous panorama of the
Grose Valley and Bridal Veil Falls. Although many walks
start from the centre, one of the most popular, **The Grand
Canyon**, begins from Evans Lookout Road at the south
end of town, west of the Great Western Highway. The village of Blackheath itself offers some good browsing in
antique shops.

The Zig Zag Railway

Map 2, B6. Departures from Clarence Mon–Fri 11am, 1pm & 3pm, Sat, Sun & holidays 10.30am, 12.15pm, 2pm & 3.45pm. From the Zig Zag platform add 40min to these times; $12; to check times call ℂ6353 1795.

Beyond Blackheath, drivers can circle back towards Sydney via the scenic **Bells Line of Road**, which heads back east through the fruit- and vegetable-growing areas of Bilpin and Kurrajong to Richmond, with growers selling their produce at roadside stalls. Situated 35km along the road at Clarence is the **Zig Zag Railway**. In the 1860s engineers were faced with the problem of how to get the main western railway line from the top of the Blue Mountains down the steep drop to the Lithgow Valley, so they came up with a series of zigzag ramps which fell into disuse in the early twentieth century, to be relaid by rail enthusiasts in the 1970s. Served by old steam trains, the picturesque line passes through two tunnels and over three viaducts. You can stop at points along the way and rejoin a later train. CityRail runs regular services between Sydney and Lithgow (via Katoomba and Mount Victoria) and will stop at a Zig Zag platform on request – remember to ask the guard to let you off.

Accommodation

Glenella 56 Govett's Leap Rd ℂ4787 8352, fax 4787 6114. Guesthouse in a charming 1905 homestead, surrounded by a beautiful garden. Rooms are furnished with antiques. Light breakfast $5 extra. ⑤–⑥.

Jemby-Rinjah Lodge 336 Evans Lookout Rd ℂ4787 7622, fax 4787 6230. Award-winning accommodation, calling itself an "eco-lodge", with

good links with National Park rangers and bushwalks organized
for guests who stay in distinctive timber cabins, with wood fires,
in bushland near the Grose Valley. Cabins sleep up to six people;
no linen but duvets supplied. ⑤, weekends ⑥.

Kanangra Lodge 9 Belvedere Ave ℂ4787 8715, fax 4787 7563.
Small, peaceful B&B with four rooms, all en suite, in a 1930s brick
house backing onto bush. Also offers open fireplaces in cosy
lounges. Run by a friendly couple who offer lots of local info. ⑥.

MOUNT VICTORIA

Secluded and homely **Mount Victoria**, one train stop on
from Blackheath, is the last mountain settlement proper,
and the only one with an authentic, unspoilt village feel.
There's a great old pub, the *Imperial*, and the best scones on
the mountain at the *Bay Tree Tea Shop*. Mount Victoria is
also fondly regarded for its quaint tiny **cinema**, Mount Vic
Flicks, Harley Avenue, off Station Street (ℂ4787 1577), in a
public hall, where the patron introduces the varied films
and defends his choice (Thurs–Sun, daily during school
holidays; cheaper tickets Thurs). Several antique shops and a
cluttered antiquarian and secondhand bookshop are worth a
browse. Some short **walks** start from the Fairy Bower
Picnic area, a ten-minute walk from the Great Western
Highway via Mount Piddington Road: get details from any
Blue Mountains tourist office.

Accommodation and eating

Victoria and Albert Guesthouse Station St ℂ4787 1241, fax
4787 1588.
Classy but friendly place with Art Deco features. Rooms are large
and there's a bar, civilized verandah café (Thurs–Sun 10am–5pm),
highly recommended restaurant (dinner nightly) in a wonderful old

Mountain activities

Canyoning is the big thing in the mountains: Blue Mountains Adventure Company, 84a Main St, Katoomba (℗4782 1271), offers beginners' canyoning and abseiling trips for $89–99 (full day, including lunch), rock-climbing, mountain-biking and caving. Within the handy outdoor equipment shop, Paddy Pallin, the Australian School of Mountaineering, 166b Katoomba St (℗4782 2014), is Katoomba's original **abseiling** outfit, offering abseiling courses (daily; $79 including lunch) plus a programme of canyoning, climbing and bush-survival courses. It also sells all camping gear and a good range of topographic maps and bushwalking guides. Great Australian Walks (℗9555 7580), offer **guided walks** in the Jenolan Caves area and along the 42-kilometre-long Six Foot Track from Katoomba to Jenolan Caves. High 'n' Wild Mountain Adventures, 3/5 Katoomba St (℗4782 6224), has a consistently good reputation for beginners' abseiling courses ($49 including lunch) plus canyoning ($65), rock-climbing ($55) and wilderness walks (from $49).

Cycle Tech, Gang Gang Street, opposite Katoomba CityRail (℗4782 2800), rents **mountain bikes** ($15 half-day, $25 full day). You can go horse riding with The Packsaddlers, Green Gully, Megalong Road, Megalong Valley (℗4787 9150; 1hr $20 or longer overnight rides), or Werriberri Trail Rides, Megalong Road, Megalong Valley (℗4787 9171), who offer **horse riding** for all abilities, pony rides for children and two-day camp-outs.

dining room, pool, spa and sauna. Breakfast included. ②, weekends ③.

Hotel Imperial Station St ℗4787 1233, fax 4787 1461.
Good-value, filling and tasty bistro meals can be eaten in the foyer, ballroom, verandah or garden of this classic old-fashioned country-style pub. Meals daily 8am–8.30pm. Spa and en-suite

rooms, shared bathroom options, and backpacker rooms. B&B rooms ④–⑦, weekends two-night packages only ⑦–⑧, dorms $20.

Bay Tree Tea Shop Station St. 10.30am–5pm; closed Wed–Fri. Family-run place in a converted Victorian cottage, and the best place in the mountains for scones and pots of real leaf tea.

THE JENOLAN CAVES

The **Jenolan Caves** lie 30km southwest across the mountains from Katoomba on the far edge of the Kanangra Boyd National Park – over 80km by road – and contain New South Wales' most spectacular limestone formations. There are nine visitable caves with entry prices ranging from $12 to $20 (daily, guided tours every 30min 9.30am–5pm). If you're coming for just a day, plan to see one or two caves: the best general cave is the Lucas Cave ($12), but a more spectacular one is the Temple of Baal ($14). Visitors are treated to stalactites and stalagmites that have dripped into weird contortions and have been given names, such as the "Sword of Michael" and "Gabriel's Wing". The system of nine limestone caves is surrounded by the **Jenolan Caves Reserve**, a fauna and flora sanctuary with picnic facilities and walking trails to small waterfalls and lookout points.

Ring Fantastic Aussie Tours (℡4782 1866) for details of transport and tours from Katoomba.

Accommodation

Forest Lodge 7km southeast of the caves on Caves Rd, Oberon Plateau ℡6335 6313.
Peaceful and pleasant place where all rooms are en suite and rates include a cooked breakfast. ⑤.

Jenolan Caves House Jenolan Caves ℭ6359 3304, fax 6359 3388.

This rather romantic old hotel found fame as a honeymoon destination in the 1920s. Make sure you get one of the characterful older rooms; food in the restaurant is good and plentiful. ⑤, en-suite ⑥, weekend ⑦.

Porcupine Hill Jenolan Cabins Oberon Rd, 5km west of Jenolan Caves ℭ & fax 6335 6239.

Modern, prize-winning place. Very reasonably priced well-equipped two-bedroom timber cabins with wood-fires accommodate six (bring your own linen) – all with magnificent bush views. ④.

Royal National Park

Beyond Botany Bay and Port Hacking, the Princes Highway and the Illawarra railway hug the edge of the **Royal National Park** for more than 20km, a huge nature reserve right on Sydney's doorstep, only 32km from the city. Established in 1879, it was the second national park to be founded in the world (after Yellowstone in the US). The railway between Sydney and Wollongong marks its western border, and from the train the scenery is fantastic – streams, waterfalls, rock formations and rainforest flora fly past the window. On the eastern side, from Jibbon Head to Garie Beach, the park falls away abruptly to the ocean, creating a spectacular coastline of steep cliffs broken by creeks cascading into the seas and little coves with fine sandy beaches.

Transport and information

Frequent CityRail **trains** leave Central Station stopping at Loftus, Engadine, Heathcote, Waterfall or Otford, good starting points for walking trails. The Sydney Tramway Museum at Loftus (p.324) provides a Parklink service on an old Sydney **tram** (Sun & public holidays hourly 9.15am–4.15pm; Wed on demand 9.30am–3.30pm; 30min; $4 return). An hourly **ferry** from Tonkin Street Wharf near Cronulla CityRail (p.132) crosses Port Hacking to the small settlement of **Bundeena** at the park's northeast tip (Cronulla National Park Ferries ✆9523 2990; April–Oct Mon–Fri 8.30am–5.30pm; Nov–March Mon–Fri 5.30am–6.30pm except 12.30pm, Sat & Sun 8.30am–6.30pm; $2.40); narrated cruises of Port Hacking are also available (Mon, Wed, Fri & Sun 10.30am; 3hr; $10).

You can **drive** in or exit at three points off the Princes Highway, near Loftus, Waterfall and Stanwell Park ($7.50 entry; gates open 24-hour), with roads to beaches at Garie Beach, Wattamolla and Bundeena (Garie and Wattamolla gates shut around 8pm). Coming in at the northern end near Loftus, you can visit the **NPWS Visitor Centre** (daily 8.30am–4.30pm; ✆9542 0648), by the Parklink tram terminus, or it's a 2km walk from Loftus CityRail; for a scenic drive, exit just south of Otford at **Stanwell Park** on Laurence Hargrave Drive, where you can watch hang-gliders swooping down from the top of Laurence Hargrave Lookout.

Sydney Tramway Museum

Map 2, D7. Wed 9.30am–3.30pm, Sun 10am–5pm; last entry one hour before closure. $10 includes unlimited tram rides. Parklink only $4 return. Loftus CityRail.

Trams operated in Sydney for a century, until 1961, and examples of the old Sydney fleet, including a Bondi tram, as well as trams from around the world, including ones from San Francisco, Nagasaki and Berlin are on display here. You can also ride a tram on the three-kilometre line which heads via bushland towards Sutherland. Another two kilometre track heads into the park to the NPWS office (above), offering an easy 1km path to a lookout. There's a kiosk and picnic facilities at the museum.

Walks and beaches

The ultimate trek is the spectacular 26km **Coastal Walk**, taking in the entire coastal length of the park. Give yourself two days to complete it, beginning at either Otford or Bundeena, camping overnight at one of several bush camps en route. Undertaking part of the route is also satisfying, such as the popular trail from **Otford** down to beachfront **Burning Palms** (2hr one-way; no camping). To begin the Coastal Walk from Bundeena, beyond the ferry wharf follow Loftus Street 1km to the national park gate. A pleasant half-day walk to pretty sheltered **Little Marley Beach** for a swim and a picnic (2hr one-way) is one shorter option – or head down a pathway to **Jibbons Beach**, a 30-minute stroll along which will bring you to some rock engravings of the Dharawal people, one of about eighty **Aboriginal art sites** around Port Hacking.

The easy 1km **Bungoona Path** from the tram terminus and NPWS Centre to the Bungoona Lookout boasts panoramic views and is wheelchair-accessible. Not far south, reachable by road, **Audley** is a picturesque picnic ground on the **Hacking River**, where you can rent a boat or canoe for a leisurely paddle. Deeper into the park, on the ocean shore, **Wattamolla** and **Garie beaches** have good surfing waves (both patrolled summer weekends and school holidays). Wattamolla has extensive grassy picnic grounds on the banks of Wattamolla Creek and a kiosk; about a 30-minute walk uphill, part of the creek has been dammed to form an idyllic waterhole, perfect for a swim on a hot day. The less pretty, shadeless Garie Beach has a Surf Life Saving Club and a kiosk.

A good book to buy is the *Royal National Park on Foot* by Alan Fairley ($8.95; Enviro Books), and try to get a copy of the *Royal National Park* map ($5.50); both available at the NPWS Visitor Centre (opposite).

Camping, accommodation and supplies

There's a small, very basic but secluded YHA **youth hostel** inside the park 1km from Garie Beach (book in advance at YHA head office ☏9261 1111; key collected from there or at Waterfall; $7), with no electricity or showers. There are also six designated **bushcamps** which have no facilities or drinking water – most popular of these is **Curracurrong**, a pretty little bay with popular campsites along Curracurrong Creek near Wattamolla. Open fires are banned so bring a cooking stove, and either your own water or sterilizing tablets. The campsites require a permit (free) from the NPWS Visitor Centre (see p.334): book at least a week in advance if you can, or for more spontaneity, phone up to check site availability. The NPWS also have a campsite with hot showers and toilets at the **Bonnie Vale Camping Ground** just west of Bundeena within the park, on the shores of the Hacking River (site $10 per night). For more comfort, *Bundeena Caravan Park* (☏9523 9520; cabins ①–②), also has cabins, and the settlement has a general store and café.

CONTEXTS

A brief history of Sydney

Pre-history and Aboriginal occupation

The first European settlers who arrived at Botany Bay in 1788 saw Australia as *terra nullius* – empty land – on the principle that Aborigines didn't "use" the country in an agricultural sense. However, decades of archeological work, the reports of early settlers and oral tradition have established a minimum date of forty thousand years for human occupation, and evidence that Aboriginal peoples shaped and controlled their land as surely as any farmer.

In the area around Sydney, there were about 3000 Aboriginal inhabitants at the time of colonization, divided into two tribes organized and related according to complex kinship systems, and with two different languages and several dialects: the **Eora**, who settlers called the coast tribe, and the **Dharug**, who lived further inland. Common to the two tribes was a belief that land, wildlife and people were an interdependent whole, engendering a sympathy for the natural processes, and maintaining a balance between population and natural resources. Legends about the mythical **Dreamtime**, when creative forces roamed the land, provided **verbal maps** of tribal territory and linked natural features to the actions of these Dreamtime ancestors.

The early records of the colony mainly describe the lifestyle and habits of the **Eora people**, whose staple diet being fish and seafood made temporary camps close to the shore, usually sleeping in the open by fires. Even in the winter they went naked. Shaping canoes from a single piece of bark they would fish on the harbour using fish hooks made from shells attached to fishing lines of bark fibre or spear-fished from rocks with multipronged wooden spears spiked with kangaroo teeth. The fish diet was supplemented by the hunting of kangaroo and other game and gathering plants such as yams. Besides storytelling and ceremonial dancing, other cultural expression was through **rock engraving**, usually of outlines of creatures such as kangaroo and fish.

The first Europeans

Although earlier attempts had been made to locate and map the continent, by the Dutch, Spanish and French, it was only with the *Endeavour* expedition headed by Captain **James Cook** that a concerted effort was made. Cook had headed to Tahiti (where scientists observed the movements of the planet Venus), then mapped New Zealand's coastline before sailing west in 1770 to search for the Great Southern Land.

The British arrived at **Botany Bay** in April of 1770; Cook commented on the Aborigines' initial indifference to seeing the *Endeavour* but when a party of forty sailors attempted to land, two Aborigines attacked them with spears and had to be driven off by musket fire. The party set up camp for eight days, where botanist **Sir Joseph Banks** studied, collected and recorded specimens of the unique plant and animal life. Continuing up the Queensland coast, after entering the treacherous passages of the Great Barrier Reef, running aground and stopping for six weeks to repair the *Endeavour*, Cook successfully managed to navigate the rest of the reef, finally claiming Australia's eastern seaboard – which he named **New South Wales** – on August 21 1770.

Founding of the colony of NSW

The outcome of the American War of Independence in 1783 saw Britain deprived of anywhere to transport convicted criminals; they were temporarily housed in prison ships or "hulks", moored around the country, while the government tried to solve the problem. Sir Joseph Banks advocated Botany Bay as an ideal location for a **penal colony** that could soon become self-sufficient. The government agreed and in 1787 the **First Fleet**, carrying over a thousand people, 736 of them convicts, set sail on eleven ships under the command of Captain **Arthur Phillip**. Reaching Botany Bay in January 1788, they expected the "fine meadows" that Captain Cook had described. What greeted them was mostly swamp, scrub and sand dunes which Phillip deemed unsuitable for his purposes, moving the fleet north, to the well-wooded **Port Jackson**.

In the first three years of settlement, the colonists suffered erratic weather and **starvation**, soil which appeared to be agriculturally worthless, and Aboriginal hostility. The Eora's land had been invaded, half of their numbers wiped out by smallpox, and they were also starving as the settlers shot at their game. When supply ships did arrive, they usually came with hundreds more convicts to further burden the colony.

It was not until 1790, when land was successfully farmed further west at **Parramatta**, that the hunger began to abate. To ease the situation, Phillip granted packages of farmland to marines and former convicts before he returned to Britain in 1792. The first **free settlers** arrived in 1793, while war with France reduced the numbers of convicts being transported to the colony.

The Rum Corps and Governor Macquarie

After Phillip's departure in 1792, the military, known as the **New South Wales Corps** (or more familiarly as "the rum corps"), soon became the supreme political force in the colony. Headed by **John Macarthur**, they soon manipulated the temporary governor, Major Francis Grose, into becoming the governor's strong arm. Exploiting their access to free land and cheap labour, they became rich farm-owners and virtually established a currency based on their monopoly, rum. Events culminated in the **Rum Rebellion** of 1808, when merchant and pastoral factions, supported by the military, ousted mutiny-plagued Governor **William Bligh**, formerly of the *Bounty* who had attempted to restore order. Britain finally took notice of the colony's anarchic state, and resolved matters by appointing the firm-handed Colonel **Lachlan Macquarie**, backed by the 73rd Regiment, as Bligh's replacement in 1810. Macquarie settled the various disputes – Macarthur had already fled to Britain – and brought the colony eleven years of disciplined progress.

Macquarie has been labelled the "Father of Australia", for his vision of a country that could rise above its convict origins; he implemented enlightened policies towards former convicts or **emancipists**, enrolling them in public offices. The most famous of these was **Francis Greenway**, the convicted forger who he appointed civil architect, and with whom Macquarie set about an ambitious programme of public buildings and parks. But he offended those who regarded the colony's prime purpose as a place of punishment.

In 1821 Macquarie's successor Sir Thomas Brisbane was instructed to segregate, not integrate, convicts. To this end, New South Wales officially graduated from being a penal settlement to a new British Colony in 1823, and convicts were used to colonize newly explored regions – Western Australia, Tasmania and Queensland – as far away from Sydney's free settlers as possible. By the 1840s the transportation of convicts to New South Wales had ended (the last shipment of convicts arrived in Van Dieman's Land in 1853).

The Victorian Era

Australia's first **goldrush** occurred in 1851 near Bathurst, west of Sydney. Between 1850 and 1890 Sydney's population jumped from 60,000 to 400,000; terrace houses were jammed together, and with their decorative cast iron railings and balconies, they remain one of Sydney's most distinctive heritage features. The first railway line, to Granville near Parramatta, was built in 1855. However, until the 1880s tramway system most people preferred living in the city centre within walking distance of work.

During this Victorian era Sydney's population became even more starkly divided into the haves and the have-nots: self-consciously replicating life in the mother country, the genteel classes took tea on their verandahs and erected grandiloquent monuments such as the Town Hall, the Strand Arcade and the Queen Victoria Building in homage to English architecture of the time. Meanwhile, the poor lived in slums where disease, crime, prostitution and alcoholism were rife. An outbreak of the plague in The Rocks in 1900 made wholesale **slum clearances** unavoidable, and with the demolitions came a change in attitudes. Strict new vice laws meant the end of the bad old days of drunken taverns and rowdy brothels.

Federation, WWI and WWII

With **Federation** in 1901, the separate colonies came under one central government and a nation was created. Unhappily for Sydney, Melbourne was the capital of the **Commonwealth of Australia** until Canberra was built in 1927 – exactly halfway between the two rival cities. The **Immigration Act** was the first piece of legislation to be passed by the new parliament, reflecting the nationalist drive behind federation. The act heralded the **White Australia policy** – greatly restricting non-European immigration right up until 1958.

With the outbreak of **World War I** in 1914, Australia promised to support Britain to "the last man and the last shilling", and there was a patriotic rush to enlist in the army. This enthusiasm tapered with the slaughter at **Gallipoli** – when 11,000 **Anzacs** (Australian and New

Zealand Army Corps) died in the eight-month battle in Turkey – and began the first serious questioning of Anglo-Australian relationships. The aftermath of Gallipolli is considered to be the true birth of Australian national identity.

As the **Great Depression** set in 1929, Australia faced collapsing economic and political systems; pressed for a loan, the Bank of England forced a restructuring of the Australian economy. This scenario, of Australia still financially dependent on Britain but clearly regarded as an upstart nation, came to a head over the 1932 controversy over England's "**Bodyline**" bowling technique at an international cricket series at the **Sydney Cricket Ground**. The loan was virtually made conditional on Australian cricket authorities dropping their allegations that British bowlers were deliberately trying to injure Australian batsmen during the tour. In the midst of this troubled scenario, it was a miracle that construction continued on the **Sydney Harbour Bridge**, which opened in 1932.

During **World War II**, Labor Prime Minister **John Curtin**, concerned about Australia's vulnerability after the Japanese attack on Pearl Harbor, made the radical decision of shifting the country's commitment in the war from defending Britain and Europe to fighting off an invasion of Australia from Asia. In February the Japanese unexpectedly bombed Darwin, launched **submarine raids** against Sydney and Newcastle, and invaded New Guinea. Feeling abandoned by Britain, Curtin appealed to the USA, who quickly adopted Australia as a base for co-ordinating Pacific operations under **General Douglas MacArthur**, who made his headquarters in Sydney at the Grace Building, on York Street (now the *Grace Hotel*).

The postwar generation

Australia came out of World War II realizing that the country was closer to Asia than Europe, and began to look to the USA and the Pacific, as well as Britain, for direction. **Immigration** was speeded up, fuelled by Australia's recent vulnerability. Under the slogan "Populate or Perish", the government reintroduced assisted passages from Britain – the "ten-pound-poms" – also accepting substantial numbers of European refugees. The new European migrant populations ("New Australian"), a substantial number of Italians, Greeks and Eastern Europeans among them, colonized the inner city, giving it a more cosmopolitan face.

Anglo-Australians took on board postwar prosperity during the conservative **Menzies era** – Robert Menzies remained Prime Minister from 1949 until 1966 – and headed for the suburbs and the now affordable dream of their own home on a plot of land. Over the next few decades, Sydney settled into comfortable suburban living as the red-brick, fibro and weatherboard bungalows sprawled west and southwards into the new suburbs, while the comfy parochialism of the Menzies years saw Australian writers, artists and intellectuals leave the country in droves.

1965 to the present

Immigration continued in waves, with a large influx of people from postwar Vietnam and Southeast Asia aided by Gough Whitlam's liberal government. Noticeably concentrated ethnic enclaves include a vibrant Vietnamese community at Cabramatta, a Filipino focus in Blacktown and an emerging Chinese community in Ashfield, resulting from the thousands of Chinese students who the Prime Minister **Bob Hawke** allowed to remain in Australia on humanitarian grounds after the Tian'anmen Square massacre in 1989.

Other developments were more concrete. When the restrictions limiting the height of buildings was lifted in 1957, the development of Sydney's high-rise skyline really took off. Notable high-rise office blocks include the 183-metre-tall Australia Square Tower (1961–1967), and the 244-metre-high MLC Centre (1975–1978) designed by Sydney's most prominent architect, **Harry Seidler**. The AMP Sydney Tower (1981) is – at 259m – the tallest and most recognizable structure in the skyline. But it's the **Sydney Opera House** which can claim to be both the most striking and controversial of Sydney's postwar buildings, originally designed by the Danish architect Jørn Utzon in 1957 and finally opening in 1973.

This building boom saw many heritage buildings unthinkingly demolished. The NSW Premier, Robin Askin (1965–1974), was keen for many residential areas of the inner city to make way for new office blocks and hotels. People began protesting against developments and a radical union, the Builders' Labourers Federation (BLF) put might behind the dissent. The BLF secretary, Jack Mundey, coined the term **Green Ban**, meaning the withdrawal of union labour for projects opposed by the community and potentially damaging to the environment. In November 1971 a Green Ban was placed on demolition of The Rocks: two-thirds of the city's most historic area would be redeveloped if the Sydney Cove Redevelopment Authority had had its way. In October 1973, non-union workers poised for demolition were stopped by 80 members of the Rocks Resident Action Group. A compromise in 1975 saw some development but the residential areas were extended and historic buildings restored.

Askin's development schemes were set aside by Labor Premier **Neville Wran** in 1976, but pressure for a bicentennial project saw a fortune spent on the controversial **Darling Harbour redevelopment**, which opened in 1988, a commercial extravaganza of shops, restaurants, a casino and tourist attractions. Environmentalists were particularly opposed to the ugly monorail trundling above the city streets and providing little more than a tourist link.

When Sydney beat Beijing in 1993 for the **2000 Olympics**, the city rejoiced. But in January 1994 the world watched stunned as the future Olympic city went up in flames: front page images of the two icons of Australia, the Opera House and the Harbour Bridge were silhouetted against an orange, smoke-filled sky during the **Black Friday** bushfires, which destroyed 250 homes and cost four lives.

In 1995 a NSW Labor government was elected. In preparation for the Olympics Premier Bob Carr's unenviable task was to co-ordinate the city's biggest infrastructure project since the construction of the Harbour Bridge, with more than $2.5 billion of public money being spent on major road and rail projects, including a $630 million rail link from the airport to the city, and a $93 million rail link to Olympic venues at the $470 million Homebush Bay site. At the same time, a rash of luxury apartment developments seem to be taking over characterful harbourfront locations, to the wrath of Sydneysiders. The East Circular Quay Apartments, or "The Toaster" (see p.52), is smack bang by the Opera House, and went up despite hot protest. If luxury development continues apace, Sydney Harbour may no longer be a working port, and a substantial part of its charm and vigour will have disappeared.

Books

We've given the publishers of each book, where available, in the United Kingdom (UK), the United States (US), and Australia (Aus); many Australian published books are only available there. A good Web site to check out is that of Gleebooks (*www.gleebooks.com.au*) with a host of recent reviews of Australian literature; specific titles can be ordered via email (*books@gleebooks.com.au*) and posted out. O/p signifies an out-of-print – but still highly recommended – book which you should be able to find in a library. University Press is abbreviated as UP.

History and politics

Meredith and Verity Burgmann *Green Bans, Red Union* (University of NSW Press Aus). The full political ins and outs of the Green Bans of the 1970s – when radical NSW Builders' Labourers Union, led by Jack Mundey, resisted developers' plans for The Rocks and other areas of Sydney.

Ann Coombs *Sex and Anarchy: The Life and Death of the Sydney Push* (Viking Aus). The Sydney Push are part of the Sydney legend, a network of anarchists and bohemians who met up at pubs through the conservative 1950s and 1960s, experiencing the sexual revolution a generation before mainstream society and influencing everyone from Germaine Greer to Robert Hughes.

David Day *Claiming A Continent: A History of Australia* (Angus & Robertson Aus). The freshest general and easily readable history available. Day looks at Australia's history from a contemporary point of view, with the possession, dispossession and ownership of the land – and thus issues of race – central to his narrative.

Tim Flannery (ed) *Watkin Trench 1788* (Text Publishing Aus). A reissue of the two accounts Trench, a captain of the marines who came ashore with the First Fleet, wrote and published: "A Narrative of the Expedition to Botany Bay" and "A Complete Account of the Settlement of Port Jackson". Trench, a natural storyteller and fine writer, was a young man in his twenties, and the accounts brim with youthful curiosity.

Alan Frost *Botany Bay Mirages: Illusions of Australia's Convict Beginnings* (Melbourne UP Aus). Historian Frost's well-argued attempt to overturn many long-cherished notions about European settlement.

Robert Hughes *The Fatal Shore* (Harvill Press UK; Random US; Pan Aus). A minutely detailed epic of the origins of transportation and the brutal beginnings of white Australia.

Grace Karskens *The Rocks: Life in Early Sydney* (Melbourne UP Aus). Karskens detailed social history draws a vivid picture of Australia's earliest neighbourhood from 1788 until the 1830s.

Peter Murphy and Sophie Watson *Surface City: Sydney at the Millennium* (Pluto Press Aus). This 1997 study written by two urban planners looks close-up at contemporary Sydney in fascinating detail, from its gay culture to council corruption, through city development battles and multiculturalism.

John Pilger *A Secret Country* (Vintage UK, Aus). Australian-born Pilger challenges the country's sunny self-image with accounts of dirty dealings: mistreatment of Aborigines, racist immigration policies, British nuclear experimentation, Vietnam and the cosy mateship among politicians and industrialists.

Henry Reynolds *The Other Side of the Frontier* and *The Law of the Land* (both Penguin Aus). A revisionist historian demonstrates that Aboriginal resistance to colonial invasion was both considerable and organized.

Portia Robinson *The Women of Botany Bay* (Macquarie Aus). After painstaking research into the records of every woman transported

HISTORY AND POLITICS

from Britain between 1787 and 1828, as well as the wives of convicts who settled in Australia, Robinson is able to tell us just who the women of Botany Bay really were.

Ann Summers *Damned Whores and God's Police* (McPhee Gribble Aus). Stereotypical images of women in Australian society are explored in this ground-breaking reappraisal of Australian history from a feminist point of view.

Biography

Jill Ker Conway *The Road from Coorain* (Minerva UK; Vintage US). Conway's extraordinary, hardworking childhood, on a drought-stricken Outback station in New South Wales during the 1940s, is movingly told, as is her equally fraught battle to establish herself as a young historian in sexist, provincial 1950s Sydney.

Robin Dalton *Aunts Up the Cross* (William Heinemann Aus). Dalton, a prominent London literary agent, spent her childhood in the 1920s and 1930s in Kings Cross, in a huge mansion peopled by the eccentric aunts (and uncles) of the title.

Dulcie Deamer *The Queen of Bohemia* (University of Queensland Press Aus). Dulcie Deamer, Kings Cross resident for half a century, wrote this memoir in her seventies, attempting to capture the bohemian literary and artistic community of Sydney in the roaring twenties. Deamer, a standout with her theatrical outfits, dancing and imaginative rituals, reigned undisputed queen of all the other eccentrics of the period.

Dorothy Hewett *Wild Card* (Virago UK o/p; McPhee Gribble Aus o/p). Playwright, poet and novelist, Hewett is one of Australia's more unconventional and outspoken writers. Her autobiography explores her life between 1923–1958: the beautiful, passionate writer threw her energies into the Australian Communist Party and into her love life, challenging political and sexual convention. She moved to Sydney, where she lived in working-class areas and took a job in a factory – on which she based her novel *Bobbin' Up* (Virago UK).

Clive James *Unreliable Memoirs* (Picador UK; Knopf US o/p). The expat satirist humorously recalls his postwar childhood and adolescence in Sydney's southern suburbs.

Travel and specialist guides

Michael Duffy, David Foster et al, *Crossing the Blue Mountains: Journeys Through Two Centuries* (Duffy & Snellgrove Aus). Eleven personal accounts of crossing the Blue Mountains west of Sydney, including Gregory Blaxland's famous expedition with Wentworth and Lawson in 1813 where they found a route across; Charles Darwin's visit in 1836 as part of his five-year world trip on the *Beagle*; and contemporary novelist David Foster's reflections on wilderness, solitude and eucalypts as he walks from Mittagong to Katoomba.

Alan Fairley *Sydney's Best Bushland Walks* (Envirobook Aus). The "Top 30" walks detailed – which include nature notes and maps – are all accessible by public transport.

Kangaroo Press publish a useful series of special interest guides including *Seeing Sydney By Bicycle* by Julia Thorn, *Sydney by Ferry and Foot* by John Gunter, and *Uncovering Sydney: Walks into Sydney's Unexpected and Endangered Places* by Graham Spindler.

Paul Knox *Guide to Parks of Sydney* (University of New South Wales Press Aus). A landscape architect writes of Sydney's outdoor spaces, from Barrenjoey Head at Palm Beach to Bare Island at Laperouse.

Jan Morris *Sydney* (Penguin UK, Aus). An insightful and informative account of Australia's favourite city by one of the world's most respected travel writers.

Ruth Park *Ruth Park's Sydney* (Duffy & Snelgrove Aus). By one of Australia's most loved storytellers, author of *The Harp in the South* trilogy set in Surry Hills. Park's impressionistic and personal look takes the form of a walking guide full of anecdotes and literary quotations.

Tyrone Thomas *100 Walks in NSW* (Hill of Content Aus). Forty-six of the walks cover the area detailed in this book, with tracks on the Central Coast, in the Royal National Park and the Blue Mountains.

Sydney in fiction

Inez Baranay *Pagan* (Angus and Robertson o/p). Set in bohemian 1950s Kings Cross (and based on the life of the painter Rosaleen Norton, who was rumoured to be a witch), an affair between an artist and a famous European conductor causes scandal.

Rosa Cappiello *Oh Lucky Country* (University of Queensland Press Aus o/p). A powerful novel of the migrant experience from a young woman's point of view in the Sydney of the 1970s, translated from the Italian.

Peter Carey *Bliss* (Faber & Faber UK; Random US; University of Queensland Press Aus). Carey's first novel, and one of his best: a story, somewhere between fantasy and reality, of a Sydney ad executive who drops out to New Age New South Wales.

Peter Corris *The Empty Beach* (Unwin UK, Aus). Australia's answer to Raymond Chandler. This is one of a series of Cliff Hardy detective stories, all set in a glittering but seedy Sydney. Private eye Hardy investigates murder and exploitation in a Bondi old people's home.

Eleanor Dark *The Timeless Land* (HarperCollins Aus o/p). A historical novel which recounts the beginnings of Australia.

Delia Falconer *The Service of Clouds* (Picador US, Aus). This poetically written novel, romantic in its sensibility and literary in its intent, dwells on the Blue Mountains landscape in all its moods, covering the period 1907–1926, as pharmacy assistant Eureka Jones falls in love with Harry Kitchings, "a man who takes pictures of clouds".

Kate Grenville *Lillian's Story* (Picador UK; Harcourt Brace & Co US; Allen & Unwin Aus). The tragicomic tale of Lillian Singer is loosely based on the life of Bea Miles, the eccentric, Shakespeare-spouting, tram-stopping, taxi-hijacking Sydney bag lady.

David Ireland *City of Women*. Ireland creates weird visions of Sydney; here it's a futuristic, violent place from which men have been banished. *Archimedes and the Seagle* provides a delightful philosophical discussion between a dog and a bird as they roam The Domain and Woolloomooloo (Penguin UK, Aus).

Linda Jaivin, *Eat Me* (Chatto UK; Broadway BDD US; Text Publishing Aus). A successful first novel billed as an "erotic feast"; opens with a memorable fruit-squeezing scene (and this is only the shopping) as three trendy women (fashion editor, academic and writer) hang out in Darlinghurst cafés and swap stories of sexual exploits – though we never quite know who is telling the truth.

Louis Nowra *Red Nights* (Picador Aus). To Nelson Taylor it appears as if "Sydney is drowning"; in fact, it is he who has been shot and is sinking below the surface of the harbour. The past 24 hours are relived, roaming through Sydney's underworld, as the once powerful Taylor, desperately tries to turn his luck.

Ruth Park *The Harp in the South* (Penguin Aus). First published in 1948, this first book in a trilogy is a well-loved tale of inner-Sydney slum life in 1940s Surry Hills. The spirited Darcy family's battle against poverty provides memorable characters, not least the Darcy grandmother with her fierce Irish humour.

Dorothy Porter *The Monkey's Mask* (Hyland House UK, Aus). This novel in verse is a detective thriller and a fine piece of erotica. A tough lesbian private investigator trawls through the Sydney literary scene on the hunt for a murderer of a young student. Disturbing, full of suspense – and very witty.

Christina Stead *For Love Alone* (Virago UK; Harcourt Brace & Co US o/p; Imprint Aus). Set largely around Sydney Harbour in the 1920s, where the late author grew up, this novel follows the obsessive Teresa Hawkins, a poor but artistic girl from an unconventional family, who scrounges and saves to head for London and love.

Kylie Tennant *Ride on Stranger* (Imprint Aus). First published in 1943, this is a humorous portrait of Sydney between the two world wars, seen through the eyes of a newcomer.

Art and architecture

Wally Caruna *Aboriginal Art* (Thames and Hudson UK, US). An excellent illustrated paperback introduction to all styles of Aboriginal art.

Philip Drewe *Sydney Opera House* (Phaidon Press UK; Chronicle Books US). A study of one of the world's most striking pieces of contemporary architecture, designed by Jørn Utzon, with detailed photographs and notes.

Robert Hughes *The Art of Australia* (Penguin Aus). The internationally acclaimed art historian, author of *The Shock of the New*, cut his teeth on this seminal dissection of Australian art up to the 1960s.

Food, wine, facts and fauna

Jean-Paul Bruneteau *Tukka: Real Australian Food* (Angus & Robertson Aus). Bruneteau arrived in Australia in 1967 as a child from France, and is passionate about the use and understanding of native Australian foods. A wide-ranging fusion of well-researched history and botany as well as a cookbook.

Bill Coppell *Australia in Facts and Figures* (Penguin Aus). Subtitled "Vital Statistics on the Country and its People", this has all you ever wanted to know, including how many people really have been eaten by sharks.

Mark Shields and Huon Hooke *The Penguin Good Australian Wine Guide* (Penguin Aus). A handy book for a wine buff to buy on the ground, with the best wines and prices detailed to help navigate you around a "bottle shop".

Peter and Pat Slater *Field Guide to Australian Birds* (Weldon Aus). Pocket-sized, and the easiest to use of the many available guides to Australian birds.

INDEX

ROUGH GUIDES: Travel

ROUGH GUIDES: Mini Guides, Travel Specials and Phrasebooks

MINI GUIDES

Antigua
Bangkok
Barbados
Big Island of Hawaii
Boston
Brussels
Budapest
Dublin
Edinburgh
Florence
Honolulu
Lisbon
London Restaurants
Madrid
Maui
Melbourne
New Orleans
St Lucia

Seattle
Sydney
Tokyo
Toronto

**TRAVEL
SPECIALS**

First-Time Asia
First-Time Europe
More Women Travel

PHRASEBOOKS

Czech
Dutch
Egyptian Arabic
European
French

German
Greek
Hindi & Urdu
Hungarian
Indonesian
Italian
Japanese
Mandarin
  Chinese
Mexican
  Spanish
Polish
Portuguese
Russian
Spanish
Swahili
Thai
Turkish
Vietnamese

AVAILABLE AT ALL GOOD BOOKSHOPS

ROUGH GUIDES:
Reference and Music CDs

REFERENCE
Classical Music
Classical:
  100 Essential CDs
Drum'n'bass
House Music

World Music:
  100 Essential CDs
English Football
European Football
Internet
Millennium

**ROUGH GUIDE
  MUSIC CDs**
Music of the Andes
Australian
  Aboriginal
Brazilian Music
Cajun & Zydeco
Classic Jazz
Music of Colombia
Cuban Music
Eastern Europe
Music of Egypt
English Roots
  Music
Flamenco
India & Pakistan
Irish Music
Music of Japan
Kenya & Tanzania
Native American
North African
Music of Portugal

Jazz
Music USA
Opera
Opera:
  100 Essential CDs
Reggae
Rock
Rock:
  100 Essential CDs
Techno
World Music

Reggae
Salsa
Scottish Music
South African
  Music
Music of Spain
Tango
Tex-Mex
West African Music
World Music
World Music Vol 2
Music of Zimbabwe

SYDNEY 2000

The XXVII Olympics

The XXVII Olympics

SEPTEMBER 15 TO OCTOBER 1 2000

The modern Olympic movement began at the **Modern Olympic Games** in 1896 in Athens, inspired by the ancient Greek athletic festival which began in 766 BC in Olympia. Instead of receiving gold medals, winners were awarded an olive branch, symbol of power and vitality. To show how times have changed since 1896, women were not allowed to compete, only thirteen countries were officially represented (compared to the 198 today), sailors had their own swimming event, and a professor from Oxford University competed in the tennis doubles – he didn't win but composed an Olympic Ode which he recited at the victory ceremonies.

....

Australia is one of the five nations that have attended every summer Olympic Games since 1896 – the four other most games-enthused are Britain, France, Switzerland and Greece.

....

Australia is one of the twelve Olympic nations of Oceania and it's through this Pacific region that the **Olympic torch** will be carried after it is traditionally lit in Olympia, in May

2000. After being carried around Greece for ten days, it will be flown to Guam, then journey for twenty days to Australia via American Samoa, the Cook Islands, Micronesia, Fiji, Nauru, New Zealand, Papua New Guinea, the Solomon Islands, Tonga, Vanuatu and Samoa, arriving at Yulara Airport in the Northern Territory, near Uluru (Ayers Rock). The first Australian torch-bearer is Aboriginal Australian and former Atlanta women's hockey gold medallist Nova Peris Kneebone; it will be relayed to 2499 other escorts over the hundred-day journey through every state of the nation, from desert to beach, hopping on the *Indian Pacific* train across the Nullarbor Plain, and taking a ride in a Bondi life-saving boat, to arrive at the Olympic Stadium in Homebush Bay to light the cauldron for the opening ceremony on Friday September 15. Other games symbolism involves the three very cheesy official **mascots** – Olly, Syd and Millie (think about it) – cuddly cartoon versions of native critters, in order, of a kookaburra, a platypus, and an echidna.

This is not the first time Australia has hosted the Olympics. Back in 1956 that honour fell to Melbourne, and the home base must have provided a great boost for the Australian Olympians, who won the country's biggest ever pile of gold medals, thirteen in all.

SYDNEY OLYMPIC PARK

The Olympic site at **Homebush Bay**, situated on the Parramatta River, roughly 14km west of the Harbour Bridge, on the **Parramatta River**, is virtually the geographical heart of Sydney. The Olympic grounds are accessed by a fast RiverCat service and a new rail link. The site has a long industrial history, having seen life as a saltworks, abbatoir, brickworks, naval armaments depot and waste dump.

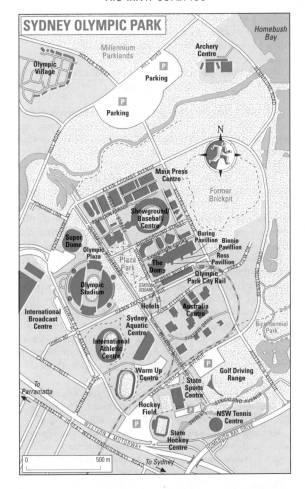

Sydney's successful bid was accompanied by environmental guidelines, with a strong waste management strategy and a desire to clean and green the contaminated site.

Since 1896, Australia has won a total of 123 medals, 40 of them gold.

The $470 million Olympic project at Homebush Bay is centred around the 110,000-seat **Olympic Stadium**, the largest ever, which will witness the opening and closing ceremonies, track and field events, and marathon and football finals. Other new projects on site are the 16-court New South Wales Tennis Centre, and an indoor multi-use arena, the SuperDome. The new Sydney Showground, completed in 1996, acts as a funfair during the Royal Easter Show, and its pavilions and showground will host various events (the showground becomes the Baseball Centre during the games). A green-friendly **Athlete's Village** will house over 15,000 athletes and officials. Alongside the village a new solar powered suburb, **Newington**, is being built for private tenants who will already be in occupation during the Olympics. Two on-site hotels will have their own restaurants, bars and coffee shops. Besides building work there is the landscaping of the grounds – many trees taken off site during building will be put back on, and ninety-five percent of plants will be native. A large percentage of the site is being created as the 440-hectare **Millenium Parklands**.

With its small population base, Australian Olympic athletes are disproportionately successful. The sport they most succeed at is swimming, not surprising coming from a nation of water babies who developed and popularized freestyle in the Victorian era (commonly known as "Australian crawl").

The pentathlon is set to be contested across the road from the Olympic site at the huge **Bicentennial Park**; more than half of the expanse is conservation wetlands. The Visitor Centre (✆9763 1844) at the park can give details of around 8km of cycling and walking tracks, and on weekdays at 1.30pm an "Explorer Train" tours the wetlands.

More sporting venues are being erected on Sydney's western outskirts: a $41 million cycling velodrome at Bankstown, a $30 million Shooting Centre in Liverpool, an $11 million softball centre in Blacktown and a $37 million Equestrian Centre at Horsely Park. Other Olympic events around town will take place at more picturesque locations, like the beach volleyball at Bondi Beach and sailing at the revamped Rushcutters Bay Marina. The marathon will commence at North Sydney, cross the Harbour Bridge and finish at the Olympic Stadium, while the road cycling races will terminate amidst beach and café culture at Bronte. Darling Harbour will be quite a focus, with basketball at the Entertainment Centre, boxing, judo, table tennis and taekwondo at the Exhibition Centre, and weightlifting at the Convention Centre. Moore Park will see football events in the Sydney Football Stadium and fencing in the former Showground pavilions. Further afield, water polo will be held at the revamped Ryde Pool complex, mountain-biking at Fairfield City Farm while rowing events will take place at Penrith Lakes.

It was only at Montréal in 1976 that the Australian contingent did not receive any gold medals. So scandalized was the sport-obsessed nation that the Federal government set up the Australian Institute of Sport (AIS) in the nation's capital Canberra in 1981 to train elite athletes for future games; it can be visited on daily tours led by AIS athletes (✆6252 1444 for details).

FACTS AND FIGURES

The main **public transport** to the site is the $93 million rail link to the **Olympic Park Station**. During the Olympic period, ticket holders are entitled to free transport on CityRail trains, with the network extending as far north as Newcastle and south to Wollongong; special Olympic bus services will also be free. No private vehicles will be allowed on the site during the Olympics, and even taxis will be banned from within a certain radius, leaving public transport as the only alternative. Around 10,000 athletes and 5000 team officials will pour into the country, as well as something like 9000 staff of 175 foreign broadcasters, and then there are the expected quarter of a million spectators, with ticket sales (*www.sydney.olympic.org.au/*) hoping to generate around half a billion Australian dollars.

The Andrew "Boy" Charlton pool at The Domain (see p.282) was named after the champion swimmer, a Manly local who turned seventeen at the 1924 Olympic Games in Paris, winning a gold medal for the 1500-metre freestyle. He was beaten at the 400-metre event by Johnny Weissmuller, who famously went on to play Tarzan in Hollywood films.

SOCOG, the committee organizing the games, are assuring that there will be enough **accommodation** to house all the visitors. They have commandeered fifty percent of hotel rooms in the city to house officials and media and have made deals with the contracted hotels to keep the prices of the remaining rooms at fair and equitable levels. However, other hotels and accommodation places are free to raise their prices as high as they like and there have been reports of places like caravan parks planning to charge upwards of $350 a night for a van that would normally cost around $60.

There are contingency plans to anchor cruise ships to increase capacity.

If you want to check out where the main Homebush action will be before the event, you can visit the site, though only a couple of the Olympic venues. The **Homebush Bay Information Centre** (daily 9am–5pm; free; ℅9735 4800), housed in a red-brick former abattoir building dating from 1907, features up-to-the-minute information about the development of the site and its facilities. There's a separate souvenir shop (daily 10am–4pm) selling Olympic paraphernalia such as pricey "Sydney 2000" T-shirts and the rest. Head for Australia Avenue to the **State Sports Centre** (daily 8.30am–10pm; ℅9763 0111; 24hr information line ℅1902/260 690, 50¢ per minute), where you can visit the **NSW Hall of Champions** (same hours as centre; free) devoted to the state's sporting heroes. The Hall of Champions is closed when events are being held at the State Sports Centre, so call the latter before setting out. Australia Avenue is home to the **Sydney International Aquatic Centre** where you can go for a swim outside of Olympic time (see p.283).

To get out to the Olympic site before the Olympics, from Strathfield Station you can take bus #401–404 to the Homebush Bay Olympic Centre, the State Sports Centre and the Athletic Centre (every 15–30min between 6am and 10pm; 10min); on weekends the #401 service is only offered in the evenings (every 30min, 6.35–10.05pm) and you should take the train to Olympic Park Station. Bus-only **tours** of the Olympic site, providing information about current facilities and those planned, leave the Homebush Bay Information Centre every half-hour from 10am to 1pm ($5; 45min; entry to sites and venues isn't included; ℅9735 4800 for more information). You can take a combined RiverCat Cruise from Circular Quay to Homebush Bay and a bus tour at the Olympic Park site

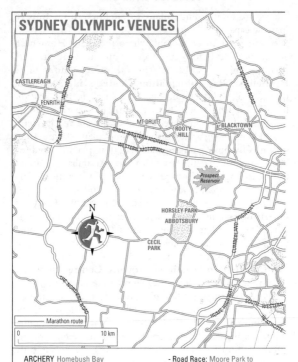

SYDNEY OLYMPIC VENUES

CASTLEREAGH

PENRITH

MT DRUITT · ROOTY HILL · BLACKTOWN

GREAT WESTERN HIGHWAY

WESTERN MOTORWAY

Prospect Reservoir

HORSLEY PARK
ABBOTSBURY

N

CECIL PARK

SOUTH WESTERN

— Marathon route

0   10 km

ARCHERY Homebush Bay
ATHLETICS Homebush Bay
BADMINTON Homebush Bay
BASEBALL Homebush Bay and Blacktown
BASKETBALL Homebush Bay
BEACH VOLLEYBALL Bondi Beach
BOXING Darling Harbour
CANOEING/KAYAKING Castlereagh
CYCLING - Mountain biking: Abbotsbury
         - Velodrom: Bankstown

- Road Race: Moore Park to
               Bronte Beach
- Time Trials: Moore Park
DIVING Homebush Bay
EQUESTRIAN Horsley Park
FENCING Darling Harbour
GYMNASTICS Homebush Bay
HANDBALL Homebush Bay
HOCKEY Homebush Bay
JUDO Darling Harbour

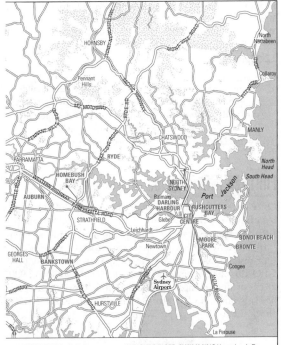

MARATHON North Sydney to Homebush Bay	**SYNCHRONISED SWIMMING** Homebush Bay
PENTATHLON Homebush Bay	**TABLE TENNIS** Homebush Bay
ROWING Castlereagh	**TAEKWONDO** Homebush Bay
SAILING Rushcutters Bay	**TENNIS** Homebush Bay
SHOOTING Cecil Park	**TRIATHLON** City Centre
SOCCER Homebush Bay Prelims - interstate	**VOLLEYBALL** Homebush Bay Darling Harbour
SOFTBALL Rooty Hill	**WATERPOLO** Homebush Bay and Ryde
SWIMMING Homebush Bay	**WEIGHTLIFTING** Darling Harbour
	WRESTLING Darling Harbour

including a visit to the information centre (Mon–Fri 10am, 11am, noon, 1pm, 1.30pm; tour 1hr; $15; tickets from Wharf 5; ℭ9207 3170); an extended weekend tour also includes the Aquatic Centre (Sat & Sun 10.35am & 12.25pm; $22).

Sydney will also host the much smaller Sydney 2000 Paralympic Games (October 18–29), when 400 disabled athletes from 125 countries will compete in 18 sports. For more information, consult the organizing body's Web site: *www.paralympic.com.au*

FURTHER INFORMATION

Once in Sydney you can find out more about the Olympics by checking out various IBM-sponsored **Olympic Information Kiosks** in prominent places around town. For more serious information, contact the Sydney Organising Committee for the Olympic Games (SOCOG), GPO Box 200, Sydney, NSW 2001 (ℭ9297 2000, fax 9297 2817) or the Olympic Co-ordination Authority, GPO Box 5341, Sydney, NSW 2001 (ℭ9228 3333, fax 9228 5551), or check the useful Olympic Web site: *www.sydney.olympic.org*

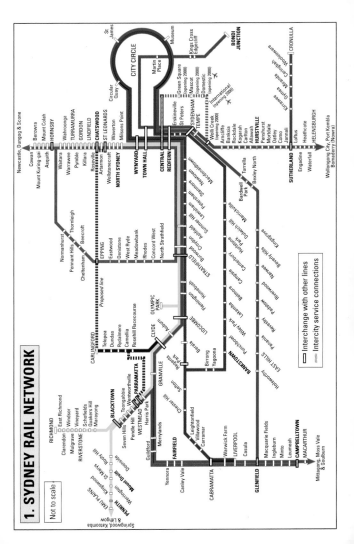

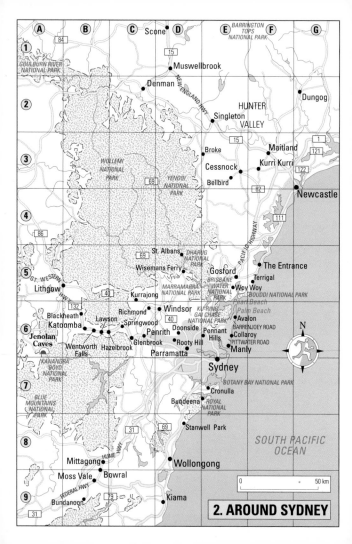

2. AROUND SYDNEY

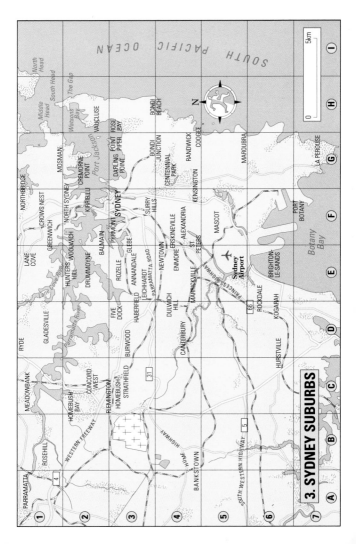

3. SYDNEY SUBURBS

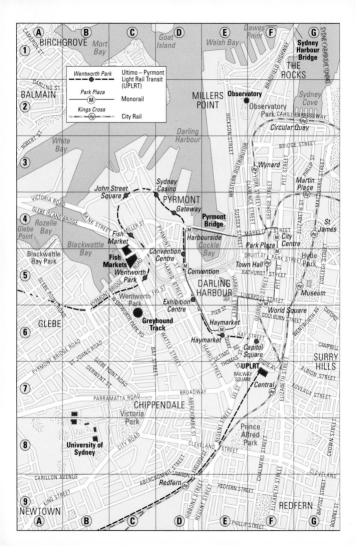

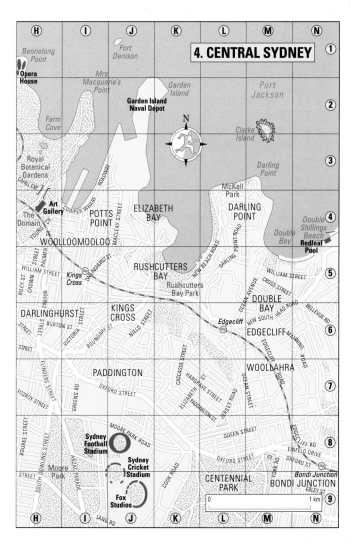

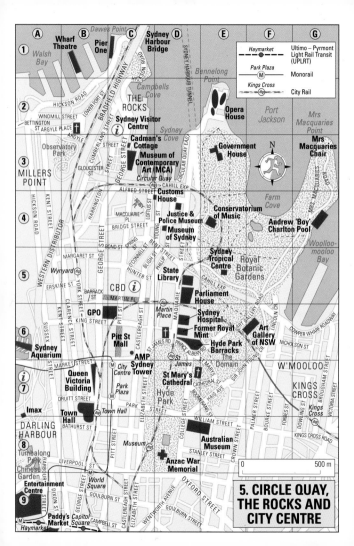

A
B
C
D
E
F
G
1
2
3
4
5
6
7
8
9
Dawes Point
Wharf Theatre
Pier One
Sydney Harbour Bridge
Walsh Bay
HICKSON ROAD
SYDNEY HARBOUR TUNNEL
Bennelong Point
Haymarket
Ultimo – Pyrmont Light Rail Transit (UPLRT)
Park Plaza
Monorail
Kings Cross
City Rail
Campbells Cove
THE ROCKS
HICKSON ROAD
LOWER FORT ST
BRADFIELD HIGHWAY
WINDMILL STREET
BETTINGTON ST
ARGYLE PLACE
ARGYLE
Sydney Visitor Centre
Opera House
Port Jackson
Mrs Macquaries Point
Sydney Cove
Cadman's Cottage
STREET
CUMBERLAND STREET
Observatory Park
Museum of Contemporary Art (MCA)
GEORGE STREET
CIRCULAR QUAY EAST
Government House
N
Mrs Macquaries Chair
GLOUCESTER ST
STREET
MILLERS POINT
Circular Quay
CAHILL EXP
MRS MACQUARIES ROAD
ALFRED STREET
Customs House
Farm Cove
HICKSON ROAD
KENT STREET
HARRINGTON
REIBY PL
LOFTUS ST
MACQUARIE PL
YOUNG ST
Justice & Police Museum
Conservatorium of Music
Andrew 'Boy' Charlton Pool
WESTERN DISTRIBUTOR
BRIDGE STREET
Museum of Sydney
GEORGE STREET
BOND ST
SPRING ST
O'CONNELL ST
BENT STREET
Woolloomooloo Bay
MARGARET ST
BLIGH ST
PHILLIP ST
STREET
Sydney Tropical Centre
Royal Botanic Gardens
Wynyard
HUNTER ST
State Library
ERSKINE ST
YORK STREET
CBD
CAHILL EXP
BARRACK ST
MARTIN PL
MACQUARIE
Parliament House
ART GALLERY ROAD
CLARENCE STREET
KENT STREET
GPO
PITT ST
CASTLEREAGH ST
Martin Place
Sydney Hospital
KING STREET
LINCOLN CR
SUSSEX
Former Royal Mint
Art Gallery of NSW
COWPER WHARF ROADWAY
Pitt St Mall
ST JAMES RD
PRINCE ALBERT RD
Hyde Park Barracks
NICHOLSON ST
Sydney Aquarium
STREET
AMP Sydney Tower
St James
The Domain
MARKET STREET
City Centre
ST MARYS
SIR JOHN YOUNG CR.
W'MOOLOO
Queen Victoria Building
St Mary's Cathedral
CATHEDRAL ST
BROUGHAM STREET
Park Plaza
ELIZABETH STREET
Hyde Park
HAIG AVE
KINGS CROSS
VICTORIA STREET
DRUITT STREET
BOOMERANG ST
PARK STREET
COLLEGE STREET
PALMER STREET
BOURKE STREET
FORBES ST
DOWLING ST
Kings Cross
Imax
Town Hall
Town Hall
WILLIAM STREET
DARLING HARBOUR
BATHURST ST
PITT STREET
CROWN STREET
KINGS CROSS ROAD
Australian Museum
Museum
Tumbalong Park
STANLEY STREET
LIVERPOOL ST
Anzac War Memorial
Chinese Garden
HARBOUR STREET
0
500 m
Entertainment Centre
World Square
OXFORD STREET
DIXON ST
GEORGE STREET
GOULBURN ST
CASTLEREAGH STREET
ELIZABETH STREET
WENTWORTH AVENUE
GOULBURN STREET
Paddy's Market
Capitol Square
CAMPBELL ST
Haymarket
5. CIRCLE QUAY, THE ROCKS AND CITY CENTRE

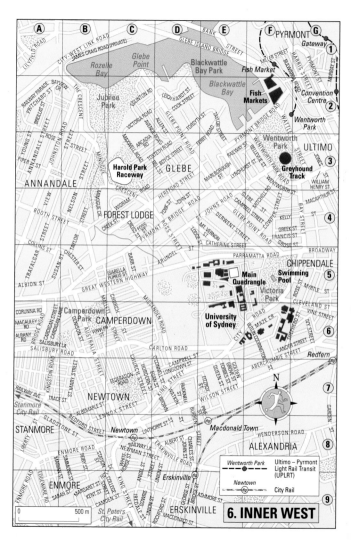

6. INNER WEST

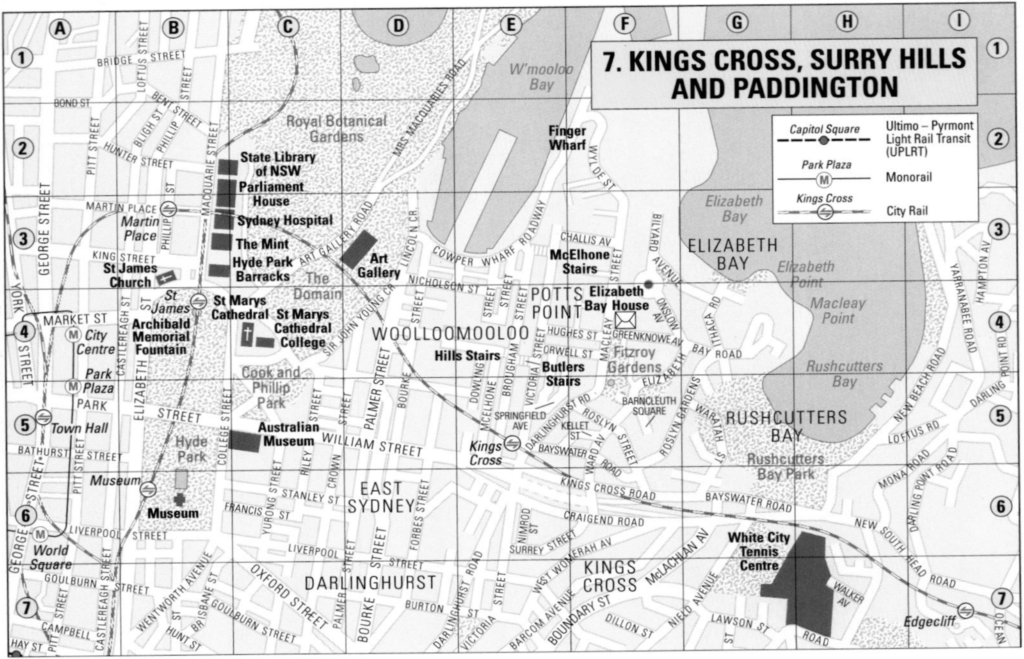
7. KINGS CROSS, SURRY HILLS AND PADDINGTON
Capitol Square
Ultimo – Pyrmont Light Rail Transit (UPLRT)
Park Plaza
Monorail
Kings Cross
City Rail
Royal Botanical Gardens
State Library of NSW
Parliament House
Sydney Hospital
The Mint
Hyde Park Barracks
The Domain
Art Gallery
St James Church
St Marys Cathedral
St Marys Cathedral College
Archibald Memorial Fountain
Cook and Phillip Park
Australian Museum
Hyde Park
Museum
Town Hall
World Square
Martin Place
City Centre
Park Plaza
W'mooloo Bay
Finger Wharf
McElhone Stairs
Elizabeth Bay House
Hills Stairs
Butlers Stairs
Fitzroy Gardens
WOOLLOOMOOLOO
POTTS POINT
ELIZABETH BAY
Elizabeth Bay
Elizabeth Point
Macleay Point
Rushcutters Bay
RUSHCUTTERS BAY
Rushcutters Bay Park
EAST SYDNEY
DARLINGHURST
KINGS CROSS
White City Tennis Centre
Edgecliff
GEORGE STREET
WILLIAM STREET
OXFORD STREET
KINGS CROSS ROAD
BAYSWATER ROAD
NEW SOUTH HEAD ROAD
MRS MACQUARIES ROAD
MACQUARIE STREET
ELIZABETH STREET
COLLEGE STREET
PALMER STREET
BOURKE STREET
CRAIGEND ROAD
DARLINGHURST ROAD
VICTORIA STREET
MACLEAY STREET
COWPER WHARF ROADWAY
NICHOLSON ST
LIVERPOOL STREET
GOULBURN STREET

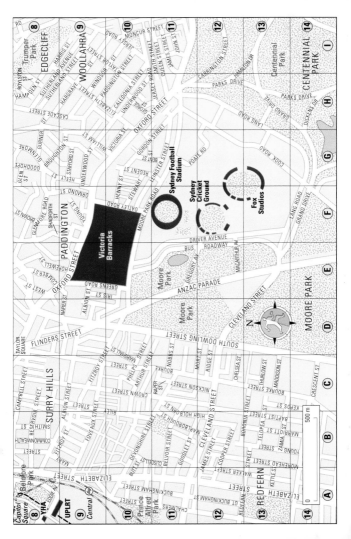

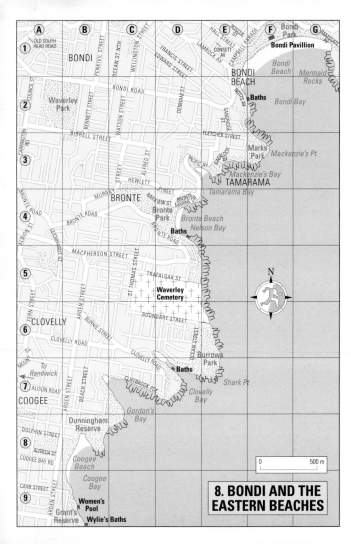

8. BONDI AND THE EASTERN BEACHES

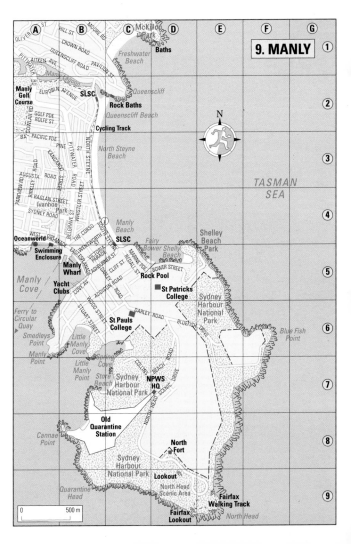

9. MANLY

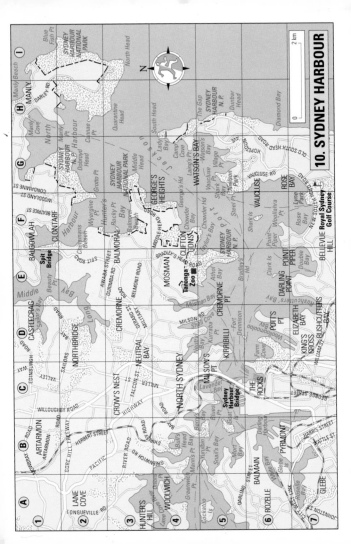

10. SYDNEY HARBOUR

0 — 2 km